D0467008

RANK
AND
FILE

RANK

AND

FILE

CIVIL WAR ESSAYS IN HONOR OF
BELL IRVIN WILEY

EDITED BY

James I. Robertson, Jr.

and

Richard M. McMurry

PRESIDIO PRESS

RANK AND FILE
CIVIL WAR ESSAYS IN HONOR OF
BELL IRVIN WILEY

Edited by
James I. Robertson, Jr.
and
Richard M. McMurry

copyright © 1976

PRESIDIO PRESS
1114 Irwin Street
San Rafael, California 94901

All Rights Reserved.

Library of Congress Catalog Card Number 76-48787
ISBN 0-89141-011-2

Printed in the United States of America by
Consolidated Printers, Inc., Berkeley, California

Cover and Book Design by Joseph M. Roter
Typesetting by The Type Shop, San Rafael, California
Binding by The Filmer Brothers Press, Co-operative Bindery,
San Francisco, California

Preface

The idea of a collection of essays honoring Bell I. Wiley first developed in January, 1972, in conversations between former graduate students Martin Abbott, Richard M. McMurry and Diffee W. Standard. The group then resolved that James I. Robertson, Jr., seemed the logical person to handle the editorial responsibilities. He promptly agreed to direct the project, and the groundwork got underway.

Letters went out to all of Wiley's doctoral students in an effort to ascertain who would be willing to contribute what to the proposed festschrift. The numerous responses and various proposals that came forth led Robertson and McMurry (who became a valuable second-in-command of the project) to conclude that some restrictions would have to be placed on subject material for the volume. Painfully the decision was made to confine the contributions to essays treating of individuals or groups primarily associated with the Civil War. Seven proposals were thus accepted. An essay on Wiley and a listing of his major publications were also to be included.

Academic duties, prior writing commitments and other impediments brought a number of delays in the individual completion of the monographs. Yet one by one they slowly began to arrive at Robertson's office. He read them for style and content, established a uniform footnoting system, and had each manuscript retyped after making editorial changes. Occasionally an essay was sent to McMurry for a second evaluation. Meanwhile, contributors Henry T. Malone, Arnold Shankman, Michael Dougan, McMurry and Robertson were independently collecting material for the all-important essay on Wiley.

The seven Civil War monographs printed herein show first of all the diversity of historical interest that Wiley was able to cultivate among his graduate students. In addition, the essays all concentrate on personalities instead of on inanimate subjects. This again is a reflection of Wiley, for he has long insisted that history is an ever-living chronicle of real people rather than a progression of statistics or the evolution of faceless nationalities.

Leading off this volume is a biographical tribute to the man who so influenced us all. If the article appears at times to become a bit sentimental, it is only because Bell Wiley was a mentor who easily and often served too as a second father. This collection of essays is an attempt to say "thank you"; yet between its covers — and between the lines of the individual contributions — is the eternal gratitude of those whom he affectionately called "my boys."

Contributors

John Porter Bloom is Editor of *Territorial Papers* and Senior Specialist for Western History at the National Archives.

Michael B. Dougan is Assistant Professor of History at Arkansas State University, Jonesboro.

Norman B. Ferris is Professor of History at Middle Tennessee State University, Murfreesboro.

Maury Klein is Professor of History at the University of Rhode Island, Kingston.

Richard M. McMurry is Professor of History at Valdosta State College, Valdosta, Ga.

Henry T. Malone is Dean of the School of General Studies, Georgia State University, Atlanta.

James I. Robertson, Jr., is Professor and Head of the History Department at Virginia Polytechnic Institute and State University, Blacksburg.

Arnold Shankman is Assistant Professor of History at Winthrop College, Rock Hill, S.C.

Willard E. Wight is Professor of Social Sciences at Georgia Institute of Technology, Atlanta.

Contents

RANK
AND
FILE

I

Bell Irvin Wiley:
Uncommon Soldier

By HENRY T. MALONE

In the summer of 1949, boxes of books began arriving in the history department at Emory University. A stream of postmen resembling the innumerable carriers of a bush-country safari spent days delivering Bell Irvin Wiley's private collection to the campus in Atlanta's suburbs.

It proved to be a most appropriate introduction. Scores of graduate students and thousands of undergraduates at Emory learned early in their association with Wiley that the professor followed a bibliographic orientation in the pursuit of knowledge. All historians deal in books; but somehow Wiley's profound respect for the printed page and his remarkable encyclopedic mental catalogue set him apart. Yet the enormous respect that Wiley disciples feel for their mentor is based on much more than a collection or knowledge of books.

Wiley's distinguished contributions to the literature of the Civil War and related subjects have brought an international reputation. His sparkling lectures, close personal counseling and painstaking, demanding direction of theses and dissertations have been the hallmark of his professorial career.

His interest and writings concentrated on the ordinary people of North and South. He described leadership roles and assessed performance. Presidents, cabinet members, congressmen, governors and mayors walk the Wiley pages as do all ranks from generals and admirals to privates and seamen. Wiley edited memoirs, letters and personal narratives. He prowled through countless libraries, special collections, museums, attics

1

and archives. He pored over thousands of manuscripts, diaries, letters, reminiscences, notes, journals and interviews. The relentless and meticulous examination of the printed page, the scribbled scrap, the reminiscent interview—these were the steps that led scholar Wiley closer to the goal of a more complete historical picture. Asked on one occasion to give his view on the craft of writing, Wiley quoted Samuel Eliot Morison: "The historian should write as if the past were looking over his shoulder."[1]

Bell Irvin Wiley was born January 5, 1906, at Halls, Tennessee, a small town sixty miles north of Memphis in a region once noted for plantations and slave labor. His father was Ewing Baxter Wiley, a minister-teacher-farmer married to Anna Bass Wiley, also a teacher. Eleven of their thirteen children survived infancy. Bell Irvin was in the middle. Despite a near-poverty situation, the elder Wiley was determined that each of his children would have an opportunity for a college education—and he succeeded. All eleven children went to college through some form of work-study activity.[2]

The first five, including Bell, went to Methodist-oriented Asbury College in Kentucky. He studied hard but found time to become an excellent basketball player. Upon completing his work at Asbury in 1928, he began graduate studies in English at the nearby University of Kentucky. He supported himself by teaching at Asbury. That school's 1930 yearbook listed him as "Professor of Argumentation and Debate." A year later, he had attained the more exalted designation of "Assistant Professor of History and Coach of Intercollegiate Debate Team." His coaching bore fruit, for an Asbury annual noted that "under the capable supervision of Coach B. I. Wiley the debate team this year has done excellent work, gaining wide recognition and distinction. The men's team toured the East where they met some of the foremost colleges and universities of that section. The women's team went into Ohio and debated with several prominent schools. Altogether the season has been a decided success."[3]

Wiley's picture at this time portrays a thin and serious young man. Yet he was extremely popular with the students. Forty years later, one of them would remember: "I never saw Bill (we always called him Bill) without a gleaming white shirt, tie, coat—perfectly groomed. Maybe he wasn't the best-looking man on campus, but we girls thought he was—and with intelligence and charm and charisma—he was certainly the most popular. He never lacked for a word or an answer—and could converse on any subject. And he dated the most beautiful and glamorous girls on campus . . . . He was always ready to help anyone." Wiley gave many sermon-speeches in Lexington churches. Afterward he could generally be found at the Canary Cottage, where he went to drink Ovaltine and to treat his friends to frozen fruit salads.[4]

With a master's degree in English in hand, the next step in his career was doctoral study in history at Yale University. Ulrich B. Phillips, one of the school's most renowned professors, was his mentor. Tragically, Phillips contracted terminal cancer near the end of Wiley's studies. A race with time ensued over the completion of the dissertation.

A Yale classmate recalled Wiley then as "tall, thin, dark and very shy. . . extremely assiduous. He worked all the time and could seldom be inveigled into taking time off for a party." By contrast, another Yale friend remembered him as "cordial, friendly, out-going, a Southern Gentleman . . . and an altogether charming and likeable man."[5]

Young Wiley had long been interested in the Civil War, in part because of his family's background. "I grew up with the Civil War," he once told a magazine writer: "My maternal grandfather was a very young Confederate soldier in the army of Tennessee, enlisting during the Georgia campaign in the spring of 1864." The young Wiley hardly knew him, but his grandmother lived until his Yale days. "She was a splendid Christian woman, but her Christianity was never quite broad enough to embrace love of Yankees."[6] Under Phillips's tutelage at Yale the interest ripened; and his dissertation, "Southern Negroes during the Civil War," was highly regarded. Leonard W. Labaree, editor of the Yale Historical Publications series, conferred with Wiley and Phillips and determined that after some rewriting and editing, the book would be published in the series. Meanwhile, Wiley had entered the manuscript in competition for the Mrs. Simon Baruch Award of the United Daughters of the Confederacy. The winner would receive $500 in cash and $500 toward the cost of publication. Although the ladies on the Baruch Committee liked the book, they told the author that if he wanted to have the $500 for publication, the title would have to be changed to "Southern Negroes during the War Between the States." Labaree and Wiley pondered the problem, then produced a new and acceptable title. *Southern Negroes, 1861-1865* was, in Labaree's words, "short, precisely accurate, and entirely neutral as between the contending parties to the war!"[7]

Wiley was understandably proud that the dissertation became his first book so quickly. In addition, as one of his doctoral students later observed, "Wiley always considered the closing lines of that book as among his best literary prose. Moreover, it will be observed that the Daughters must not have read the text too closely." The last paragraph of *Southern Negroes, 1861-1865* states in part:

The inconsiderate and discriminatory treatment accorded Negroes in Federal military pursuits, whether as laborers or as full-fledged soldiers, is a regrettable episode in the transition of the colored race in America from slavery to freedom. In fact, the entire experience of Southern Negroes during the War of Secession was discouraging and disillusioning. The outbreak of the war and the coming of the 'Yankees' fired the hope and enthusiasm of the blacks throughout the South . . . . But whether release from slavery came early or late, it was always accompanied by unexpected hardship. Those Negroes who were assembled in contraband camps died by the thousands; those who were employed on plantations received treatment little better than that which they had received under the old regime; those who entered military pursuits were dealt with in a manner more becoming to slaves than to freedmen. In the light of all these unhappy experiences, it must have been apparent to Southern Negroes when the triumph of the North in 1865 assured the final end of slavery that the fight for real freedom had just begun.[8]

A job opportunity in Texas sent newly credentialed Dr. Wiley travelling southward. En route he learned of a vacancy at Mississippi State College for Women in Hattiesburg. He applied for and received the appointment. Almost overnight Wiley became professor and head of the history department.

During his four years at MSCW, Wiley also taught history at Peabody College in the summer. One morning in the summer of 1937, however, his custom of reading the *New York Times* while breakfasting at a Nashville drugstore received a disarming interruption. A young lady seated next to him asked to borrow a portion of the newspaper. This Peabody student, Mary Frances Harrison from Savannah, Tennessee, had gained a deep interest in politics and history from her businessman-politician father. Thus she had entered Memphis State College as a joint history-education major. She later became a Phi Beta Kappa graduate of Peabody. Nevertheless, much of her senior year in college was occupied in a courtship with the young professor she had met in the drugstore. On December 19, 1937, the couple became man and wife.

Seven months later, the Wileys arrived in Oxford, Mississippi, where the budding scholar assumed new duties as professor and head of the Department of History at the University of Mississippi. The newlyweds found life in Oxford particularly pleasant because of the friendliness and genuine charm of a neighbor, novelist William Faulkner. Wiley regularly "hobnobbed in field and stream" with Faulkner. Their friendship blossomed in part because "young Bell didn't constantly bring up the great novelist's work."[9]

During the following years Bell Wiley plunged into a direction of research which would establish him firmly in the ranks of leading students of the American Civil War. In spite of many hundreds of thousands of pages on the war already published, and more on the way, an important story remained to be told. It was one whose raw material was not easily acquired. What was usually described as the life of the common soldier of the Confederacy consisted of specific individuals whose life stories were available and from whose experiences generalizations had been drawn. But to Bell Wiley the true account of Johnny Reb would not be told until the countless pages of unpublished manuscripts scattered across the United States could be read and analyzed.

This is the stuff of which *The Life of Johnny Reb* (1943) and its companion volume, *The Life of Billy Yank* (1952), are made. Wiley examined over 30,000 documents in the preparation of the two books. He combed libraries, visited private homes and kept the mails busy with inquiries and manuscript material. A Julius Rosenwald Fellowship, Rockefeller Foundation Postwar Fellowship and Social Science Research Council Grant enabled him to complete the expensive research and long months of writing.

The Life of Johnny Reb examines critically every phase of Civil War soldier life as revealed in published and unpublished letters, diaries, memoirs and reminiscences, and in official records. Some of the book's chapter titles suggest the thoroughness of investigation and method of presentation: "Heroes and Cowards," "Breaking the Monotony," "From Finery to Tatters," and "Blue Bellies and Beloved Enemies." Similarly, the pages of *The Life of Billy Yank* detail the everyday existence of men in blue in such chapters as "Southward Ho!," "The Depths of Suffering," "Toeing the Mark" and "Hardtack, Salt Horse and Coffee." Wiley's conclusions about Johnny Reb are interestingly and poignantly portrayed:

> The average Rebel private belonged to no special category. He was in most respects an ordinary person...middle-class rural, largely nonslaveholders... lacking in polish, in perspective and in tolerance, but he was respectable, sturdy and independent . . . .
>
> He had a streak of individuality and of irresponsibility that made him a trial to officers during periods of inactivity. But on the battlefield he rose to supreme heights of soldierhood.
>
> He was far from perfect, but his achievement against great odds in scores of desperate battles through four years of war is an irrefutable evidence of his prowess and an eternal monument to his greatness as a fighting man.[10]

The concluding chapter in his volume on Billy Yank is a moving essay comparing Northerners and Southerners as fighters, as citizens and as men. Wiley noted the hatred of the enemy which characterized both sides at the outset of the war and which, for some, lasted throughout the conflict. He showed how contempt and loathing diminished in favor of new feelings of sympathy for men similarly caught in a terrible war because of political actions, of new respect for bravery and gallantry, of surprised discovery of character and manliness. As to comparisons, Billy Yank enjoyed greater literacy, was more interested in politics and was more pragmatic. Yet he also was less emotionally religious, less rural, less imaginative and less concerned with the war.[11]

Wiley attributed Johnny Reb's better showing in battle during the first two years "in the main to better leadership." As this advantage was overcome, however, it is apparent that "on the basis of the whole war record it cannot be said that the common soldier of one side was any better or any worse [as a] fighter than the one who opposed him." Differences, Wiley argued, were far fewer than similarities: "They were both Americans, by birth or by adoption, and they both had the weaknesses and the virtues of the people of their nation and time . . . . Their conduct in crisis compared favorably with that of more privileged groups and revealed undeveloped resources of strength and character that spelled hope for the country's future."[12]

A significant byproduct of Wiley's research on *Johnny Reb* and *Billy Yank* was his preparation for republication of nearly a dozen classic Civil War narratives. These memoirs range from a private's front-line experiences to a Confederate congressman's letters and a woman's account of life in wartime Richmond. Six of these works were reprinted in facsimile by McCowat-Mercer Press, in Jackson, Tennessee. They became the nucleus of the Sources, Monographs and Reprints in Southern History series of which Wiley served as general editor.

In addition to *Southern Negroes*, *The Life of Johnny Reb* and *The Life of Billy Yank*, other Wiley works portray customs and behavior in the wartime South. In 1943, Louisiana State University invited him to give the annual Fleming Lectures. Wiley presented three addresses around the theme, "The Plain People of the Confederacy." The following year, the Louisiana State University Press issued the lectures in book form. Birmingham-Southern College's Henry T. Shanks declared the volume to be "a highly entertaining and . . . penetrating analysis of the life of the formerly neglected common people of the Confederacy."[13]

Another group of lectures, analyzing causes of Confederate defeat, was published in 1956 by Memphis State College Press under the title,

The Road to Appomattox. Wiley then collaborated on two books with his close friend, Hirst D. Milhollen, curator of the photographic collection of the Library of Congress. Wiley contributed the sparkling prose, and Milhollen supplied the little-known but highly revealing photographs for the oversized pictorial studies: *They Who Fought Here* (1959) and *Embattled Confederates* (1964).

Wiley's penchant for collecting the written words of statesmen, commoners, orators, editors, generals and the like also blossomed in a documentary text for American history classes. *American Democracy*, which appeared in 1961, was a useful tool that he coedited with former Emory graduate student, J. Rogers Hollingsworth.

Another Wiley collaboration made a much grander impact. In 1963, the U.S. Civil War Centennial Commission in Washington, D.C., directed its officers — Allan Nevins (chairman), James I. Robertson, Jr. (executive director) and Wiley (chairman of the executive committee) — to undertake an annotated bibliography of the major Civil War books. Nevins and Wiley agreed to handle organizational and promotional aspects; Robertson, one of Wiley's doctoral graduates, assumed the chores of managing editor. Fifteen historians were engaged to assemble titles and commentaries on as many categories.

The result was a monumental compilation: *Civil War Books: A Critical Bibliography* (two volumes, 1967-1969). More than 5,000 titles were analyzed in a novel manner. Photographic reproductions of Library of Congress cards, with brief annotations in typescript added at the bottom of each card, were arranged two columns to the page. The whole work was made more useful by a name-, subject- and cross-referenced index at the end of Volume Two. The annotations presented succinct summaries of content and generally provided brief critiques in pungent and incisive language. One reviewer asserted that the set would become "recognized as a lasting memorial of the Civil War Centennial Commission while serving as an indispensable aid in the reading and writing which memorialize the War itself."[14]

Wiley's undying interest in Southern common folk emerged in print again in 1975 with the publication of *Confederate Women*. A volume in Greenwood Press's Contributions in American History, the work demonstrates anew Wiley's earlier observation that "on the homefront there were far more Scarletts huffing and puffing, than Melanies, whining and down-at-the-mouth."[15]

During World War II, Wiley's career took a new turn and provided him with the opportunity to write about modern warfare. In 1943, while anticipating his draft notice, a fortuitous referral by the chancellor of the

University of Mississippi to the commanding general of the U.S. Second Army rescued Wiley from enlisted status to a first lieutenancy on Gen. Benjamin Lear's staff. Commissioned on March 19, 1943, Lieutenant Wiley was first stationed in Memphis as staff historian. After writing a preliminary history of the Second Army, he journeyed to Washington to become assistant historical officer of army ground forces. He worked under the direction of Kent R. Greenfield and enjoyed the novelty of writing military history as it happened.

His efforts resulted in two well-received and oft-consulted works. Wiley, Greenfield and R. R. Palmer produced *The Organization of Ground Combat Troops* (1947); with Palmer and W. R. Keast, Wiley wrote *The Procurement and Training of Ground Combat Troops* (1948). By the end of World War II, Wiley held a lieutenant colonel's rank as well as the Legion of Merit. He subsequently became a colonel in the reserves. Since 1954, he has served as occasional consultant to the historical section of the Joint Chiefs of Staff.

In September, 1946, the Wileys departed the capital for Baton Rouge, where the historian had been appointed head of that department at Louisiana State University. The long trip southward was especially trying for Mrs. Wiley, for she was in the final stages of pregnancy. In November, 1946, George Bell Wiley was born. The Wiley life-style of the previous nine years now underwent necessary change. He continued his usual heavy schedule of teaching, directing theses, writing articles and preparing book reviews but, with the birth of a child, concentrated research posed a momentary problem.

His major effort at this time was *The Life of Billy Yank*. This meant extensive travels to depositories throughout the North. In the preparation of *The Life of Johnny Reb*, Mary Frances Wiley had contributed full-time labor in research and typing. Wiley fully acknowledged this in the preface to his book: "Mary Frances Wiley, my wife, contributed so vitally to the research and writing as to deserve a co-author's rating, and it is only her firm refusal that prevents this recognition."[16]

With young George to tend, her research role necessarily diminished. Yet a combined effort was still evident. Arriving at a library or archives, Bell would pore over the records in the morning and note material to be copied, while Mary Frances minded George. In the afternoon, the positions reversed. She copied records while he babysat and reviewed the material. Thus, the Wiley station wagon toured research facilities on long weekends, holidays and vacations.[17]

One of Wiley's most enjoyable research stops was in Atlanta where a number of Civil War veterans resided in the Confederate Soldiers' Home.

The superintendent willingly gathered about twenty of the old soldiers on the front lawn to talk with the historian. Wiley first queried them on such matters as food, supplies, uniforms and the like. Then he gingerly asked: "What about camp followers? The problem of prostitution?"

The chief spokesman for the group drew himself up and indignantly replied: "Sir, I would have you know that we didn't have that kind of man in the Confederate army!"

In describing this event to a reporter, Wiley added: "My hunch that Confederate soldiers were like soldiers of all other wars was confirmed when I found in the National Archives a monthly health report on the Tenth Alabama. Sixty-two new cases of gonorrhea were reported, and six new cases of syphilis."[18]

On December 18, 1954, Mary Frances gave birth to a second son, John Francis. As the family grew, so did Wiley's stature. In 1949 he was appointed professor of history at Emory University. There he spent the next twenty-five years. More than one lucrative offer came his way in that time; yet with the exception of an endowed chair at Midwestern University, he gave the invitations little thought. He had fallen too much in love with Emory and Atlanta.

Emory was just then launching its doctoral program in history. In the years that followed, Wiley rapidly matured as a scholar and teacher of national reputation. The high esteem that he now enjoyed is apparent in reviews of one of his most provocative books, *The Road to Appomattox*. The University of Colorado's Hal Bridges wrote that "this excellent study in causation is for those who seek the facts, not the myths, of Confederate history." T. Harry Williams called the study "a seminal work" and added: "Here, in a little more than a hundred pages, is one of the best analyses you can get of the Lost Cause and why it was lost." The most laudatory comments of all, however, came from the distinguished William B. Hesseltine: "When Bell Wiley speaks on the subject of the Southern Confederacy, it behooves all men to listen. Dr. Wiley . . . has studied, as no man has done, the plain folk of the Confederacy and the common soldier in the Confederate army, and he has come, through those studies, to a penetrating insight into the lives and thoughts of the Southern people in the days when they were at war."[19]

In February, 1955, Wiley returned to the University of Mississippi as a lecturer in Civil War history. He received the accolades of his peers later that year by being elected president of the Southern Historical Association. (A true "organization man," he rarely misses the annual meetings of the several historical associations to which he belongs.) During the periods of October, 1964-January, 1965 and May-July, 1966, and under the auspices of the U.S. State Department, Wiley was American Specialist Lecturer in the British Isles, Denmark, Norway, France, Austria, Germany, Yugoslavia and Italy. His occasional summer teaching assignments have taken him far afield. In 1964 he taught at the University of Colorado and the following year at the University of Alaska. His most enjoyable summer stint came in 1967 at the University of Hawaii. However, one of his graduate students at that time still recalls (with mock revulsion) "those garish shirts from Hawaii he brought back and inflicted on us all for *several* years."[20]

In his career, Wiley has lectured at more than 150 colleges and universities in this country and at fifty schools in foreign nations. "Prof. Wiley probably knows as much Southern history as any man alive," a reporter observed on his return from Europe. "He is neither partisan to nor apologist for the region—nor, he declares, 'have I ever found any occasion to be!'"[21]

His most prestigious off-campus appointment occurred in the 1965-1966 academic year, when he served as Harmsworth Professor of American History at Queen's College, Oxford University. His wife observed that while Wiley had happy and rewarding experiences in England, in one regard "he was terribly frustrated. The English students were not responsive in class and although he invited them to come to his office with queries or conversation, he sat and sat and none came."[22]

While in England, Wiley gave three lectures on British television. His inaugural Harmsworth address, "Lincoln and Lee," was subsequently published by Clarendon Press.

In 1960 he was one of twelve Emory faculty members elevated to Charles Howard Candler professorships. The Candler professorships, named in honor of a longtime chairman of the Emory Board of Trustees, honored "professors selected for outstanding teaching ability, productive scholarship and distinguished service to the University in furthering the cause of higher education." In 1970 Wiley was one of four Emory professors named to appear in *Outstanding Educators of America*. In the summer of that year he lectured in the annual Kyoto Summer American Studies Seminar in Japan and participated in a social studies conference in New Zealand.

Wiley once told *Atlanta Constitution* reporter, Harold Martin: "I teach better when I am writing, I write better when I am teaching." Indeed, thousands of undergraduates in lecture classes and hundreds of master's and doctoral students who experienced Wiley's impact in classroom and seminar can attest to the excellence of a great teacher whose instructional performance seemed to become better as each book or article appeared. In the autumn of 1973, Martin visited a class of 200 under-graduates which Wiley was addressing at Emory. The reporter observed how attentive listeners were as they heard of plain people North and South, black and white, all caught up in the maelstrom of the war. The campus newspaper later headlined the event: "No Dry Eyes in Classroom."[23]

Whether in occasional large-group lectures or in everyday appearances to a small class of students, Wiley remains a master teacher; the lecture material carefully and meticulously organized; multi-paged outlines given to students and followed closely in lectures; each topical outline accompanied by bibliographic suggestions ranging from adequate to extensive. In addition to the outlines, lists of sources and clear organization, another characteristic that Wiley's students have known and enjoyed is his resonant voice delivering sparkling prose. Wiley's lectures, like his writings, are studded with the well-chosen word, the dramatic phrase, the graphic sentence, and — especially — the colorful excerpt. A few examples are illustrative.

Of Southern attitudes about the possible effect that the establishment of an independent Confederacy would have on slavery, he states: "No longer would slavery be exposed to the abusive knocks of Yankee statesmen and to the malicious machinations of Northern abolitionists; but basking in the light of a warming Southern sun, hedged about by a circle of admiring friends, it would recover from the accumulated bruises of eight decades of unhappy association with cruel and misunderstanding partners, and attain a strength hitherto unknown."[24]

Wiley's greatest enjoyment when lecturing comes in quoting from the letters and diaries of semiliterate Civil War soldiers. There, he firmly believes, is the clearest and most human picture of the war's pathos, suffering, drama, color and humor. His books on Johnny Reb and Billy Yank abound with such quotations. These range from picturesque similes — Yankees were "thicker than lise on a hen and a dam site ornarier" — to poignant commentaries on individuals — "The Major is a hell of a man to go on a . . . [detail] with he dont no enough to learn a dog to bark."

The worse the grammar and spelling, the more Wiley relishes the quotation. He is particularly fond of the statement of an Ohioan who, upon hearing that his beloved sister back home was associating with a man of questionable morals, exploded in anger and wrote her: "Alf sed he heard that you and hardy was a runing to gether all the time . . . that orney thefin, drunkerd, damned card playing Sun of a bich . . . the god damned theaf and lop yeard pigen tode helon, he is too orney for hel . . . i will Shute him as shore a i Sea him."

Among Wiley's favorite nuggets was a letter from a Georgia soldier who, in the short span of two sentences, went from a pronouncement of marital devotion to the possibility of extramarital activity. "If I did not write and receive letters from you I believe that I would forgit that I was maryed I don't feel much like a maryed man but I never forgit sofar as to court enny other lady but if I should you must forgive me as I am so forgitful."[25]

Anyone who ever experienced a Wiley examination could well argue that he or she had been subjected to a military interrogation. Few graduate students were prepared for the meticulousness of the objective portion of one of Wiley's finals. (How many Civil War students can identify Juan A. Quintero—an item that unexpectedly appeared on a 1963 exam?) The story still circulates of the young man who, along with his stunned classmates in 1950, looked at the long sheet of questions on a Wiley test and then blurted out, "My God! I believe I have memorized the wrong set of minutiae!"[26] On the other hand, such examinations usually included a subjective portion on which the majority of the grade was based. Moreover, Wiley customarily graded on a curve and always demonstrated scrupulous fairness in compiling final averages.

Graduate students had first claim on Wiley's time. He was a hard taskmaster with his doctoral candidates. Because he himself practiced exhaustive research, skillful organization, impeccable prose and incisive interpretations, he expected the same of those who were to be his reflection. His master's degree was in English, not history. Hence, he demanded good grammar and lectured constantly against such evils as overly long sentences and the excessive use of adjectives. "During my days at Emory," one student likes to recall, "I supported my family by working in a local funeral home. Yet in four years I never saw anything any bloodier than one of my dissertation chapters after Dr. Wiley's red pencil had done its work!"[27]

Wiley continually exhorted his students to search attics, basements, old trunks and the like for Civil War material. Initial scoffing at such activity soon gave way to excitement as a number of heretofore unknown collections came to light. Included in the discoveries were letters of Samuel F. B. Morse, U. S. Grant and Abraham Lincoln.[28]

Countless examples exist of personal assistance far beyond the limits of usual professor-student relationships. "No one in the academic world has had a greater influence on my work and career," confessed a former student now at a North Carolina college. He added that Wiley "read and criticized my dissertation chapter by chapter, leaving me with no doubts as to the direction in which I should be working." The care and attention he gave to his majors from first-day indoctrination to departure for the first job is a common remembrance among all of his doctoral candidates. A typical comment is: "I appreciate the pains he took with me, the assistance, the suggestions, the guidance."[29]

Bell Wiley's deep personal concern for his students also included their families. Vivid memories prevail of a Wiley phone call to an anxious wife to announce that her husband had passed his oral examinations. Caring for people is a Wiley trademark. His basic humanity was an ever-present factor in handling students and their problems. "In all of my dealing with Wiley," a former student observed, "I think the thing that has always impressed me most has been the fundamental decency and humaneness of the man."[30]

Another characteristic has been his strong interest in helping libraries. Emory's Candler Library benefitted enormously from Wiley's aggressiveness in working for its betterment. The associate university librarian recently commented: "Dr. Wiley as a faculty member was a reference librarian's ideal. He made heavy use of the library and of the services of the reference department, and his students were inspired to do the same. He, of course, was thoroughly familiar with the resources of the library and developed in his students an expertise which meant that these resources would be exploited thoroughly . . . . He developed the collections covering the Civil War period of American history so effectively that it is one of the strongest collections at Emory. But above all, he was vitally concerned more about financial support. . . . This cause became a crusade for him, especially during his last few years at Emory, and he left no path unexplored, no means untried . . . and the library is still benefitting."[31]

His impact as a teacher was such that even the most seasoned graduate student often had difficulty taking notes during a dramatic or inspiring lecture. One of his students, now a private school headmaster, doubtless spoke for many of his classmates when he stated: "I could go on indefinitely, but in sum, I can only say that he was my teacher and remains today one of my best friends. Out of the many teachers I have had or that all of us have had, how many can you count like Bell Wiley?"

Another former student put it more succinctly: "He was such an inspiration to me that as long as I live, and as intimate as our friendship has been, I still will always call him 'Dr. Wiley.'"[32]

In 1957, Wiley's talent for stimulating, planning and directing historical efforts found a national showcase. President Dwight D. Eisenhower appointed him to the U.S. Civil War Centennial Commission. Wiley was the only Southerner among ten citizens-at-large who served with the president, vice-president, speaker of the house, four senators and four congressmen. In rapid and progressive fashion, he became chairman of the commission's committee on historical activities and chairman of the commission's executive committee.

These new duties made little dent in his historical productivity. In 1960 he completed a twenty-four-page booklet, *Why Georgia Should Commemorate the Civil War*, for the Georgia Department of State Parks. In February, 1961, he received nationwide attention with the publication in *Life* magazine of his article, "Soldier Life North and South." Early in May, 1962, he appeared on the ABC-TV network show, "Meet the Professor." While in Texas the following year to address the annual meeting of the Texas Historical Association, Wiley presented two lectures on the common soldiers in a television course. This series, "American Civilization by Its Interpreters," was televised numerous times throughout the United States.

He has understandably been the recipient of a host of honors. Included among them are five honorary degrees: Litt. D., Lincoln College, 1959; D.H.L., Jacksonville University, 1961; L.L.D., Tulane University, 1961; Litt. D., Asbury College, 1965; and L.L.D., University of Kentucky, 1968. Wiley, however, has never rested on his laurels. Today he is an active member of two associations separately publishing the papers of Ulysses S. Grant and Jefferson Davis. In 1969 he was selected as chairman of the advisory board of the National Historical Society, which is closely allied with the two periodicals *American History Illustrated* and *Civil War Times Illustrated*.

Throughout life's tribulations, and for Wiley some have been agonizingly severe, he has nevertheless exhibited an ever-smiling disposition. His laugh is infectious. The personal habits developed at Emory were as unique as the man. He customarily arose before dawn and rode a bicycle to his Emory office. There he would work diligently at research for two hours or more, then pedal home to join his family for breakfast. The lanky professor would remount his bicycle, an old English model, and wheel rapidly down East Clifton Road to the campus and work. At midday came lunch and a short rest at home. As in the morning, steady work filled the afternoon. He would cycle home around 5 P.M. He jealously prized the early evening hours with his wife and sons, and he was rarely receptive to any intrusions or outside interruptions in that period. By 9 P.M. he was generally in bed.

His chief hobbies were book-collecting and sports. He is an avid fan of the Atlanta Hawks and Atlanta Falcons. He became well known among graduate students for such dishes as vegetable soup, hamburgers and crowder peas. Wiley took great delight in discussing the merits of one of his favorite dishes: Tennessee River Blue Channel Catfish. He loathes yardwork.[33]

Collecting books was his most absorbing pastime. Wiley avidly pored over every secondhand book catalogue he could obtain. He built his personal library with the eager determination that he exercised in research. As a result, his collection quickly overflowed into all empty spaces in the Emory Department of History. Floor-to-ceiling bookcases covered his office walls and were crammed full; Wiley volumes covered another wall in the departmental seminar room; his set of the *Official Records* reposed in Dr. J. Harvey Young's office; the remaining volumes were shelved in at least one other office — as well as amid stationery, pencils and other items in the departmental supply room. It became well-nigh impossible to walk through the history wing without encountering a bloc of the Wiley collection.

Born and raised amid religious surroundings, Wiley has retained strong sinews of Christianity. He embraced his parents' Methodism until he reached manhood. The orderliness and formalism of the Episcopal Church were partly responsible for his subsequent confirmation in that faith. He has since been a regular worshipper at Anglican services and takes pride still in being the Episcopal godfather to the son of one of his students.[34]

Wiley has always maintained a pace that would break all but the stoutest of historians. His March 1973 schedule belied the fact that he was entering his sixty-seventh year. In the first half of that month he addressed Wofford College students on "The Changing South, 1930-1973," the Twin Cities Civil War Round Table in Minneapolis on "Mary B. Chesnut and Her *Diary from Dixie*," the ladies' night program of the Chicago Civil War Round Table on "Women of the Lost Cause," the Baton Rouge Civil War Round Table on the same subject, the Jackson, Mississippi, Civil War Round Table on "Johnny Reb and Billy Yank," and an audience in St. Louis on "Mary Boykin Chesnut and Other Confederate Women." During March 17-20, Wiley was in Mexico City. He proceeded thence to the Henry E. Huntington Library in Pasadena to do research. While in California, he attended a meeting of the National Archives Advisory Council (on which he has represented the Southern Historical Association since the council's formation).[35]

Work with Civil War Round Tables has been a continuing hobby for Wiley. He was among a small group of men who met in the autumn of 1949 and established the Atlanta CWRT. Wiley was an active force in the steady growth and interesting program activity of the Atlanta group and served in 1959-1960 as its president. In April, 1959, the Washington,

D.C., CWRT presented Wiley with its Gold Medal Award for outstanding achievement in the field of Civil War history.

Only a few years later, he became entangled for the first time in large-scale controversy. Wiley's sympathies for blacks had been obvious as far back as his graduate days at Yale. His dissertation had treated of that oppressed race; both his research and his career centered around the adversities of America's plain people. He was proud of his acquaintance with such Negro leaders as Robert Russa Moton and George Washington Carver. Speaking of these pioneers in Negro education, Wiley once asserted: "It would be impossible for a fair-minded man to hold that these learned leaders should ride in the back of a bus. Knowing them and other Negroes of their kind has been the most important single influence in helping me break away from the pattern of segregation and to achieve an emancipation of my own."[36]

It is hardly surprising, therefore, that Wiley was an early activist on behalf of the Negro cause; and when the civil rights issue exploded in the early 1960s, he became outspoken in his support. This action cost him many friendships in his native South. Although he effectively concealed it, these losses were painful blows.

He appeared to take a reverse stand on the race issue a decade later. Yet those unacquainted with Wiley did not know the sanctity he had always attached to principle.

In the winter of 1970, dissension swept across the Emory campus over the issue of the admission of black students. The *Emory Wheel* in February devoted several pages to various faculty views. Wiley was a leading spokesman in the newspaper debate. He reminded readers that he had been "one of a relatively small group on the faculty which many years ago began to work for the integration of Emory." For several years he had actively supported "full equality for black Americans socially, politically and economically." Such support brought him "threatening letters and . . . menacing phone calls." Nevertheless, Wiley wrote, he now felt compelled to speak out against the university's proposal to admit twenty blacks whose academic credentials were below current Emory standards.

A two-column statement of principle then followed. Wiley argued that the proposal posed "a threat to the academic excellence that has characterized Emory over the years." The school's admission standards should not be lowered for any special group." To do so "will be self-defeating" because blacks previously admitted under regular standards had "more than their share of academic difficulty" already. Wiley feared that with such exceptional admissions the faculty would be pressured "to go easy" on grades. On this point he was firm. "I do not want to be called a racist if I am unwilling to pass a student whom my better judgment tells me, I should fail."[37]

Long a Wiley blind spot has been his belief that others shared his passion for scholarly objectivity. Sometimes his bluntly honest assessments left biased audiences less than enthusiastic. Such reactions occurred at both extremes of the political spectrum. At an historical conference in Atlanta, blacks were noticeably unhappy with Wiley's detailed reporting of white attitudes toward Negroes in the Civil War. On another occasion the program chairman of a Southern white organization angrily left the rostrum in the middle of a Wiley lecture when the description of Johnny Reb became pointedly graphic.[38]

The Emory controversy over the admission of blacks was still smoldering when Wiley became embroiled in another public dispute. He had been an active member of the group planning the dedication ceremonies for the newly completed Stone Mountain Memorial. He had given reluctant endorsement to the selection of President Richard Nixon as principal speaker at the observances. Suddenly the situation soured. Nixon withdrew and named Vice-President Spiro Agnew to speak in his stead.

Having as a presidential substitute a man who had publicly and repeatedly criticized the "effete corps" of dissenting youth was a development that Wiley could not accept. "I was abhorred," he stated, "mainly because I knew . . . that Agnew's coming would be upsetting to the students." Wiley then inserted an historical analogy. "There is the inconsistency of having a man like Agnew dedicating a monument whose central figure is Robert E. Lee. Agnew is the antithesis of everything that Lee stood for as I see it."

Wiley was unsuccessful in blocking Agnew's appearance at Stone Mountain. His publicized opinions provoked a heavy volume of mail. One anonymous writer asserted that "the only insult to the memorial is by having ingrates and reds like you in our college system." Another unidentified correspondent urged Wiley to resign from Emory. Only few letters of support came forward.[39]

In his last years at Emory, Wiley became even closer to his undergraduates by reviving a custom of earlier teaching: personally conducted bus trips to Civil War sites. His 1972 Civil War class, for example, toured the Shiloh battlefield and intermediate sites of historical interest. Early in 1973, seeking as always to connect the past with the present, Wiley took a colloquium studying "History of Negroes in America" to Atlanta's Grady Hospital. There the class reverently interviewed 111-year-old John Stinson, born a slave in Talbot County, Georgia.

The year 1974 marked Wiley's forty-sixth year in the historical profession and a quarter century of service to Emory University. He retired from Emory after giving the 1974 summer commencement address. Yet retirement has only opened new doors for Wiley's energies. He has already served as visiting professor at Agnes Scott College, the University of South Carolina and Tulane University. Other teaching commitments are scheduled. Two books have appeared since retirement, and at least one other is in production. Book reviews and short essays continue to flow from his ever-busy pen. Few historians have been so blessed with the long, productive and highly successful career that he has known. An additional and substantial measure of his fame lies too in the successes of his students, for their efforts reflect the meticulous research, paternal criticism, careful attention to grammar and unceasing pursuit of scholarship that the master imparted.

Above these accomplishments, however, is the firmly established fact that Wiley is—and will remain for years to come—the premier authority on the heretofore faceless masses of the 1860s. Where Johnny Rebs and Billy Yanks are concerned, he has firmly adhered to his conclusion that "it was these men and their kind whose strength was the bedrock of their respective causes and whose greatness made their war one of the most inspiring in the history of embattled humanity."[40]

Bell Irvin Wiley gave new life to the Civil War's common folk—and he did it in an uncommon way.

NOTES

[1] Gene Moore, "Focus: Bell I. Wiley," *Georgia Magazine*, March 1972, 57.

[2] *Who's Who in America* (Chicago, 1975), II, 3303; biographical sheet supplied by Emory University News Bureau; conversations between Henry T. Malone and Mrs. Mary Frances Wiley (hereafter cited as M.F. Wiley conversations). Of Wiley's ten brothers and sisters, three became full-time laborers in Methodism: Robert and Patrick as clergymen and Pansy as a minister's wife. Bessie Wooten married an architect and Frances an affluent farmer. Owen became a dentist, John a businessman and Miller a civil servant. James, like his brother Bell, went into teaching. When Ewing, Jr., was unable to afford medical school, he earned an R.N. degree and ultimately became administrator for an oil refinery hospital.

[3] Hazel Elson Wagers to Richard M. McMurry, November 6, 1975; *Asburian* (1930), 107, 144; Ibid. (1931), 21. From experiences with the debate team came Wiley's earliest publications: "Splitting the Team Has Advantages" and "Bridging the Gap between the Decision and the No-Decision Type of Debate."

[4] Testimony of a former Asbury student to Richard M. McMurry.

[5] Thomas E. Drake to Henry T. Malone, September 25, 1973; William Huse Dunham, Jr., to Henry T. Malone, June 2, 1973.

[6] Moore, "Focus: Bell I. Wiley," 44.

[7] Leonard W. Labaree to Henry T. Malone, May 31, 1973.

[8] Michael B. Dougan to James I. Robertson, Jr., July 18, 1975; Bell I. Wiley, *Southern Negroes, 1861-1865* (New Haven, 1938), 344.

[9] M.F. Wiley conversations; Moore, "Focus: Bell I. Wiley," 11.

[10] Bell I. Wiley, *The Life of Johnny Reb* (Indianapolis, 1943), 347.

[11] Bell I. Wiley, *The Life of Billy Yank* (Indianapolis, 1952), 346-61.

[12] Ibid., 361.

[13] *Journal of Southern History* X (1944), 225.

[14] *Atlanta Journal-Constitution*, May 18, 1969.

[15] M.F. Wiley conversations; Moore, "Focus: Bell I. Wiley," 11; Emory University fact sheet.

[16] Wiley, *The Life of Johnny Reb*, 13.

[17] M.F. Wiley conversations.

[18] Moore, "Focus: Bell I. Wiley," 51.

[19] *Virginia Magazine of History and Biography* LXV (1957), 510; *Baton Rouge Morning Advocate*, November 18, 1956; *Jackson* (Tennessee) *Sun*, December 2, 1956.

[20] Michael B. Dougan to James I. Robertson, Jr., July 18, 1975.

[21] *Atlanta Journal-Constitution*, March 21, 1965.

[22] M.F. Wiley conversations; Moore, "Focus: Bell I. Wiley," 11; *Emory History Newsletter*, April, 1967.

[23] Harold Martin, "Dr. Wiley's War," in *Atlanta Constitution*, January 10, 1974.

[24] Bell I. Wiley, "The Movement to Humanize the Institution of Slavery during the Confederacy," *Emory University Quarterly* V (1949), 207.

[25] Wiley, *The Life of Johnny Reb*, 205; *The Life of Billy Yank*, 185-86; "A Time of Greatness," *Journal of Southern History* XXII (1956), 6.

[26] Testimony of Henry T. Malone.

[27] Testimony of James I. Robertson, Jr.

[28] Undated memorandum of Arnold Shankman.

[29] Richard H. Haunton to Henry T. Malone, May 30, 1973; Michael B. Dougan to Henry T. Malone, March 26, 1973.

[30] Richard M. McMurry to Henry T. Malone, March 22, 1973; Arnold Shankman to Malone, March 22, 1973; testimony of Henry T. Malone.

[31] Ruth Walling to Richard M. McMurry, August 28, 1975.

[32] Emmett Wright, Jr., to Henry T. Malone, March 5, 1973; testimony of James I. Robertson, Jr.

[33] Richard M. McMurry to James I. Robertson, Jr., July 11, 1975; undated memorandum of Arnold Shankman.

[34] James I. Robertson, III.

[35] *Emory Campus Report*, April 23, 1973. Later that year he travelled to Brazil in order to collect information on Confederate expatriates.

[36] *Atlanta Journal-Constitution*, March 21, 1965.

[37] *Emory Wheel*, February 19, 1970.

[38] Testimony of Henry T. Malone.

[39] *Emory Wheel*, May 19, 1970.

[40] Wiley, "A Time of Greatness," 35.

II

Thomas C. Hindman:
Arkansas Politician and General

By MICHAEL B. DOUGAN

In 1854, as the Arkansas legislature assembled in Little Rock, a small, dapper, almost beardless young man with his long hair greased back arrived at the capital to begin his brief but exciting political career as Arkansas's leading antebellum, fire-eating demagogue. Mobility on the American frontier was nothing new. That a man might be born in one state, raised in another and make his career in yet a third was fairly common in nineteenth-century America. Nevertheless, the choice of Arkansas in 1854 was, for Thomas Carmichael Hindman, Jr., out of the ordinary.

Arkansas's geography, high mountains and extensive swamps — all arranged to thwart economic development — made internal improvements a vital necessity. Unfortunately, when Arkansas entered the Union in 1836, it chartered two banks whose subsequent bankruptcy left the state financially incapacitated for over half a century. In the absence of decent roads and reliable streams, pioneers avoided Arkansas until the late 1850s, when the best cotton land elsewhere in the South had been taken. Beginning in the middle of the decade, Arkansas witnessed a flood tide of development that brought Thomas C. Hindman, Jr., to the state.

During that first visit to the capital, Hindman made it clear that he came not to see but to conquer. He would not defer to the older, wiser leadership known locally as the Dynasty: the Conway, Johnson, Sevier and Rector clan who had arrived in territorial days and governed ever since.[1] Hindman's object was power; his desire for it demanded instant gratification. He would not begin as prosecuting attorney and work his way up as legislator, elector and judge, finally aspiring to be governor or congressman. When Hindman arrived in Little Rock he already expected to be obeyed in all things. The legislators were startled by this impulsive newcomer on the floor who was giving orders, marshaling votes and acting as if the capitol were his. Hindman's arrogance led to hard feelings and culminated in a violent encounter a few days before adjournment. Hindman, one editor decided, initiated a new kind of political warfare, "a wholesale denunciation of every one who does not truckle to his mandates and implicitly obey his behests."[2]

Thomas Carmichael Hindman was born on January 28, 1828. He was the son of a well-to-do Mississippi planter who died in an 1856 cotton gin accident. Young Hindman was educated at the Classical and Commercial High School of Lawrenceville, N.J. At the outbreak of the Mexican War, he enlisted as a lieutenant in the Second Mississippi Infantry. During his brief military experience, his regiment performed only guard duties in northern Mexico. Hindman nevertheless managed to get into trouble; the regimental records of August, 1847, show him under arrest.[3]

Upon returning to Mississippi after the war, Hindman studied law and was admitted to the bar. Although he remained an attorney until his death, nothing suggests that the profession of law was for him any more than a convenient stepping-stone into politics. In the wake of the Mexican War, Mississippi political life stood sharply divided between Henry S. Foote, who supported the Compromise of 1850, and Jefferson Davis, who opposed it. Hindman, following Davis in espousing state rights and Southern nationalism, represented Tippah County in the state legislature. In light of his subsequent career, it appears that young Hindman had no strong concern for theoretical issues. He was no legalist or diligent student of the Constitution. Probably he disliked the North (his speeches indicate as much), but as an ambitious man he needed a cause. State rights and slavery were *the* causes in the South for a bright young man of slaveholding antecedents. Initially, however, Hindman found that his cause did not prosper. The big planters, fearful of change, content with the Compromise of 1850 and Whigs by inclination, generally did not espouse the doctrines so carefully prepared for them. In the mid-1850s, Foote's star was ascendant; Davis, although still a national figure, was out of favor in Mississippi. Thus, political circumstances prompted the young man with ambition to seek a new start. A feud between the Hindman and Faulkner families, culminating in the murder of Robert

Holt Hindman by William C. Faulkner, may also have made it expedient for Thomas Hindman to depart.[4]

For whatever causes, the year 1854 found Hindman scouting. He visited Helena, Arkansas, and probably other posts as well, but Helena beckoned. In June, 1854, he made the town his home and was admitted to the local bar.[5] Helena in the 1850s foresaw a great future as the emporium of east Arkansas, if only she could tap the interior with a railroad. Then she could displace her rival on the Chickasaw Bluffs and become the leading town in Arkansas. In the early stages of Hindman's Arkansas career, he paid lip service to local boosterism. Yet his ambitions were higher than merely serving the merchant and his chimerical iron horse.

From the beginning, Hindman plunged into the local political affray. He served as secretary and chairman of local meetings, as speech maker and even as editor pro tem of the local organ.[6] Moreover, he found time in the fall of 1856 to woo and marry the daughter of Henry L. Biscoe, who was a wealthy planter-speculator, a trustee of the defunct Real Estate Bank and a member of the Whig and Know-Nothing parties. Although initially opposed to the match (it was said that he sent his daughter to St. Agnes in Memphis but Hindman followed, visiting her disguised as her Uncle Peter), Biscoe apparently became reconciled to it and at times even publicly supported his son-in-law. Mollie Hindman, a capable judge of the ladies noted, "would be right pretty if her chin was not so long."[7]

The marriage may not have been a happy one, but politically it was important. Biscoe was associated with powerful elements in the state who had no desire to settle their bank debts and no love for the ruling Dynasty. The young couple's honeymoon was, significantly, spent on a visit to the seat of power at Little Rock.

The political issue that catapulted the young aspirant to fame was the formation of the Know-Nothing party. With the demise of the national Whig party following the Compromise of 1850, anti-Democratic sentiment needed a new facade. In Arkansas, many young Democratic politicians were dissatisfied with Dynasty or "family" dictation and were looking for a chance to revolt. Know-Nothingism, with its trappings, symbols and slogans totally unrelated to the pressing problems of the day, offered an opportunity. Thus, for a few brief moments, rural Anglo-Saxon Arkansians, many of whom had probably never seen a foreigner or a Catholic, were led down the primrose path of political heresy.

Secrecy facilitated Know-Nothing penetration into Democracy. When a nominally Democratic legislature first passed and then repealed a set of resolutions critical of nativism, it gave Hindman the opportunity to claim that because the horrid oaths of these midnight assassins had penetrated the Democratic inner sanctum, a housecleaning must take place. To save the people, Hindman took to the stump in northern Arkansas. He organized Democratic Associations to counter the covert menace. These bodies were to consist of all loyal Democrats who came forward and took a public oath. Democrats who failed to take the oath were to be ostracized and denied political office.

This program served Hindman in two ways. It gave him a gripping issue with the masses, and it provided the instrument for grass roots support all over north Arkansas. The *True Democrat*, a "family" organ, noted: "He has been making speeches in all the counties in the northeastern part of the State. He is an eloquent speaker, a ready debater, a man of talents and of courteous manners. Though but a young man, he has already achieved a brilliant reputation."[8]

Such instinting work demanded its reward. Hindman was thereupon selected to serve as a delegate to the national convention.[9] His goal was the congressional seat held by A.B. Greenwood of Bentonville. In 1856, the northern congressional district ran from Indian Territory in the northwest to Helena on the Mississippi River. Greenwood, from the northwest, represented the yeoman rather than the planter, the hills rather than the delta. By 1856, Hindman had emerged as the candidate of the planters. His paper, the *Helena State Rights Democrat*, argued: "Give the man who struck the first blow at Know Nothingism in Arkansas, an opportunity to finish the work that *himself* began."[10]

When the congressional nominating convention met at Batesville, Greenwood, who had been unopposed two years earlier, found himself locked in a tie with Hindman through 277 ballots. On Saturday morning, after an all-night session failed to break the tie, Hindman entered the room, addressed the delegates and withdrew his name. He claimed that his duty to the party outweighed his personal ambitions and that the worst sin was to be a disorganizer.[11]

Hindman took out his frustrations back in Helena by launching a bitter attack on W.D. Rice, a former Phillips County legislator who had turned Know-Nothing. Rice responded first in the press; then, on May 24, 1856, he ambushed Hindman on the streets of Helena. In the melee that followed, Hindman was shot through the right breast; his friend and companion Patrick Cleburne was pierced through the lungs; James T. Marriott, a friend of Rice, lay dead in the streets; and Rice fled town. A grand jury refused to hand down indictments. Hindman, missing the

Cincinnati Democratic National Convention, returned home to Mississippi to recover.[12]

A good duel never did a politician any harm. In Arkansas, it once elevated a second-rate man (Solon Borland) to the U.S. Senate. Thus, with renewed prestige, Hindman in 1858 was selected without opposition to succeed Greenwood. Hindman's arrival in Washington coincided with an acute political crisis: the election of a speaker of the House. Northern disgust with President Buchanan's Kansas policy cost the Democrats control of the House. Yet no other group was strong enough to elect one of its members. Hindman aggravated the crisis. The freshman congressman announced that he desired the destruction of the country and would change his vote to prevent a speaker from being chosen. On the forty-fourth ballot, conservative New Jersey Republican William Pennington was elected. Hindman, amid great confusion, shouted that a Black Republican had been chosen by Know-Nothing votes.[13] His belligerent attitude attracted attention. His colleague, Samuel "Sunset" Cox, recalled that Hindman seemed "perpetually anxious to have a duel."[14]

Hindman's own practical contribution to the sectional crisis consisted of a set of resolutions: a reopened slave trade, federal protection of slavery in the District of Columbia as well as the territories, congressional acceptance of any proslavery territorial constitution, free travel with slaves through any free state, a denial of representation of any state interfering with the recovery of fugitive slaves, an absolute negation by the slave states on all future legislation and state appointment of federal officials within the state. All amendments were to be unamendable and irrepealable. These resolutions were not designed to open debate but to close it. As Hindman stated, "I shall under no circumstances vote for halfway measures."[15]

Hindman's main concern during his first term was the patronage issue. Upon his arrival in Washington, he discovered that most of the state's patronage was locked up in the hands of Senator Robert Ward Johnson, the leading "family" member. Hindman wanted that power. He began his move by insisting that representatives, elected directly by the people, had a better right to it than did senators.[16] At the same time, somewhat contradictorily, he began canvassing for elevation to the Senate. His target was Helena's own William King Sebastian, the "milk and cider" man, who was invulnerable largely because he was inoffensive.[17]

Hindman's attack began when he asserted that ex-Know-Nothings had participated in the renomination of Sebastian. Claiming to be a Simon-Pure Old Line Democrat, Hindman launched a daring revolt against the state machine. Hindman's attack was well timed. The legislature had voted to cut taxes rather than to settle the bank debts and at Christmas had taken a per diem payment. When Governor Elias N. Conway opposed these moves, a lively war erupted. The per diemists, led by Speaker Ben T. DuVal of Sebastian County, allied themselves with Hindman. No revolt could hope to succeed without a newspaper in the capital. Hence Thomas C. Peek, editor for hire, arrived fresh from editing a Douglas organ in Illinois and assumed the tripod of the *Old Line Democrat*. So that there would be no misunderstanding the reason for its creation, the first issue mentioned Hindman by name thirty-eight times.[18]

The founding of the *Old Line Democrat* was the high-water mark in Hindman's career. In late 1859 and early 1860, he began to encounter unexpected obstacles. The quarrel between Congressman Hindman and Senator Johnson reached the point where Hindman announced that he would come to Little Rock and denounce the members of the "family" to their faces. The fateful day arrived. Senator Johnson exerted himself to be there, but Hindman never appeared. His press reported that family illness forced him to leave for Mississippi. Public opinion thought he had backed down. Johnson branded him "a bully and an imposter to the ranks of honor."[19] A near duel in Washington between the two men did not redeem Hindman's reputation.[20]

At the same time, it came to light that Hindman himself had been the author of the glowing "Viator" letters that appeared in the press after each of his public appearances. When his initial denials proved useless, Hindman lamely claimed that he only did what all congressmen did in revising their speeches for the *Globe*.[21] Thus, by 1860, Hindman was stymied. No Democrat revolt threatened his congressional seat, but his chances for further advance had been seriously curtailed.

On the other hand, Hindman's success demonstrated that the "family" was vulnerable. In April, 1860, when a packed Democratic State Convention chose Richard H. Johnson, the senator's brother and the *True Democrat* editor, to be the gubernatorial candidate, a ground swell of discontent began. In May, Henry M. Rector, formerly a lower echelon "family" man, announced as an independent candidate. With no Whig in the running, Johnson's carefully wrought nomination proved to be "not worth a fingersnap."[22]

It was rumored that Hindman had engineered Rector's announcement and promised to stump the state for him. If so, relations between the two soured. Hindman was out of the state during the gubernatorial canvass, and his future cooperation with Rector was limited. However, the *Old Line Democrat* became Rector's paper for the duration of the campaign. Its editor, Thomas C. Peek, cemented an alliance with Rector's niece.[23]

While the state pot was simmering, the national caldron was boiling. Hindman was not a delegate to the Charleston convention of disharmonious Democrats. Yet when that body disintegrated and a divided Arkansas delegation returned home, Hindman took action. At Dover his carefully controlled congressional nominating convention declared all delegates' seats vacated. Hindman and his friends were then selected to fill them. The other congressional nominating convention also elected new men to replace the Douglas delegates, the old delegates refused to give up their seats, and a Douglas convention at Madison selected a new slate of pro-Douglas men to replace the fire-eaters.[24] When all these groups gathered at Baltimore, the anti-Douglas men banded together as the Regular Arkansas Delegates to the exclusion of the Madison group. Tempers ran high. Hindman had another encounter, this time with Dr. William Hooper. No duel took place, presumably because a Douglas man could not be a gentleman.[25] When the Baltimore convention seated the Douglas groups, the Southern extremists bolted again, met at Richmond and nominated John C. Breckinridge.

Defending Breckinridge in Arkansas was easy. The Douglas men were denounced as national disorganizers, while the Constitutional Unionists were Whigs. Both groups were no better than Black Republicans. Hindman consistently upheld Breckinridge as the candidate of National Democracy and denied the charges of disunion. Hindman, a hostile editor observed, showed "great elasticity and tact both as a debater and a dodger."[26] The tactic succeeded. The yeoman farmer, having imbibed Democracy with his mother's milk, put Breckinridge across in Arkansas.[27]

Immediately upon the news of Lincoln's election, Hindman began to press for immediate secession. In this he was joined by Governor Rector (the victor over Richard H. Johnson in August), Senator Johnson, Albert Pike and a smattering of lesser figures. Since the greater national issues made the split in secessionist ranks unseemly and costly, Hindman and Johnson mended their feud. Rector was left politically isolated. The *Old Line Democrat* ceased existence. Work began in earnest to get a reluctant state legislature to authorize a state convention.[28] In Washington for the session of Congress, Hindman voted to condemn the conduct of Major Robert Anderson at Fort Sumter. Otherwise he was inactive.[29]

At home the people approved the calling of a convention but elected Unionists to it. That body rejected secession until the firing on Fort

Sumter forced them to change their minds. On May 4, 1861, with Hindman present, Arkansas severed its tie with the Union.[30] The convention, which then drew up a new constitution and otherwise sought to reorder things, struck out against Governor Rector. A military board was created to limit the governor's war power. Hindman, it was asserted, was the author of the bill whose purpose was to prevent the convention from deposing Rector altogether. Hindman received little credit from Rector, who considered the board an act of "supererogation" and railed at it throughout his term. In a second step, the convention provided for a new election in 1862 of certain state officers. Among those who would lose two years from their terms was the governor.

For Thomas C. Hindman the Civil War was a godsend. Although his political career was blocked on the state level, his newfound friendship with the Dynasty and his old friendship with Jefferson Davis offered him national scope if he could establish a military reputation. Only thirty-three years old, he was nevertheless a seasoned veteran in promoting his own advancement. A hostile newspaper had once pronounced him "fit to command a sortie but not a regiment." The war gave Hindman the opportunity to test that prediction.[31]

Hindman secured a colonel's commission from the Confederacy and began recruiting his regiment. Eventually his unit ballooned to a larger size and became Hindman's Legion. Arming the men was a problem, for private purchase of weapons was virtually impossible. Yet the state had recently bought some arms, and there were more in the arsenal at Little Rock. Hindman applied to Rector for these state weapons only to find that the governor was planning to keep them for state defense. Thrown back on his own resources, Hindman kept the wires hot until the Confederacy sent the requested shipment. Not only had the split between the colonel and the governor widened, but Hindman had discovered first-hand how state rights could impede the war effort.[32]

Hindman and his men were anxious to see action. However, instead of being sent to the "seat of war" at Richmond, they and the Arkansas state army were assigned to the command of Gen. William J. Hardee. At Pitman's Ferry in northeast Arkansas, the impeccable Hardee drilled Hindman's men. The transfer of the state army to Hardee became embroiled in politics and personal ambitions, and it ended a failure. Of the state troops at Pitman's Ferry, 805 remained after the transfer. The rest of the Arkansas troops were in Missouri, having recently contributed to the Confederate victory at Wilson's Creek. When they returned to Arkansas, Hardee sent Hindman across the mountains to act as his agent and to receive the troops. Again problems arose, and Hindman found himself with eighteen men. Hindman attempted to recruit a new regiment from the shattered remnants of the state army. When that failed, he rejoined Hardee. The general responsible for the protection of Arkansas thereupon transferred most of his force to Kentucky.[33]

In Kentucky Hindman received promotion to brigadier general — even though he had hardly heard any firing. All sung his praises. There "could not be a better selection made in this state," wrote Gen. Ben McCulloch.[34] However, the new brigadier was still unable to drill his brigade, and Hardee had to make periodic visits to give him pointers.[35]

The Confederacy's hold on Kentucky and central Tennessee was short-lived. During the southward retreat, Hindman attracted attention by declaring martial law in Murfreesboro, Tennessee. Apparently unrebuked for this military encroachment on civil authority, Hindman came to believe that in emergencies the military must be given a free hand even at the expense of the civil authorities.[36] He participated gallantly at the battle of Shiloh, where his horse was blown to pieces beneath him. Following the battle he was promoted to major general.[37]

In May, 1862, Senator Johnson arrived in General Beauregard's camp at Corinth, Mississippi, with a grim tale. In order to strengthen the Army of Tennessee, Gen. Earl Van Dorn, who had followed Hardee to Arkansas and had subsequently been defeated at Pea Ridge, removed his entire army across the Mississippi. This left Arkansas undefended in the face of the Federal advance of Gen. Samuel Curtis. The main Federal force was already at Batesville, and scouting parties were within thirty-five miles of Little Rock. The Richmond authorities had done nothing. Beauregard, who alone could save Arkansas, must act.[38]

On May 26, 1862, Hindman, ready and anxious for independent command, was assigned to Arkansas. Impressing supplies, raiding the Memphis banks and commandeering steamboats, Hindman arrived just in time. For the next ninety days he had things his own way. He caused all the cotton in the state to be collected and burned on the approach of the enemy. He raised new regiments (without authority) by enforcing his own version of the conscript act that prohibited the use of substitutes. When the governor tried to create a new state army, Hindman threatened to take every man and impress every supply. He caused new manufactures to be started, martial law to be enforced and prices to be fixed. A host of new offices — provost marshals — sprang into existence. When discontent arose in his conscript army, Hindman had men executed without benefit of trial. In all of this, Hindman claimed he was supported by all except "tories, speculators, extortioners, and deserters, and a few smaller politicians." As a result, Curtis was forced to retire to

Helena. There he sat in virtual isolation as the Confederacy reasserted itself on the Missouri border.[39]

Soon new troubles enveloped Hindman's head. Blunt orders to Gen. Albert Pike in Indian Territory outraged that sensitive constitutionalist. Pike, ignored, abused and robbed of his supplies at every turn, exploded in letters addressed to the War Department and the press. In purple prose, Pike attacked Hindman as a tyrant and robber. Pike compared him unfavorably to the Duke of Alva and Abraham Lincoln. Hindman thereupon arrested Pike for treason. The ensuing controversy led the War Department to appoint Gen. Theophilus H. Holmes to quiet the controversy. Once in Arkansas, however, Holmes sided with Hindman, continued martial law, rearrested Pike and defended Hindman's policies to President Jefferson Davis.[40]

As a subordinate officer to Holmes, Hindman was not happy. Holmes had responsibility for the defense of the Mississippi Valley and Indian Territory and for the recapture of Missouri. These three objectives so divided Holmes's enfeebled mind that he ended up being ineffective in all three. Hindman sensed this; and although his personal relations with "Old Granny" remained pleasant, his evaluation of what needed to be done varied greatly from that of Holmes. In late fall, 1862, Hindman convinced Holmes that the time had come to strike a blow in northwest Arkansas. He received reluctant permission to launch a campaign on the condition that, whatever its result, Hindman would return to Little Rock after the fighting. The subsequent and ill-fated Prairie Grove campaign was doomed from the start. It was criminal foolishness to launch a campaign at the onset of winter in the absence of such needed supplies as food, shoes, clothing and munitions.[41]

Hindman's plan was to catch Federal Gen. James G. Blunt's forces before the other Federal army under Gen. Francis J. Herron could offer reinforcements. Yet Hindman's barefoot army moved too slowly, and this allowed Herron to join Blunt on the battlefield. At Prairie Grove, south of Fayetteville, Federal and Confederate armies fought to a bloody standoff. One Arkansas regiment "distinguished" itself by deserting en masse to the enemy. Otherwise, Hindman's conscript army proved itself. The next day a truce was called to bury the dead. Under its cover, Hindman successfully retreated. There was no more ammunition and no more food, and bitterly cold weather had arrived. The retreat to Little Rock proved to be more costly than the battle. Meanwhile, the Federals crossed the mountains, raided Van Buren, destroyed stores and munitions and completed the devastation of Confederate morale.[42]

The hue and cry against Hindman mounted. "Hindman has been

weighed and found wanting," one hostile paper proclaimed.[43] Unhappy with Holmes and distressed at the pending collapse of his work, Hindman applied for a transfer. In February, 1863, he left Arkansas to serve on the Court of Inquiry investigating the fall of New Orleans.[44] During his period of control in Arkansas, he had demonstrated that his main object was to win the war. He would trample down state rights, his raison d'etre as a prewar politician, without hesitation. His advocacy of the total war, including the use of guerrillas, the mobilization of the civilian population, a scorched-earth policy and unified central control could produce results. Yet Hindman failed to grapple with the practical political problems.

Many Confederates put their theories ahead of Confederate success and preferred defeat and failure to a tainted victory. Others put their pocketbooks first and cried out for their cotton, slaves or produce. Hindman's chance to redeem himself at Prairie Grove failed; but his system, although patently illegal by Richmond standards, was never completely dismantled either by Holmes or his successor, Kirby Smith.[45]

On August 13, 1863, after the clamor had subsided, Hindman returned to active duty as commander of a division in the Army of Tennessee.[46] At this stage of the war, that unfortunate army was under the command of Gen. Braxton Bragg in north Georgia. Hindman and Bragg promptly came to odds when Hindman failed to carry out certain of Bragg's orders at McLemore's Cove.[47] On the heels of this occurred the battle of Chickamauga, in which Hindman was conspicuous for gallantry. Yet no sooner had the battle ended than a new feud erupted between Bragg and his generals. Hindman was relieved from duty on September 29, 1863.[48] Compared to Bragg's controversy with Gens. D.H. Hill and Leonidas Polk, Hindman's encounter was a mere skirmish. In November, Hindman was restored to command.[49] In a December reorganization of the army, he even became a corps commander.[50]

Besides quarreling with Bragg, Hindman also became embroiled in the famous slave-arming controversy initiated by his Arkansas friend, Gen. Pat Cleburne. The ever active Cleburne read his remarkable proposal to an assemblage of officers that included Hindman. Gen. Joseph E. Johnston, Bragg's replacement, squelched further discussion. Yet Gen. W.H.T. Walker was determined to have Cleburne disciplined. He demanded of Hindman his opinion of Cleburne's proposal. Hindman replied that all the officers were bound to respect the privacy of the discussion. He would avow his personal opinion only "at the proper time and in the proper way" and "not on compulsion of this sort."[51]

Hindman's support of Cleburne no doubt rested in part on friendship;

but at the same time, both men were dedicated to winning the war. If Hindman demonstrated his disregard for the shibboleth of state rights, Cleburne merely indicated his of the already dying institution of slavery. The proposals of both were eventually vindicated but only by halfway measures. Significantly neither man, from that date forward, received any promotion. Indeed, the unpromoted Cleburne, probably one of the five best generals in the Confederacy, went to his death the next year at the battle of Franklin even as lesser men advanced beyond him. Meanwhile, Hindman's name could not be mentioned in Congress without causing an uproar.

Hindman's career as a corps commander was brief. In February, 1864, the Army of Tennessee received the dubious accretion of corps commander John Bell Hood. Hindman returned to the division level.[52] He offered his resignation, but the president refused to accept it.[53] Thereafter his relations with Hood went sour. "I can never give an order but that you have some suggestion to make," complained Hood. "Yes," responded Hindman, "because you never give me an order with any sense to it."[54]

On July 17, 1864, Hood replaced Johnston as commander of the Army of Tennessee. At that time Hindman was absent, recuperating from a wound. When Hood suggested that Hindman would never rejoin the army, the Arkansian was relieved from command. Shortly thereafter, Hindman left for the Trans-Mississippi.[55] He petitioned to be assigned a command there but was told there were already too many major generals across the river. When rumor leaked of Hindman's request, Arkansas's influential congressman, A.H. Garland, made it clear that his return would not be welcomed.[56] No new assignments followed.

Hindman ultimately moved with his family to Texas (probably San Antonio) for the duration of the war. When the news of the surrender came, Hindman issued an address that apparently called for good Southerners not to surrender but to seize the arms and supplies of the defunct Confederacy and strike for Mexico.[57] Hindman himself moved to Monterrey, together with his slaves (who then left him). He learned Spanish, began to practice law and planted coffee.[58] However, Mexico did not agree with Mrs. Hindman. She disliked Catholicism, refused to cross herself and wanted her children brought up Presbyterians. "She told Hindman they must get away from Mexico," a friend recalled.[59] In the amnesty papers is a note of disdain when she wrote of her husband: "He failed in Mexico even to make a support."[60] With no serious persecution facing ex-Confederates, the Hindmans returned to Helena.

Once back in Arkansas, Hindman refused to attend quietly to his business. Again he engaged in politics. He opposed radicals led by Governor Powell Clayton and soon was involved in a feud with that powerful and dangerous leader. Moreover, he advocated a policy of participation in politics in opposition to many ex-Confederates, including Albert Pike, who wanted to avoid any recognition of carpetbag-scalawag legitimacy.[61] On September 29, 1868, in the midst of the hot election campaign of 1868, Hindman was sitting with his family when a musket loaded with buck and ball was fired through the window. The charge struck him point-blank. In considerable pain, Hindman made a short speech and asked all to forgive him and his murderer. Eight hours later, he died.[62]

The Democratic press immediately claimed that Hindman's unknown assassin was working for the Loyal League, that it was a white man who had been paid $800 for the work and that this person was now in Mexico.[63] Powell Clayton, indirectly implicated, retorted that Hindman had been killed by his brother-in-law, Cameron Biscoe, because of Hindman's plan to divorce his wife.[64] Finally, in the hills it was rumored that the assassination was an act of revenge for some wartime deed.

At this distance, it is impossible to conclude which story is true. Nevertheless, the circumstantial evidence favors the brother-in-law theory. Hindman's actions following the shot were those of a man who knew who shot him and why. Had politics been the motive, he would hardly have been in a forgiving mood. His son, Biscoe Hindman, excising his Biscoe relatives from his will, left his large estate to the University of Arkansas, Helena, and the Prairie Grove memorial. Yet by whoever's hand, a man violent in word and deed met a violent death.

As an antebellum politician, Hindman might appear as a typical Southern state rights fire-eater were it not for his wartime record. Politically he was less than honest, for he was an opportunist seeking fame and power from the ballot box. His brittle manipulation of the voters, his abilities as a debater and his willingness to resort to force mark him as an instance of the degradation of democratic dogma in the Old South.

As a general, Hindman deserves more attention than he has received. Most military historians look with a jaundiced eye upon what they designate as "political" generals. Stanley F. Horn, for instance, claimed that Hindman "possessed no visible qualifications" for high command.[65] The only battle he directed, Prairie Grove, was not an overwhelming success. Yet an unknown obituarist observed that "as a military man he has been underrated," for his "well-known notoriety as a *politician* always disabled him as a general."[66]

To his credit, Hindman was farsighted. His dedication to victory led him to the conclusion that total war was the answer, but his attempt to apply it failed. His devotion to the cause was not universally shared. The means at his disposal were insufficient to enforce conformity. As an exponent of total war, he would perhaps have been of more service to the Confederacy in high political office. But whether as politician or general, his basic personal shortcomings would have ultimately caused him to fail. Behind the shortened leg, the nervous style, the hyperbole and the grand gesture was a man whose constant need to prove himself amounted to a fatal flaw. Truly Thomas Carmichael Hindman was the Arkansas Hotspur.

NOTES

[1] See Brian G. Walton, "The Second Party System in Arkansas, 1836-1848," *Arkansas Historical Quarterly* XXVIII (1969), 120-55; Michael B. Dougan, "A Look at the 'Family' in Arkansas Politics, 1858-1865," Ibid. XXIX (1970), 99-111; Lonnie W. White, *Politics on the Southwestern Frontier: Arkansas Territory, 1819-1836* (Memphis, 1964); Margaret Ross, *Arkansas Gazette: The Early Years* (Little Rock, 1969).

[2] *Helena Democratic Star*, February 1, 1855; *Des Arc Citizen*, March 21, 1860; Charles E. Nash, *Biographical Sketches of Gen. Pat Cleburne and Gen. T.C. Hindman* (Little Rock, 1898), 149-50. The *Fayetteville Arkansian*, February 10, 1860, a hostile source, claimed that after the shooting Hindman ran down the floor shouting for protection.

[3] Biscoe Hindman, "Thomas Carmichael Hindman," *Confederate Veteran* XXVII (1930), 97-100; D.Y. Thomas, "Thomas Carmichael Hindman," *Dictionary of American Biography* V, Pt. 1, 61-62; Hindman file, Military Service Records, National Archives. Apparently the matter was not serious, for shortly thereafter he was sent on detached service.

[4] Hudson Strode, *Jefferson Davis, American Patriot, 1808-1861* (New York, 1955), 230-89. The romantic version of his relations with the Faulkner family is presented in Maud Marrow Brown, "William C. Faulkner, Man of Legends," *Georgia Review* X (1956), 421-38. More accurate is Victor Hoar, "Colonel William C. Faulkner in the Civil War," *Journal of Mississippi History* XXVII (1965), 42-62. Hoar pointed out that during the war, when Faulkner sought promotion, Hindman wrote a supporting letter. The novelist's views of his great-grandfather are found in William Faulkner, *Sartoris* (New York, 1929).

[5] *Helena Democratic Star*, June 14, 1854.

[6] Ibid., July 5, 1854; May 31, August 30, September 13, October 4 and November 29, 1855; *Helena State Rights Democrat*, July 30, 1857. His most remembered accomplishment was a giant barbecue at which Hindman spoke in his "usual nervous style," *Helena Democratic Star*, November 29, 1855.

[7] Mrs. T.J. Gaughan (ed.), *Letters of a Confederate Surgeon* (Camden, 1960), 114; *Little Rock True Democrat*, October 30, 1855; *Des Arc Citizen*, December 21, 1859.

[8] Nash, *Biographical Sketches*, 151-52; *Helena Democratic Star*, May 31, 1855; *Little Rock True Democrat*, June 12, 1855; February 12, 19 and 26, 1856. "So far he has certainly shown great resolution and perseverance in overcoming the difficulties of getting along at this season of the year," the February 12, 1856, *True Democrat* stated. Yet his luck did not hold. Two years later, a storm-blown tree toppled on his buggy and shattered his thigh. This accident left him with one leg shorter than the other and compelled him to wear a boot with a high heel. Nash, *Biographical Sketches*, 75; *True Democrat*, December 18, 1855.

[9] *Helena State Rights Democrat*, May 22, 1856

[10] Ibid., April 10, 1856.

[11] Ibid., May 22, 1856.

[12] Ibid., May 29 and June 5, 1856. Of the causes of this incident, Nash stated: "It was said by Henry Mooney, a whig, that Hindman had stripped every vestige of political clothing from Rice and left nothing but his naked deformity. Rice left the court house in a very angry mood." Nash, *Biographical Sketches*, 63-69.

[13] *Congressional Globe*, Thirty-sixth Congress, First Session, 654.

[14] Samuel Sullivan Cox, *Three Decades of Federal Legislation* (Providence, 1885), 96. One politician recalled: "It was unfortunately one of the evils of the times that political distinction and promotion often followed a fight, which made young men often seek them." Nash, *Biographical Sketches*, 150.

[15] *Congressional Globe*, Thirty-sixth Congress, Second Session, 78-79, 1864.

[16] *Little Rock True Democrat*, December 28, 1858.

[17] *Des Arc Citizen*, June 8, 1859; *Little Rock Arkansas State Gazette and Democrat*, June 13, 1857. Hereafter cited as *Little Rock Gazette*. Sebastian was not a secessionist and, commented Senator Johnson, was never "consulted by the leading men engaged in the secession movement." See John Mula, "The Public Career of William King Sebastian," (Master's thesis, University of Arkansas, 1969).

[18] *Little Rock Old Line Democrat*, September 15, 1859. This excessive laudation, a Dynasty paper reported, would "sicken and disgust an Eastern Sultan." Ibid., February 2, 1860.

[19] *Fayetteville Arkansian*, December 23, 1859.

[20] Ibid., January 6, 1859; *Des Arc Citizen*, January 4, 1860. Robert Toombs and Roger Pryor mediated the dispute.

[21] *Little Rock True Democrat*, February 29, 1860; *Des Arc Citizen*, December 7, 1859; *Little Rock Old Line Democrat*, February 9, 1860.

[22] *Litle Rock Gazette*, June 2, 1860.

[23] Nash, *Biographical Sketches*, 153-54, states that "he supervised and engineered all." See also *Little Rock Old Line Democrat*, July 24, 1860.

[24] *Van Buren Press*, May 25, 1860; *Little Rock True Democrat*, May 12 and 19, June 2, 1860.

²⁵ *Fayetteville Arkansian*, July 7, 1860.

²⁶ *Little Rock Gazette*, September 8, 1860.

²⁷ Diary of Judge John W. Brown, October 10 and November 6, 1860, microfilm, University of Arkansas. "The people of the county have been sadly blinded by falsehood and appeals to their Democratic prejudices so as to lose sight of the great issue in the contest, and most of the Democrats voted accordingly."

²⁸ *Little Rock Old Line Democrat*, December 20, 1860; *Little Rock Gazette*, December 29, 1860; *Fayetteville Arkansian*, February 8, 1861.

²⁹ *Congressional Globe*, Thirty-sixth Congress, Second Session, 281.

³⁰ U.S. War Department (comp.), *War of the Rebellion: A Compilation of the Official Records of the Union and Confederate Armies* (Washington, 1880-1901), Ser. I, I, 690. Hereafter cited as *Official Records*; unless otherwise noted, all references are to Ser. I.

³¹ *Batesville Democratic Sentinel*, December 13, 1859.

³² Nash, *Biographical Sketches*, 208-9. *Official Records*, III, 588.

³³ *Official Records*, III, 609-10, 616, 618, 716; XIII, 31; *Little Rock Gazette*, July 20, 1861. Hindman's detailed activities can be followed in the Thomas C. Hindman Papers, Record Group 109-121, National Archives. See also *Little Rock True Democrat*, November 7, 1861; Nathaniel Cheairs Hughes, Jr., *General William J. Hardee, Old Reliable* (Baton Rouge, 1965), 79-82.

³⁴ *Official Records*, IV, 489; LIII, 740.

³⁵ Ibid., IV, 489.

³⁶ *New Orleans Daily Picayune*, March 7, 1862.

³⁷ William G. Stevenson, *Thirteen Months in the Rebel Army* (New York, 1959), 88; Marcus J. Wright, *Arkansas in the War, 1861-1865* (Batesville, 1963), 62.

³⁸ Robert G. Hartje, *Van Dorn: The Life and Times of a Confederate General* (Nashville, 1967), 162-72.

³⁹ *Official Records*, X, Pt. 2, 547. What Hindman, Johnson and Beauregard did not know was that Richmond created a new department that same day and appointed Gen. John B. Magruder to command it. Ibid., IX, 713. However, Magruder never assumed command. In September, Congress inquired of the secretary of war about Hindman's assignment, and the secretary replied that he knew nothing of it. Ibid., Ser. IV, II, 73.

⁴⁰ Ibid., XIII, 874. T.H. Holmes to Jefferson Davis, August 28, 1862, Theophilus Holmes Papers, Duke University.

⁴¹ The Richmond authorities failed to consider the defense of the Mississippi River as a whole. Instead, one general defended one side and another the other. When Secretary Randolph told Holmes (without telling Davis) that Holmes could march to the aid of Vicksburg, Davis confronted Randolph with charges of encroaching on the president's powers. Randolph thereupon resigned. See Robert L. Kerby, *Kirby Smith's Confederacy, The Trans-Mississippi South, 1863-1865* (New York, 1972), 431-32; Burton J. Hendrick, *Statesmen of the Lost Cause* (New York, 1939), 325. As for Holmes, his minister wrote, his "memory, will,

judgment, all debilitated to a degree which incapacitates him for any efficient administration." Henry C. Lay to Mrs. Lay, February 18 and 24, 1863, Henry C. Lay Papers, *Arkansas Gazette* Foundation Library. Kirby Smith came to believe that Holmes had softening of the brain. Thomas C. Reynolds, memorandum, August 27, 1863, Johnston Collection, Tulane University; *Official Records*, XXII, Pt. 1, 139. The only recent student of Hindman concluded: "Scholfield was more aware of the limitations within which he had to work, than was Hindman." Bobby Leon Roberts, "Thomas C. Hindman, Jr.: Secessionist and Confederate General" (Master's thesis, University of Arkansas, 1972), 100.

⁴² *Official Records*, XXII, Pt. 1, 79, 139, 143; John N. Edwards, *Shelby and His Men* (Cincinnati, 1867), 110-30.

⁴³ *Little Rock Arkansas Patriot*, January 8, 1863. Hindman subsequently attempted to show that he was still trusted by his men. *Official Records*, XXII, Pt. 2, 895-96. *The Patriot*, March 14, 1863, did not agree. Significantly, both the "family" *True Democrat* and the opposition *Gazette* continued to support him.

⁴⁴ *Official Records*, VI, 555-643; XXII, Pt. 2, 780. 895-96. The War Department even began addressing Hindman as brigadier general! Ibid., VI, 555. Seddon, who replaced Randolph, told Kirby Smith that Hindman was "perfectly odious" and the army "disaffected and hopeless." Ibid., XXII, Pt. 2, 802.

⁴⁵ Hindman anticipated most of the steps taken by Holmes's successor, Kirby Smith. See Kerby, *Kirby Smith*.

⁴⁶ *Official Records*, XXX, Pt. 4, 495.

⁴⁷ Stanley F. Horn, *The Army of Tennessee* (Norman, 1953), 283; Thomas L. Connelly, *Autumn of Glory: The Army of Tennessee, 1862-1865* (Baton Rouge, 1971), 175-84; *Official Records*, XXX, Pt. 2, 309-10.

⁴⁸ *Official Records*, XXX, Pt. 2, 309-10.

⁴⁹ Ibid., 311.

⁵⁰ Ibid., XXXI, Pt. 3, 833.

⁵¹ Ibid., XXXII, Pt. 2, 537; LII, Pt. 2, 594; Irving A. Buck, *Cleburne and his Command* (Jackson, Tenn., 1959), 188-200.

⁵² *Official Records*, XXXII, Pt. 2, 812.

⁵³ Ibid., LII, Pt. 2, 646-47.

⁵⁴ J.C. Higdon, "Hindman's Reply to Hood," *Confederate Veteran* VIII (1900), 69.

⁵⁵ *Official Records*, XXXVIII, Pt. 5, 5, 926, 953.

⁵⁶ Ibid., 926; LXI, Pt. 2, 1031, 1042.

⁵⁷ Ibid., IXVIII, Pt. 2, 767.

⁵⁸ Ted R. Worley (ed.), "A Letter Written by General Thomas C. Hindman in Mexico," *Arkansas Historical Quarterly* XV (1956), 365-68.

⁵⁹ Nash, *Biographical Sketches*, 216.

⁶⁰ Roberts, "Hindman," 156.

⁶¹ Thomas S. Staples, *Reconstruction in Arkansas, 1862-1874* (New York, 1923), 170.

⁶² *Little Rock Gazette*, September 29, 1868.

[63] Ibid., October 4 and November 21, 1868.
[64] Powell Clayton, *Aftermath of the Civil War in Arkansas* (New York, 1915), 91-96.
[65] Horn, *Army of Tennessee*, 251.
[66] *Little Rock Gazette*, September 29, 1868.

III

Rise to Glory:
A Speculative Essay on the
Early Career of John Bell Hood

By RICHARD M. McMURRY

A 1960 issue of the *Army Quarterly and Defence Journal* contained an article by Lieutenant Colonel Alfred H. Burne entitled "General J.B. Hood." This essay attempted to answer the question, "Was Hood a general of strategical ability?" Burne's conclusion was a surprising yes. The justification for this answer was a quick and superficial survey of the 1864 campaigns in Georgia and Tennessee during which Hood commanded the Confederate Army of Tennessee. Burne dismissed any consideration of Hood's career prior to assuming command of the army as irrelevant to the question of the general's ability as a strategist. "It would therefore be [a] waste of time to examine Hood's early military career," Burne wrote, "for he was a West Point cadet with only eight years' commissioned service and he had never commanded an independent army till, on the 18th [of] July, 1864, he took over J.B. [*sic*] Johnston's defeated army of Atlanta."[1]

Both Burne's premise and conclusion are questionable. An examination of the general's life, although greatly hindered by a lack of information, indicates that Hood's early career was not unimportant. In fact, the general's career as an army commander and strategist cannot be satisfactorily explained without a consideration of the factors that shaped his mind and personality prior to the day he assumed command of an army and, for the first time, attempted to devise and implement strategy.

The major obstacle to interpreting Hood's early career is a lack of evidence. Little is known of either his boyhood years or his family. Only relatively limited information is available about his adult life prior to the second year of the Civil War when he emerged as a prominent Southern general.[2] This paucity of evidence stems in large part from the fact that Hood seems to have been a man who wrote few personal letters. He probably was not close to his parents or other relatives, and he did not marry until 1868. Furthermore, his father died in 1857, and during the Civil War most of his family lived behind Union lines in Kentucky. Thus, there were few people to whom he would or could write regularly.

Any study of Hood's pre-1864 career is further hampered by the poor quality of much of the available evidence. Hood proved such an easy target for Civil War biographers and historians that much of his story has been distorted. For instance, Hood had been so spectacularly unsuccessful as an army commander that he could be labeled incompetent without much risk to those who would make him a scapegoat. Moreover, Hood's early death in 1879 left a clear field for those who, in the 1880s and 1890s, desired to criticize him. Because of the limited evidence, therefore, any evaluation of Hood's early career must rest in large part upon reasoned speculation. Nevertheless, grounds exist for reaching the tentative conclusion that much of what Hood did as a commanding general grew out of his earlier experiences. This essay is an attempt to define those experiences and to explore their possible influence upon Hood's later career.

John Bell Hood was born on June 29, 1831, in Owingsville, Bath County, Kentucky. He spent his early years on his father's farm near Mount Sterling in Montgomery County, some thirty miles east of Lexington in the Bluegrass region. The time and place of his birth and his boyhood environment combined to make him unique among the eight men who served the Confederacy as full generals. He was the only one born in the Old South — in effect, he was the only true Southerner among them. This play on words is, nonetheless, of much importance in explaining Hood's career.

Historians are generally agreed that in the 1820s and 1830s the people of the South first began to sense a real awareness of their region's separate identity and of themselves as a distinct people. This development was largely the product of the South's economic difficulties in those decades and of the Southern reaction to the abolitionist crusade and to Northerners' criticisms of slavery. As the Southern people coalesced through this new understanding of themselves, they gradually abandoned their earlier devotion to the liberal ideals of Thomas Jefferson.

They began increasingly to follow leaders who stressed the uniqueness of their region and the necessity of conformity in defense of the South and all her institutions. The ultimate result of this change was to produce the Southerner — a person progressively more isolated from the ouside world and filled with erroneous and unrealistic ideas about both himself and the North.

The Southern people were thus increasingly submerged in romanticism and emotionalism. In this frame of mind they created and apparently came to believe the myth of Southern chivalry — that white Southerners were the descendants of the feudal, Norman aristocracy of England and, as such, were characterized by all of the virtues associated with true aristocrats. Such a belief influenced their actions in almost every area of endeavor.[3] John Bell Hood was the only full general of the Confederacy born and raised in this environment.[4]

In the 1780s, Hood's grandfather had moved from Virginia to Kentucky. His father, John W. Hood, was a frontier doctor who prospered during the 1830s and 1840s. He broadened his holdings until he owned more than 600 acres of land and perhaps as many as thirty slaves.[5] Dr. Hood also traveled often to Philadelphia to study medicine and to present his own theories on the causes and cures of various diseases.[6] Nothing is known of his personality, but he may have been one of the common types of the Old South, the arriviste, the nouveau riche, the man successful enough to purchase land and slaves, who envisaged his family rising from frontier conditions into the ranks of the planter aristocracy.

Though speculation, it seems certain that young John Bell Hood grew up in a family that did not know poverty and in an environment that was much influenced by the rapidly developing romanticism of the South. The Bluegrass region in which he spent his youth was the most Southern-oriented part of Kentucky. That state was still very much under the spell of Virginia, from which many of her people had come and which remained the ideal of Southern chivalry.[7] Perhaps, because of the family's recent rise to affluence, the Hoods were more than ordinarily affected by the desire to be Southern. It thus appears that the romantic, unrealistic atmosphere of the Old South was the first factor that shaped the career of General Hood.

Furthermore, Hood never left this environment. His experiences at West Point and in the United States Army took place in similar surroundings that were not conducive to realistic thinking. Nor, so far as the evidence shows, did he ever undergo any personal experience that might have led him to question the assumptions of Southern romanticism. While such things cannot be precisely documented, perhaps some of

Hood's conduct as an army commander owed at least a part of its origin to the romanticism of the South of the 1830s and 1840s and to the environment in which he grew up, one that encouraged immaturity and adolescence.

Historian Charles Fair has recently advanced the thesis that some generals fail because they too perfectly represent the era and society from which they come. In other words, a general's strategy is often dictated by the nature of his society. A general who is too far out of line with his nation's ideals will not be given high command, regardless of his abilities. Conversely, an incompetent general, if he reflects a society's values, can rise to high command — even if his rise results in disaster. Such, it seems, was the case with Hood. His attitude is exemplified by his 1864 plan to capture Nashville by storming the fortifications around the city with only 700 men. It would be difficult to think of a more unrealistic plan.[8]

In 1849, Hood was appointed to the United States Military Academy. His career at West Point was not spectacular. He experienced great difficulty with academic subjects and the rules and regulations of cadet life. In his senior year he came within four demerits of expulsion. He graduated in 1853, ranking forty-fourth among the fifty-two members of his class. Nevertheless, in June, 1853, he was commissioned a brevet second lieutenant in the United States Infantry.[9]

Probably the greatest importance of West Point to Hood's career lies in his early contact with Col. Robert E. Lee who, in 1852, became superintendent of the academy. Although the young cadet was probably not very close to Lee during his last year at the academy, those months may well have marked the beginning of the relationship between Lee and Hood which seems to have been the second factor in molding the general.[10]

Following graduation, Hood reported for duty with the Fourth U.S. Infantry in California where he spent about eighteen months engaged in routine duties. In August, 1855, he received orders to join the newly created Second U.S. Cavalry Regiment destined for patrol and garrison duty in Texas. For the remainder of his career in the United States Army, Hood was a member of that unit.

Transfer to the Second Cavalry renewed Hood's association with Lee, who was the regiment's lieutenant colonel. Over the next six years, Hood and Lee were often in contact. Sometimes they were the only officers stationed at a particular post, and they seem to have spent a great deal of time together. Hood later wrote that during this period they often rode together and that Lee offered him advice on such matters as marriage.[11]

These experiences probably strengthened the admiration that Hood felt for Lee. It was not unusual for young officers to esteem Lee, but one senses that Hood's admiration was especially intense. In fact, Lee may have become something of a father figure for the young lieutenant. Hood even wrote that Lee's advice on marriage "was offered with all the earnestness of a parent" and that it was "fatherly advice" that was willingly received and remembered. Lee thus seems to have become the model for Hood in very much the same way that George Washington had been the model for Lee.[12]

In selecting Lee as a model, Hood faced a dilemma. Lee was the last and best of the eighteenth-century Virginia aristocrats. His most recent biographer calls him "a product of eighteenth-century Virginia's 'golden age' extended into the first quarter of the new century."[13] Lee was a true aristocrat in the best sense of the word. Such a quality cannot be consciously assumed. It is the product of many generations and a certain indefinable attitude that comes to only a few men and then only when their minds and characters are receptive to it. As unfashionable as it may sound, it takes "breeding" to be an aristocrat.[14] Lee had it; Hood did not, and that was his problem. The young lieutenant wanted to be a Southern aristocrat, but he did not have the necessary character, self-confidence or family background. Had Hood married well and retained his father's property, later generations of Hoods might have become aristocrats. As it was, he appears, like many Southerners, to have been only an awkward young man, fresh from a well-to-do frontier family, striving to affect aristocracy. Nevertheless, the relationship with Lee and the consequent desire to imitate the Virginian comprise the second factor in shaping Hood's outlook. Some of Hood's 1864 plans to replicate Lee's manner of conducting war grew, at least in part, out of this relationship. His attacks on Sherman's armies around Atlanta, especially his plan to flank Sherman in the Battle of Atlanta on July 22, and his assault on the entrenched Federal position at Franklin, Tennessee, on November 30, are probable examples of this desire.[15]

In April, 1861, Hood resigned from the United States Army and offered his services to the Confederacy. He was commissioned a first lieutenant of cavalry and sent to Kentucky on a recruiting mission. He was soon promoted to captain of cavalry and ordered to Virginia.[16] When he reached Richmond, Hood reported to Gen. Robert E. Lee, who was assigning newly arrived officers to those areas of Virginia where they were most needed. After a brief reunion with Lee, Hood was ordered to Yorktown to report to Col. John B. Magruder as an instructor of the cavalry assembling there. Hood's promotion to major followed quickly, and by late July he was a lieutenant colonel.[17] On July 12, he was involved in a brief engagement with a party of Federals near Hampton. The Southerners captured several Northerners, and Hood won lavish praise. In September, he was elevated to colonel and given command of the Fourth Texas Infantry Regiment.[18]

Why Hood was chosen to command this regiment remains a mystery. The Fourth Texas had been accepted into Confederate service by companies. Under Confederate law, regiments accepted by companies would be commanded by officers selected by the president. After the Fourth Texas was organized at Richmond, President Jefferson Davis chose Col. R.T.P. Allen as its commander. Allen, something of a martinet, proved so unpopular with both officers and men that he was unable to exercise effective command and was soon transferred to another area. The men of the regiment wanted a commander easygoing enough to understand the undisciplined Texans but qualified to be a capable combat leader. They also expressed preference for a Texan.[19]

Davis undoubtedly wanted an officer who was qualified to command. At this juncture, someone—perhaps Lee—may have suggested Hood as the man who could solve the problem. Hood was immediately at hand, was qualified for the command, and had chosen to associate himself with Texas by "adopting" that state and listing his state as Kentucky-Texas in Confederate records. Furthermore, Hood was of striking presence, over six feet tall, and could probably defeat almost any member of the unit in a fist fight should such discipline prove necessary. If these speculations are correct, Hood was the logical choice to fill the vacancy.

Whatever the reason for his selection, Hood proved to be a superb commander. Over the next few months he molded his regiment into one of the best infantry units on either side. The assignment to the Fourth Texas may also have marked the entrance of the ungainly young officer into the upper circles of Confederate society. The lieutenant colonel of the regiment was John Marshall, a newspaperman and longtime friend of President Davis. The major was Bradfute Warwick, a young Virginian from one of Richmond's wealthiest families.[20] Marshall and Warwick may have introduced their young colonel to many of the prominent political figures who would later select him for higher commands.

In November, 1861, Hood's regiment was moved from its camp near Richmond to Dumfries, on the Potomac, where it was combined with the First and Fifth Texas Regiments and the Eighteenth Georgia to form a brigade under Brig. Gen. Louis T. Wigfall. Hood spent the winter of 1861-1862 at Dumfries, training his men and preparing for the spring campaign. In February, 1862, Wigfall resigned from the army to devote his time to the Confederate Senate. Command of the brigade normally devolved upon the senior colonel. Early in March, however, orders from

Richmond announced that Hood, who was junior to two other regimental commanders in the brigade, had been selected as Wigfall's replacement and promoted to brigadier general. Although Hood had been a capable regimental commander, no extant evidence justifies his elevation over two senior colonels.[21] It may have been that President Davis desired to promote his friend Marshall to colonel, which could only be done by elevating Hood to brigade commander. At any rate, Hood, Marshall and Warwick each stepped up one grade to fill the vacancies created by Wigfall's decision to serve in Congress rather than in the field.

Hood's promotion to brigade commander set the stage for the third experience that apparently shaped his concept of warfare—the summer battles of 1862. When the campaigns of that summer began, Hood was an unknown brigadier in Lee's army. Three months later he stood high in the ranks of Confederate heroes of the Army of Northern Virginia. Indeed, no more than four men—Lee, Stonewall Jackson, James Longstreet and J.E.B. Stuart—stood higher. Hood won this reputation by his role in three great battles of that summer: Gaines's Mill, Second Manassas and Antietam.

Gaines's Mill, fought on June 27 as part of the Seven Days campaign, proved to be especially significant in Hood's career. For that engagement Lee had concentrated the bulk of his army north of the Chickahominy River to attack what was believed to be the most exposed and weakest part of the Federal Army of the Potomac then threatening Richmond. Only a small force of Confederates remained south of the river between the bulk of the Federal army and the Confederate capital. The Southern commander took a great risk; for should he be defeated north of the Chickahominy, Gen. George B. McClellan, the Federal commander, could easily move forward and capture Richmond. On June 26, a Confederate assault against the Union position at Mechanicsville north of the river failed with heavy losses. Therefore, the stakes were very high on June 27, when the Confederates advanced against the new Union position at Gaines's Mill.

All that afternoon, Lee watched as his men attacked and then were thrown back from the strong Federal position at Gaines's Mill. By midafternoon Lee was worried. Another defeat of the Southerners north of the river might awaken McClellan to the opportunity open to him on the opposite bank. Such a setback would be disastrous to Lee and the Confederacy. As the Southern commander faced this unhappy prospect, a column of troops emerged from the woods to his rear. This was Hood's Texas Brigade and another brigade under the command of Col. Evander M. Law. Together these brigades constituted a small division under Brig.

Gen. William Henry Chase Whiting. During the early part of the battle, these troops had been lost in the woods with a column that was supposed to enter the battle on the right flank and rear of the Federal position. At about 4:30 P.M., Whiting's troops marched onto the field at the decisive place. The outcome of the battle and the career of John Bell Hood would both be changed by the events of the next few hours.

Lee directed Whiting to throw his brigades against the center of the Federal position. Almost immediately after giving this order, the commanding general encountered Hood. To his young brigadier Lee asserted that the enemy must be dislodged and asked, "Can you break his line?" Hood replied that he would try.[22]

Then, under the eyes of Lee and with the fate of the Southern cause riding on their flags, Hood's regiments, supported by Law's, advanced against the position that for so long had defied Confederate attacks. With Hood dismounted and personally leading the Fourth Texas, the infantry crossed the gap between the armies, broke the Federal lines and, just as the sun was setting, chased the Northerners from the field. The day was saved for Lee; so was his cause and his reputation. Hood and the Texans had done it — or at least they received credit for doing it.

In fact, the Federals had been worn down by the long afternoon's battle, many of their weapons had been fouled by constant use, and a brigade had been drawn out of their line and sent to reinforce another point shortly before the final attack. Furthermore, other Confederate units broke through the Northern position at about the same moment. Despite these facts (many unknown to the Southerners at the time) Hood and the Texans received the accolades for breaking the enemy's line and driving him from the field. In truth, Hood and his men had performed a brave and brilliant feat. Hood's leadership had made the assault successful and demonstrated that a forceful attack, driven home at the decisive moment, could turn the tide of battle. In addition, Hood's attack had taken place under the eyes of Lee who, from that moment forward, reserved a special place in his affection for the Texans.

Due to his success at Gaines's Mill, Hood emerged from the Seven Days battles with a much higher reputation than he had enjoyed when they began. The poor showing of other Confederates in the Seven Days left Hood as almost the only Southern general whose reputation was enhanced. Where other leaders had become exhausted or querulous or had displayed undue panic or had confused routes of march, Hood had performed well in his only assigned task. He had been ordered to attack; he had done so, and the enemy had been routed.

After the Seven Days, illness forced Whiting to go on leave. His departure put Hood, as the ranking officer present, in command of Whiting's small division. It was with this command that Hood participated in the battles of Second Manassas and Antietam. On August 30, 1862, Hood's division was posted in the center of the Confederate line on the battlefield of Manassas. His command was then a part of Maj. Gen. James Longstreet's wing of the army. In the afternoon of August 30, the Federals, commanded by Gen. John Pope, launched a massive attack against part of the Southern line. Confederate infantry and artillery fire broke Pope's charging columns. Longstreet then loosed a counterattack. Hood's men took the lead, capturing prisoners, flags and cannon. Douglas Freeman, the historian of Lee's army, evaluated Hood's performance in this battle as "magnificent" and observed that he represented the new type of officer now coming into prominence — young generals who were capable in administration, were characterized by firm, intelligent discipline and gloried in combat.[23]

Hood's finest hour as a Confederate commander came on September 17, 1862, in the battle of Antietam. In that battle Hood's small division was thrown into the fight on the Confederate left at a time when it appeared that the advancing Federals would sweep all before them. Federal Gen. Joseph Hooker's First Corps had smashed into Stonewall Jackson's position, killed, wounded or captured many of Jackson's men and shattered the Southern line. Hood's troops were rushed up to meet this threat. With fewer than 2,000 men, Hood attacked Hooker's advancing Northerners. Hood's troops were, as one historian has called them, "the finger in the dyke," holding back the Federal advance. They stopped Hooker and then, under Hood's supervision, began to drive back the Unionists. Jackson sent a messenger to ask about the situation. "Tell General Jackson unless I get help I will be forced back," replied Hood, "but I am going on while I can!"

So ferocious was Hood's attack that his men nearly routed their opponents. Only a well-served artillery battery saved the Federal right. Hooker's corps dropped out of the fight, but Gen. J.K.F. Manfield's Twelfth Corps took its place. After this action the fighting died away on Jackson's front. Hood fell back to rest his men. His casualties had been high. To an officer who asked, "Where is your division?" Hood replied, "Dead on the field."[24]

Hood's performance during the summer of 1862 had won wide attention. It had been his good fortune to fight his battles under the eyes of the three ranking commanders of the army — Lee at Gaines's Mill, Longstreet at Second Manassas, and Jackson at Antietam. In his report of the attack at Gaines's Mill, Lee recalled "the brave Texans" leading the

Southern charge, "followed closely by their no less daring comrades." Longstreet's report of Second Manassas emphasized that "the attack was led by Hood's brigades." After Antietam, Jackson, who had already expressed admiration for Hood's assault at Gaines's Mill, joined the chorus of approval. Even though Hood was not a member of his command, Jackson recommended that the young brigadier be promoted.[25]

When Lee's army was reorganized after Antietam, Hood's was one of the most deserved promotions to major general. He was given command of an enlarged division (four brigades) and assigned to Longstreet's corps. Hood's new command was but lightly engaged at Fredericksburg in December, 1862; and in the following spring, the division accompanied Longstreet on the frustrating expedition against Suffolk, Virginia.[26]

After Jackson's death in May, 1863, Hood was among the few generals whom Lee considered as a possible replacement for the great Stonewall. After selecting Richard S. Ewell and A.P. Hill as new corps commanders for the army (now reorganized into three corps), Lee paused to evaluate the Texan (as Hood was now universally regarded). Hood, Lee wrote, was a "capital officer," who would "make [a] good corps commander if necessary."[27] This was high praise indeed for a man who, only twelve months earlier, had been an unknown brigadier.

The year 1863 marked a turning point for Hood. He led his division into Pennsylvania and, on July 2, to the terrain southwest of Gettysburg. There, just as his troops were entering the battle, Hood was struck in the left arm by a shell fragment. The wound, although not serious, threw him from his horse in a state of shock.[28] He took no further part in the battle and was sent back to Virginia. He was in Richmond in September, when Longstreet's troops passed through the capital on their way west to help redeem Confederate fortunes in Tennessee and northern Georgia. In response to an appeal from some officers in his division, Hood, although not completely recovered from his Gettysburg wound, agreed to return to his command.

On September 20, Hood was advancing along Chickamauga Creek in north Georgia. He was in command of an assault column that Longstreet launched against the Federal lines. Once more, and for the last time, fortune was with John Bell Hood. Just as the Confederate advance was getting underway, a misunderstanding of orders caused the Federals to pull a division from their line at the very point where Hood's attack was to come. Into this gap dashed Hood's men. The Northern line broke and most of the Federal troops fled from the field.[29] Hood, however, was again wounded. A Federal bullet struck his right leg, so mangling the limb that it had to be amputated at the hip. First accounts of the battle reported him killed. In Virginia Lee wrote, "I am gradually losing my best men—Jackson, [Major General William Dorsey] Pender [mortally wounded at Gettysburg], Hood." The *Richmond Enquirer* lamented that any victory that cost the Confederacy the life of Hood was "most dearly purchased."[30]

After a period of rest and recovery in Georgia, Hood in mid-November made his way to Richmond. In the capital he was hailed as a great hero and exposed to the pandemonium of Richmond society, for which he was probably not ready. Few details are known of his life in Richmond during the three relaxing months in the winter of 1863-1864. Piecemeal accounts of his activities appear in the diaries and memoirs of those who knew him then, but there is little of substance in these accounts. All that can be said with certainty is that he seems to have become fairly close to President Davis, that he became engaged to Sally Buchanan Campbell Preston, daughter of Col. John S. Preston, the chief of the Confederate conscript service, and that he was promoted to lieutenant general and assigned to duty as a corps commander in the Army of Tennessee.

Accounts of Hood's relations with the president are chiefly found in the diary of Mary Boykin Chesnut, who recorded that the wounded general attended receptions at the president's mansion, dined with the president's family, used the president's carriage, and sat in the president's pew at church. By mid-January, 1864, Hood was well enough to mount a horse, and he accompanied the president on rides around Richmond.[31] Historians have attempted to make much of this relationship. Many have maintained that Hood used this opportunity to ingratiate himself with the president and his military adviser, Gen. Braxton Bragg.[32] It is difficult to evaluate most of these assertions. Knowledge of Davis's treatment of other generals in similar circumstances is lacking. However, Hood and Bragg were apparently not close friends. Bragg did not arrive in Richmond until late January or early February, 1864. Since Hood left the capital about February 15, it seems unlikely that they could have become intimate.[33]

Little concrete evidence unravels Hood's relations with Sally Preston, who was known to her friends as "Buck." Mrs. Chesnut described Sally as "the very sweetest woman I ever knew, [who] had a knack of being fallen in love with at sight and of never being fallen out of love with."[34] Hood seems to have first met the attractive Miss Preston in March, 1863, while his division was near Richmond awaiting the move on Suffolk.[35] He was with her again in the late summer of 1863, when he was in Richmond convalescing from his Gettysburg wound. Just before leaving for

Chickamauga, Hood proposed to her and "she half promised to think of it." After his Chickamauga wound, Hood believed that Sally would not marry him. When he was back with her in Richmond, however, his hopes revived. Others thought that Hood was making a fool of himself among the Richmond belles, and a friend expressed a wish to see him back in the army. Nevertheless, when Hood left Richmond in February, 1864, he and Sally Preston were engaged.[36]

As early as September, 1863, after Hood's success at Chickamauga, a movement began to secure his promotion to lieutenant general. Both Bragg, who at that time commanded the Confederate army in Georgia, and Longstreet recommended the promotion. So did Secretary of War James A. Seddon. President Davis had even written that he would promote Hood to the rank of lieutenant general.[37] Some writers have maintained that Davis decided to use Hood as an informer against Gen. Joseph E. Johnston, the president's bitter enemy and Bragg's successor as commander of the Army of Tennessee. Hood, they believed, was to furnish the president with information on Johnston's plans.[38]

Although Hood did write unauthorized letters, often criticizing Johnston, to Davis and other Confederate officials during the spring and summer of 1864, no real evidence substantiates the supposition that Davis promoted Hood with this purpose in mind. On the contrary, there was a perfectly logical reason for elevating Hood and sending him to the West. A vacancy existed in the grade of lieutenant general in the Army of Tennessee. No officer then in that army was really qualified to fill the position. At the same time, Hood's record was better than that of any living Confederate major general. Finally, Davis was convinced that the Confederacy could triumph only if its armies took the offensive. Hood was an officer whose record was built around offensive action. For the second time, Hood seemed the logical officer for Davis to promote.

As a corps commander, Hood's record was not good. During the early summer of 1864, he won no major victories and criticized his commanding officer—charges that some historians believe led to the removal of Johnston and the appointment of Hood to lead the Army of Tennessee.[38] However, Hood's record as a corps commander must be kept in perspective. No other corps commander in the Army of Tennessee did any better.

By July, 1864, Johnston had retreated from northern Georgia to the very outskirts of Atlanta, a crucial railroad and manufacturing center that in many ways was the key to holding the states of Georgia, Alabama and Mississippi under the effective control of the Confederate government. Johnston had given no sign that he would be able to stop the Federal advance that had pushed him back so far and that seemed destined to take Atlanta. Therefore, on July 17, President Davis reluctantly decided that Johnston must be removed and replaced by Hood.

Here, for the final time, Hood was the logical and perhaps inevitable choice. Lt. Gen. William J. Hardee, the senior corps commander, was not selected because he had declined command of the army the winter before. In addition, Hardee was a bitter enemy of Gen. Braxton Bragg, President Davis's military adviser. Therefore, Hardee probably could not have worked well with the Confederate government. The third corps commander of the army was Lt. Gen. A.P. Stewart, who had been made a corps commander only ten days prior to the removal of Johnston. The delay that would follow if anyone outside the army were brought in to replace Johnston dictated that the new commander had to come from the army's ranks. Hood was the only alternative.

However, the Hood who assumed command during the night of July 17-18 was not the tabula rasa that Lieutenant Colonel Burne seemed to think he was. Hood was the Southerner personified. His attitude had been shaped by his early life in the Kentucky Bluegrass by his contact with the Southern ideal of chivalry, especially as embodied in Robert E. Lee, and by his great success in the battles of 1862, which had come from direct attacks on enemy positions. Hood's virtues were those of the Southerner. He was physically brave; he was superb in leading men into battle where his large physique, his booming voice and his personal conduct could inspire his followers to deeds of great valor. Yet his Southernness was also his greatest weakness. Hood seems to have been emotional and intuitive. He was unrealistic. He did not thoroughly plan his operations. He was unaware of or unwilling to devote the necessary time to such matters as logistics. Like many Southern generals, he could not command; he could only lead. Physically, by 1864, he was incapable of close supervision of his army's battles. Thus he could not use an army to best advantage. His concept of warfare was pretty much that of the feudal knight whose glory was in battle but who fell before the more ordered armies of professional mercenaries and even of lowly townsmen who were flexible enough to introduce new tactics and weapons.

NOTES

[1] Alfred H. Burne, "General J.B. Hood," *Army Quarterly and Defence Journal*, LXXIX (1959-1960), 220-29. The long quotation is on p. 220; Burne's conclusion, on p. 228. Burne's article appeared posthumously. The writer hopes that

he is fair in using quotations that Burne probably never saw in galley proof. Several friends and colleagues have read this essay, and it has profited greatly from their advice and criticism. They, of course, are not responsible for errors of fact or interpretation.

[2] Book-length biographies of Hood are John P. Dyer, *The Gallant Hood* (Indianapolis and New York, 1950) and Richard O'Connor, *Hood: Cavalier General* (New York, 1949). Recent, shorter treatments of his life are Harold B. Simpson, "John Bell Hood," in W. C. Nunn (ed.), *Ten Texans in Gray* (Hillsboro, Tex. 1968), 55-75; Paul E. Steiner, "General John B. Hood, C. S. Army," *Medical-Military Portraits of Union and Confederate Generals* (Philadelphia, 1968), 215-36; Gerard A. Patterson, "John Bell Hood," *Civil War Times Illustrated*, IX, No. 10 (February, 1971), 12-21; Joseph B. Mitchell, "John Bell Hood," *Military Leaders in the Civil War* (New York, 1972), 193-214. Treatments of his Confederate career are in Douglas S. Freeman, *Lee's Lieutenants: A Study in Command* (New York, 1942-1944) and Thomas Lawrence Connelly, *Autumn of Glory: The Army of Tennessee, 1862-1865* (Baton Rouge, 1971).

[3] The literature on this subject is immense, and no attempt will be made to compile a complete list here. Good treatments may be found in Joseph C. Robert, *The Road from Monticello: A Study of the Virginia Slavery Debate of 1832* (Durham, 1941); Clement Eaton, *The Freedom-of-Thought Struggle in the Old South* (Durham, 1940; New York, 1964); Rollin G. Osterweis, *Romanticism and Nationalism in the Old South* (New Haven, 1949); W. J. Cash, *The Mind of the South* (New York, 1971); and T. Harry Williams, *Romanticism and Realism in Southern Politics (Baton Rouge, 1966).*

[4] With one exception, the Confederacy's other full generals were all born prior to 1820. In age, only Edmund Kirby Smith, born in 1824 in Florida, of New England parents, can be compared to Hood. Smith's family, however, was living in the South because his father had received an appointment as a federal judge. His family background separates him from the Southerners as that term is used here. See Joseph H. Parks, *General Edmund Kirby Smith* (Baton Rouge, 1954), 2-12.

[5] Dyer, *Hood*, 21, 326. Destruction of county records makes it impossible to ascertain the exact number of slaves.

[6] Ibid., 20-25.

[7] E. Merton Coulter, *The Civil War and Readjustment in Kentucky* (Gloucester, Mass., 1966), 8, 121-23; Cash, *Mind of the South*, 61-66; Garven Davenport, *Ante-Bellum Kentucky: A Social History* (Oxford, O., 1943), 15; Thomas D. Clark, *Kentucky: Land of Contrast* (New York, 1968), 3, 32, 71; Arthur K. Moore, *The Frontier Mind: A Cultural Analysis of the Kentucky Frontiersman* (Lexington, 1957), 150-51.

[8] Charles Fair, *From the Jaws of Victory* (New York, 1971), 11, 18, 21, 56-57, 270; Charles T. Quintard, *Diary*, November 27, 1864, University of the South.

[9] Dyer, *Hood*, 27-34.

[10] In his memoirs Hood wrote that he had "become very much attached" to Lee "at West Point where he was Superintendent whilst I was a cadet." J. B.

Hood, *Advance and Retreat: Personal Experiences in the United States Confederate States Armies* (Bloomington, 1959), 7. However, it seems unlikely that the relationship was very close in 1852-1853.

[11] Ibid., 7-8.

[12] Hood, *Advance and Retreat*, 8. On the Washington-Lee relationship, see Douglas S. Freeman, *R.E. Lee: A Biography* (New York, 1934-1935), I, 21-23, 44n., 109-10, 131, 169; IV, 202, 217; Clifford Dowdey, *Lee* (Boston, 1965), 34.

[13] Dowdey, *Lee*, 43.

[14] See the comments in Freeman, *Lee*, I. Chap. 10, especially p. 164; Cash *Mind of the South*, 70-72; Clifford Dowedy, *The Virginia Dynasties: The Emergence of "King" Carter and the Golden Age* (Boston, 1969), 8-9, 375-76.

[15] See Connelly, *Army of the Heartland*, 432, 502, 504; Hood, *Advance and Retreat*, Chap. 8.

[16] Service Record of Gen. John Bell Hood, National Archives; U.S. War Department (comp.), *War of the Rebellion: A Compilation of the Official Records of the Union and Confederate Armies* (Washington, 1880-1901), Ser. I, LII, Pt. 2, 68. Cited hereafter as *Official Records*, with all references to Ser. I.

[17] Freeman, *Lee*, I, 487; Hood, *Advance and Retreat*, 16-17; *Official Records*, II, 132, 576, 883; LI, Pt. 2, 122.

[18] *Official Records*, II, 296-98. Hood assumed command of the Fourth Texas on October 1, 1861. His date of rank as colonel was September 30. See Harold B. Simpson, *Hood's Texas Brigade: Lee's Grenadier Guard* (Waco, 1970), 69-73; General Order No. 1, Headquarters Fourth Texas Regiment, October 1, 1861, in the Frederic W. Pechin Collection of Civil War Papers, Civil War Miscellaneous Collection, U.S. Military History Research Collection, Carlisle Barracks, Pa.

[19] See Simpson, *Hood's Texas Brigade*, 61-62.

[20] For information on Marshall and Warwick, see Donald E. Everett (ed.), *Chaplain Davis and Hood's Texas Brigade: Being an Expanded Edition of the Reverend Nicholas A. Davis' "The Campaign from Texas to Maryland with the Battle of Sharpsburg"* (Richmond, 1863; San Antonio, 1962), 156-63; Mrs. A. Winkler, *The Confederate Capital and Hood's Texas Brigade* (Austin, 1894), 34-35.

[21] In his memoirs Hood stated that upon Wigfall's departure command of the brigade passed to Col. James J. Archer of the Fifth Texas. However, Col. William T. Wofford of the Eighteenth Georgia outranked both Archer and Hood and would normally have assumed command when Wigfall left. Unless Wofford was absent from the brigade at the time of Wigfall's departure, Hood's memoirs must be in error. Hood, *Advance and Retreat*, 20; Lillian Henderson (comp.), *Roster of the Confederate Soldiers of Georgia, 1861-1865* (Hapeville, 1958-1965, II, 614.

[22] Hood, *Advance and Retreat*, 25. For general accounts of the battle, see Freeman, *Lee*, II, 136-58; Freeman, *Lee's Lieutenants*, I, 517-37; Clifford Dowdey, *The Seven Days: The Emergence of Lee* (Boston, 1964), 221-45; Joseph P. Cullen, "Gaines's Mill," *Civil War Times Illustrated*, III, No. 1 (April, 1964), 10-17, 24.

[23] Freeman, *Lee's Lieutenants*, II, xiv, 138.

[24] Ibid., 205-09; Edward J. Stackpole, *From Cedar Mountain to Antietam, August-September, 1862* (Harrisburg, 1959), 381-88; James V. Murfin, *The Gleam of Bayonets: The Battle of Antietam and the Maryland Campaign of 1862* (New York, 1965), 211-44.

[25] *Official Records*, XI, Pt. 2, 493; XII, Pt. 2, 566; Frank E. Vandiver, *Mighty Stonewall* (New York, 1957), 309; Freeman, *Lee's Lieutenants*, II, 257.

[26] For accounts of this expedition, see Freeman, *Lee's Lieutenants*, II, 467-94.

[27] *Official Records*, XXV, Pt. 2, 811. Lee's statement, which evaluated Richard H. Anderson as well as Hood, has been quoted as singular. In the *Official Records*, the evaluation, which applied to both Hood and Anderson, is plural.

[28] John Cheves Haskell, *The Haskell Memoirs* (New York, 1960), 49-50.

[29] Glenn Tucker, *Chickamauga: Bloody Battle in the West* (Indianapolis, 1961), 260-78.

[30] *Official Records*, XXIX, Pt. 2, 743; Dyer, *Hood*, 211.

[31] Mary Boykin Chesnut, *A Diary from Dixie* (Cambridge, Mass., 1949), 349, 365, 368, 375, 379-80; Hood, *Advance and Retreat*, 67.

[32] See Dyer, *Hood*, 222-25; O'Connor, *Hood*, 174; Dowdey, *Lee*, 492; Ellsworth Eliot, Jr., *West Point in the Confederacy* (New York, 1971), 98; Stanley F. Horn, *The Decisive Battle of Nashville* (Baton Rouge, 1956), 5; Stanley F. Horn, *The Army of Tennessee* (Indianapolis, 1953), 318.

[33] *Official Records*, LII, Pt. 2, 607; James A. Seddon to Adjutant General, February 9, 1864, Hood Service Record.

[34] Chesnut, *Diary*, 280.

[35] Ibid., 296-98. This part of Mrs. Chesnut's diary is a later memoir. For information helpful in dating the events described by Mrs. Chesnut, see J. B. Polley, *A Soldier's Letters to Charming Nellie* (New York and Washington, 1908), 99-100.

[36] Chesnut, *Diary*, 341-42, 367.

[37] Longstreet to Gen. Samuel Cooper, September 24, 1863, with undated endorsement by Bragg and endorsement by Seddon, October 3, 1863, in Hood Service Record, *Official Records*, LII, Pt. 2, 555.

[38] Horn, *Army of Tennessee*, 318; Dyer, *Hood*, 228. Some writers have speculated about the psychological effects of Hood's mutilation. They contend that because of his wounds, Hood felt compelled to prove himself as a man and hence made irrational decisions. See Steiner, "Hood," 222-28, and Connelly, *Autumn of Glory*, 322. The evidence regarding Hood's psychological health is very sketchy, and any judgment about it must be highly dubious. Even if the wounds did produce such effects, they would merely constitute yet another pre-1864 factor that shaped his conduct as an army commander.

[39] See Gilbert E. Govan and James W. Livingood, *A Different Valor: The Story of General Joseph E. Johnston, C.S.A.* (Indianapolis, 1956), 310-13.

IV

Transatlantic Misunderstanding:
William Henry Seward and
the Declaration of
Paris Negotiation of 1861

By NORMAN B. FERRIS

At the outset of the American Civil War, diplomatic relations between the United States and Great Britain were in a precarious state. Fortunately, at that very moment American foreign policy passed into the hands of one of the great statesmen of the age, William Henry Seward. He had served two terms (1839-1843) as the first Whig governor of New York before advancing to the U.S. Senate. He was elected to that body first in 1849 as a Whig and then reelected in 1855 as a Republican. Always an independent thinker ahead of his time, Seward had refused to support the Compromise of 1850 because he was convinced that a higher law than the Constitution excluded slavery from American territories. He later warned that an "irrepressible conflict" would rip the nation asunder.

In 1860 he had been considered the leading candidate for the Republican presidential nomination. Yet Seward was charged with "radicalism" by political adversaries within the party, most of them former Jacksonian Democrats, Know-Nothings or ultraconservative Whigs. The anti-Seward forces succeeded in uniting behind Abraham Lincoln, a less formidable candidate whom each faction hoped to dominate once he was in the White House.

By education and experience Seward was as well qualified to conduct the nation's foreign affairs as any politically eligible contemporary—especially since most Americans with diplomatic experience had opposed Lincoln's election. His background and his power within the Republican party were instrumental in Seward's appointment as secretary of state. Seward was also well known for an intense humanitarian nationalism. He had frequently asserted that it was the glorious mission of the United States to set a compelling example as a free and prosperous society and eventually to spread its democratic system of government throughout the Western Hemisphere. American expansion was inevitable, he felt, but it should always be accomplished by peaceful means.

It was ironic, therefore, that Seward's first major task as secretary of state was not to promote national expansion but to prevent foreign intervention from destroying the American Union. In 1861, many arrogant expressions from Europe indicated the desire of some foreign powers either to meddle in the American conflict to advance their own commercial interests or to seize the opportunity to initiate adventures in Central America. An almost universal supposition among European diplomats and political leaders was that the Union was irrevocably divided; for many of them the wish was undoubtedly father to the thought. Such suppositions were likely to lead to a widespread recognition of Confederate independence—after which trade interests in the cotton states might induce armed intervention to help preserve that independence. By May, 1861, the first step in that direction had been taken in the form of a British proclamation of neutrality granting the Southern insurrectionists the rights of belligerents under international law. The British minister in Washington warned the Lincoln administration that a blockade of the Southern ports might bring the great powers into the North-South quarrel on the side of the slaveholders.

Almost from the moment he took office as Lincoln's secretary of state, William H. Seward anticipated that European governments "would naturally feel a deep anxiety about the safety of their commerce, threatened distinctly with privateering by the insurgents." Traditionally, when the United States waged war with foreign nations, letters of marque, licensing privately owned vessels to seize foreign merchant ships trading with an enemy country, supplemented a weak regular navy. Seward felt that "the danger of . . . depredation upon commerce equally by the government itself and by its enemies" would stimulate the great maritime powers of Europe to proclaim their neutrality in the developing conflict. Any declaration of neutrality by a foreign government granting belligerent rights to the Southerners would constitute a serious step toward full diplomatic recognition of the South as an independent nation. Seward therefore hastened to offer European governments assurances that "we did not desire to depredate on friendly commerce ourselves, and we thought it our duty to prevent such depredations by the insurgents in executing our own laws."[1]

From the American viewpoint, the conflict was a domestic rebellion in which neither protagonist, without being technically at war, could be classed as a belligerent under international law. Hence, neither side could legally issue letters of marque as a belligerent right, although the United States might adopt such measures as a right of internal police power. Therefore, Seward was willing to abandon the right of privateering which the United States, intending to assemble a powerful navy, no longer needed to exercise. In return, he sought an agreement among the great European maritime powers to refuse Southern privateers use of their overseas ports. Confederate President Jefferson Davis's proclamation of Confederate privateers had caused near panic in Northern shipping circles. Visions of rebel corsairs operating from West Indian bases and sweeping the seas of American merchantmen led to frantic appeals to Washington for protection. Seward could best provide such safeguards by negotiating an agreement binding the maritime powers of Europe not to interfere with the efforts of the United States to rid the world's waterways of Southern privateers.[2]

Seward hoped to accomplish this through the Declaration of Paris of 1856 — an agreement by which the European powers sought to resolve long-standing disputes over points of international maritime law. The first of four articles of the declaration bound participating governments to renounce privateering. By joining the European governments already adhering to this article, the Lincoln administration would presumably force them to close their ports to Confederate privateers as piratical vessels with no legal rights on the high seas.[3]

Seward also envisioned a long-term advantage for the United States in its adherence to the other three articles of the Paris declaration. These stipulations provided that noncontraband goods on enemy ships would be exempt from capture in wartime. Furthermore, blockades, to be respected by neutrals, had to be "maintained by a force sufficient really to prevent access to the coast of the enemy." As a probable neutral in future wars, the United States might expect to grow rich trading with the belligerents. However, its neutral rights would have to be protected by the Declaration of Paris to minimize, even entirely avert, the danger of being drawn into a foreign fray.

The secretary of state directed his ministers in Europe to ascertain whether the governments would negotiate a treaty with the United States for its accession to the Declaration of Paris. It was "eminently desirable," Seward continued, that the so-called Marcy amendment, a proposal exempting noncontraband belligerent private property from seizure aboard belligerent ships, be incorporated into the declaration. The United States government had not abandoned the idea that maritime wars ought to be limited to battles between government warships leaving all commerce, except in munitions, relatively unhindered. Yet in view of the rebellion in the South and the further possibility of war occurring in Europe at any moment over such imbroglios as the Italian and Polish questions, the United States refused to sacrifice the immediate advantages of being included among the parties to the Declaration of Paris merely because of a temporary inability to gain further immunities for private property in future wars.[4]

British Foreign Minister Lord John Russell had anticipated that the outbreak of civil war in America might lead to serious transatlantic disputes between British mercantile seafarers trading with the cotton states and American warships assigned to prevent such trade. In order to avert as much confrontation as possible, Russell and the prime minister, Lord Palmerston, decided to proclaim British neutrality in regard to the warring factions in America. At the same time, the British minister in Washington, Lord Richard Bickerton Lyons, was to seek an American commitment not to interfere with British maritime commerce, except by regular blockage of enemy ports or except in cases when a prize court could clearly establish the conveyance of contraband of war. Russell ordered Lyons to ask Secretary Seward whether the United States government would adhere to the last three articles of the Declaration of Paris. Then the British ambassador was to ascertain if the Confederate States would agree, as recognized belligerents, to observe the rules of war laid down in the last three articles of the Declaration of Paris.[5]

Russell added that the French foreign minister was reluctant to propose that the United States accede to this article because the Confederate president had already issued letters of marque to Southern privateers. As long as the Lincoln administration classified the Confederates as rebels and claimed full jurisdiction over the Southern states, a danger existed that Washington authorities might insist that foreign governments adhere to the Paris declaration and treat Southern vessels sailing under letters of marque as pirates. French and British neutrality could not be maintained under such circumstances. Hence, although Lyons would "not err in encouraging the Government to which you are accredited to . . . recognize the Declaration of Paris in regard to privateering," he was also to "understand that her Majesty's government cannot accept the renunciation of privateering on the part of the government of the United States if coupled with the condition that they should enforce its renunciation on the Confederate States."[6]

On May 18, 1861, Charles Francis Adams, selected by Seward with Lincoln's reluctant consent to represent the United States in London, had his first interview with Russell. The British foreign minister had already learned unofficially that the United States government had instructed its envoy to propose its accession to the Declaration of Paris.[7]

When Adams told Russell that he had full power to negotiate an Anglo-American agreement on neutral rights, and added that he had brought a draft incorporating the American position on the subject, Russell must have realized that Seward intended the matter of American adherence to the Declaration of Paris to be settled in London. Russell replied that Great Britain and France had already instructed their ministers at Washington upon the subject and that Lyons had been given authority "to assent to any modification . . . which the government of the United States might prefer" on the question of privateering. Hence, he anticipated "no difficulty whatever" in reaching agreement on the question there. This being the case, he said, it would be advisable to leave the question in Lyon's hands. Adams concluded that he would refrain from complicating the negotiation by proceeding any further in London, unless he should receive further instructions on the subject from his government.[8]

During his second interview with Russell on June 12, Adams mentioned the "present state of excitement in the United States" resulting from news of the British concession of belligerent rights to the Southern Confederacy. In his opinion, nothing would be more likely to diminish this growing hostility than an agreement between the two countries to prohibit privateering. This accord would show that the British did not desire to aid the Southern rebellion by extending belligerent status to this spurious class of armed vessels. At this point Russell interrupted his visitor to ask whether Adams was aware that William Lewis Dayton, the American minister to France, had proposed a negotiation in Paris based on the Declaration of 1856. Adams replied that he and Dayton had received similar instructions. However, Russell's anxiety to leave discussion of the subject to Lyons had induced Adams to abandon the subject in order to let it be handled entirely in Washington.[9]

Adams also replied that the United States asked no more of Great Britain than neutrality. Adams now believed that Russell had initially misled him into thinking that the British would consent to recognize

American adherence to all four articles of the Declaration of Paris. Indeed, that document itself stipulated that such adherence must be given indivisibly. Yet it now appeared that the British might have some ulterior purpose in excluding the article banning privateers from any Anglo-American convention.

So Adams again failed to pursue the negotiation he had been instructed to initiate. He wrote Dayton that his overtures to the British government "were not received on the ground that the negotiation belonged to Lord Lyons, to which arrangement I acceded." Yet Russell, not realizing the need for a formal convention on the subject rather than a simple executive declaration by the American government, had neglected to tell Adams explicitly that Lyons had no authority to sign a formal international convention. Had Adams realized this, he might have suggested at once that the negotiation be transferred back to London, where he had the necessary powers both to negotiate and to sign such an agreement.[10]

On June 2, 1861, Lyons received the communiques directing him to propose American adherence to the last three articles of the Declaration of Paris and to transmit the same proposal to the Confederate government at Richmond, Virginia. On the same day, Henri Mercier, the French minister in Washington, received similar instructions from his government. Consulting together on the best procedures for carrying out their orders, Lyons and Mercier agreed that "it would require very prudent management to prevent the communication with President Davis being resented here and regarded as a recognition of the Southern Confederacy." The two envoys therefore decided to "take a few days for reflexion, before definitely deciding on the mode in which our instructions should be carried out." In any case, they planned to adopt a course of action in which the positions of Great Britain and France would be "as nearly as possible identical."[11]

In the following weeks, the diplomatic problems associated with privateering assumed added complications. It was obvious that British subjects would inevitably be captured on Southern privateers. Even worse, the Lincoln administration had announced its intention to hang the crewmen of such vessels as pirates. Yet the queen's advocate had supplied the Foreign Office with an opinion that such treatment was not warranted under international law. While Lyons intended to do his utmost to save any British subject in danger of losing his life due to such "barbarity," he feared that serious complications might follow any intervention on his part.

In addition, the "dominant" people in Washington, Lyons wrote, were "in a state of mind so utterly unreasonable as to border upon frenzy." They had abandoned all prudence in the common cry to "conquer" the South with one hand and chastise Europe with the other." Hence, it was quite possible that the United States would suddenly declare war against Great Britain. In the Anglo-American war that appeared likely to result from Yankee emotionalism, Lyons stated, "We must be prepared for the employment to an immense extent of Privateers by the United States . . . whether or no the Declaration of the Congress of Paris has been previously accepted by them."[12]

Lyons and Mercier did not believe that Seward would relinquish the use of letters of marque without a commitment from England and France to treat Southern privateers as pirates. Nor did they believe that the Confederates would voluntarily give up a practice "already active and successful" against Northern shipping. Thus, they decided to "take no step in the matter" until they had further sounded out the secretary of state. In view of the latter's "present warlike tendencies," Lyons was in no hurry to propose an interview for a such a purpose.[13]

Almost a week passed before Mercier went alone to see Seward. He wished to set a time for Lyons and himself to present an official request for an explicit declaration by the United States that it would apply the principles of the second and third articles of the Declaration of Paris to the English and the French, who had already proclaimed their neutrality. Not wishing to receive official notice of the English and French concession of belligerent rights to the Southern insurgents (which would force him to say unpleasant things officially in reply), Seward told Mercier that such a visit was unnecessary. The United States, for some time, had been ready to recognize the two principles, not because of their immediate application to the Southern rebellion, but because they were in conformity with the traditional doctrines of the United States. Reminding his visitor that the United States was not fighting a war but putting down a rebellion, Seward declared that he could not agree to receive any official communication from a foreign government recognizing Southern rights to send out privateers or commit any other act reserved for lawful belligerents. He therefore insisted that Mercier and Lyons defer any formal communication of their instructions to him and be satisfied with his private perusal of them as a matter of information not requiring formal action. As for the Declaration of Paris, he hoped that an agreement to recognize American accession to all the articles of that document had already been reached in London and Paris.[14]

Both Mercier and Lyons had already learned, however, that Adams and Russell had agreed that the negotiation should be handled in Washington. Hence they thought it unlikely that any settlement of the neutral rights question would be reached in London in time to absolve them from the responsibility of obeying their instructions. Haste was advisable. Every passing day brought nearer the opening of a special session of Congress, called by the president for July 4, during which, the British minister had heard, "it was very generally supposed" that Congress would quickly pass a law proclaiming the exclusion of foreign ships from Southern ports as a right of sovereignty without further recourse to a formal blockage. In order to prevent this law from passing or at least to impede its execution, Lyons thought "that the position taken by Great Britain and France should be made distinctly known to the government of the United States without delay."[15]

After much anxious consideration of "what would be the most conciliatory form in which we could execute the instructions we had received respecting . . . maritime rights," Mercier and Lyons went to see Seward. The British minister began by observing that "the conversations which he had recently held with M. Mercier had no doubt made him sufficiently acquainted with the nature of the communication which we were instructed to make to him." The two envoys would now "be really obliged if he [Seward] would tell us in what form it would suit him best that the communication should be made."[16]

According to Lyons, Seward replied that "he could not receive from us a communication founded on the assumption that the Southern rebels were to be regarded as belligerents." He preferred instead to treat the question of neutral maritime rights in London and Paris where he had already sent detailed proposals. Moreover, although Seward would not issue a formal complaint on the subject, he did not think it was friendly procedure for two European powers to consult and act closely together upon a course to be pursued toward the United States. As for the queen's proclamation investing the insurrectionists with belligerent rights, that had been "addressed only to Her Majesty's subjects." Seward hoped that he would not be forced to recognize it officially. With these words, Seward ended the joint interview. He showed Mercier into another room for further talk with him alone, and he invited Lyons to dinner in order that he too might be at liberty to discuss the question further.[17]

Although Lyons testified that "Seward's language and demeanour throughout the interview were calm, friendly, and goodhumoured," he resented the secretary's "refusal to receive the communication, as well as the observations on the concert between Great Britain and France." Nevertheless, "the practical objects" of the interview had been obtained. Notice had been given to the American government of an Anglo-French alliance on the question of Southern belligerent rights. Also a commitment had been secured from Seward that the United States would adhere to the second and third articles of the Declaration of Paris. Therefore Lyons felt justified in allowing the conversation to terminate without insisting that the secretary of state officially "hear the communication which we were instructed to make to him."[18]

Two days later, Lyons informed Seward that the British cabinet, "without in the slightest degree recognizing the Southern government diplomatically," nevertheless insisted on its right "to hold intercourse with it more or less formally, so long as the personal safety and the interests" of British subjects living in the South "were dependent upon that government." Seward answered "that the United States government might be ignorant of such intercourse or might even shut its eyes to it," but he could never "tolerate a regular announcement" from the British government that it "intended to communicate with the Rebel government of the South." Such a statement could easily be interpreted as diplomatic recognition.[19]

Seward's stipulation provided the loophole necessary for Lyons and Mercier to transmit the proposals of their governments to Richmond. Discussing the matter later that same day, the two envoys decided to adopt Mercier's plan of instructing their respective consuls at one of the Southern ports (by means of a message sent via a British or French man-of-war) "to ascertain through the Governor of the state the views of the Southern government" on neutral rights. Because of many American press reports that France would side with the United States in any conflict with England, and because of rumors that Seward and Lincoln shared this dangerous "delusion," Lyons was anxious to let Mercier "take the lead in our communication about the Declaration of Paris."[20]

Not until July 1 did Lyons make any further effort to bring the British proposals to the attention of the Confederate government. He again let Mercier provide the impetus for action. Lyons agreed with the latter's suggestion that the new French consul for Charleston, about to pass through Washington en route to his post, ought to be the messenger for the proposals to the Southern government. Although there was a further delay when the French consular appointee failed to appear as scheduled, the propositions finally left for Charleston on or about July 5 by another messenger.

In wording his directions to Consul Robert Bunch at Charleston, Lyons made a serious error. He wrote that the Confederate States had been invested with the legal rights of belligerents by the "course of events." This status forced Her Majesty's government to seek "securities concerning the proper treatment of neutrals" from the Southern authorities." The British minister then continued: "I am authorized by Lord John Russell to confide the negotiation on this matter to you."

To apply the word "negotiation" to dealings with the Southern insurgents was a crucial mistake. No government would negotiate with another regime unless it recognized it diplomatically or was making preparations to do so. Moreover, a diplomatic negotiation was not generally considered within the permitted sphere of activity of a consul whose exequatur allowed him commercial but not political functions. Hence, even though Lyons warned Bunch to "act with great caution, in order to avoid raising the question of the recognition of the new confederation by Great Britain," and not to place himself in direct communication with the Southern government, the way was paved for misunderstanding of the venture in the Northern states. The news would eventually leak out that Bunch had been asked to induce "the government at Richmond to recognize, by an official act, the rights secured to neutrals by the second and third articles of the Declaration of Paris, and to admit its own responsibility for the acts of privateers sailing under its letters of marque." Whether the advantages of obtaining such a commitment from the Southerners would outweigh the risks of great irritation in the North, aroused by the attempted negotiation, remained to be seen.[21]

Meanwhile, on June 17, Seward had learned that the British minister was not authorized to negotiate a formal convention on the subject of neutral rights. Seward directed Adams to enter into the convention at London. Lyons's report that Seward had been informed of the misunderstanding and was sending Adams new instructions reached Russell at the end of June. The foreign minister replied that Adams "never made any proposition" based on the Declaration of Paris.[22] Adams had in fact tendered the proposition, as Russell well knew. Yet the British foreign minister was now seeking a pretext to avoid dealing with it. Not only had Lyons's warnings that Seward was trying to trap the British into a commitment to help the North wipe out Confederate privateering made Russell intensely suspicious of the American offer, but the Foreign Office had also received disconcerting news on the subject from Paris. In France, with Seward's instructions to offer total adherence to the Declaration of Paris, Dayton had informed Foreign Minister Thouvenel that he was authorized to sign a convention from his country's agreement to the four articles of the Paris declaration, but only with the addition of the Marcy amendment.

Faced thus with a proposal to change the Declaration of Paris by adding to it, Thouvenel quite properly replied that he would have to consult the other signees before acting on the American request. Meanwhile, Dayton assured Seward that he intended to hold out for the Marcy amendment because agreeing to accede to the Declaration of Paris without the amendment "would merely bind our hands as respects privateering; it would not at all . . . bind these European governments to enforce the laws of piracy" against the Southern privateers.[23]

When consulted by the French about Dayton's proposal, Russell found it unacceptable. The Marcy amendment, he stated, "would reduce the power in time of war of all States having a military as well as a commercial marine," especially England and France. It would nullify the advantage of having a large navy by preventing its use against practically all unarmed merchantmen, even those sailing under an enemy's flag and carrying enemy-owned cargoes. Moreover, the stipulation that "the privateers sent out by the so-styled southern Confederacy should be considered as pirates" would represent a departure "from the neutral character which her Majesty, as well as the Emperor of the French, has assumed."[24] Dayton had put the British on guard against the American proposals. Hence, Russell told Adams at their second meeting that the British government preferred to discuss American adherence only to the provisions of the Declaration of Paris.

Thouvenel shared Russell's sentiments about Dayton's propositions. As soon as he received word from London that they had been rejected, he informed Dayton that the French government had no power "to negotiate separately upon the application of maritime rights in time of war, any arrangement which differed from the Declaration" of Paris itself. He suggested, therefore, that Dayton would have to address his proposals to all the parties to the declaration before they could be considered by any one of them. Not being authorized to make overtures to any government except France, Dayton gladly used Thouvenel's reply to justify dropping the whole negotiation, at least until Seward had sent him further instructions on the subject.[25]

Except for Russell's brief reference to proposals made by Dayton to Thouvenel "on the basis of" the Declaration of Paris, the American minister in London was unaware of the breakdown of the negotiation at Paris. Nor did he receive any hint of the confusion at Washington on the subject until the July 9 arrival of Seward's instructions to renew the overture to Great Britain. As Adams read this communication, a feeling of "profound surprise" came over him at what appeared to have been the most tolerant construction, a most "remarkable series of misunderstandings." Adams found Russell's conduct "inexplicable," perhaps even involving some "double-dealing." The lengthy misunderstanding had now rendered it "impossible to trust the thing longer to conversation." Adams decided to send Russell a formal diplomatic note officially proposing a negotiation and so bring the matter "to a distinct issue."[26]

In an exchange of correspondence, Adams maintained that he had proposed a negotiation on the subject of neutral maritime rights at his May 18 conference with Russell, at which time the British foreign minister had suggested that the matter be left for settlement in Washington. Russell recalled (inaccurately) that he had been the one to introduce the question. He asserted that he had instructed Lyons to propose in Washington that the United States adopt the last three articles of the Declaration of Paris and that Adams had agreed for the matter to be settled in Washington.[27] On July 13, the two men finally met to unsnarl the tangle. Outwardly maintaining equanimity, Adams handed Russell a letter from Lincoln authorizing the minister to negotiate American adherence to the Declaration of Paris. Russell seemed surprised that the proposal involved nothing more. He had not realized until then, he told Adams, that the United States was disposed to agree to the first article unaltered.[28] Adams had never mentioned it. True, the American envoy replied, but this was only because he had understood that any negotiation in London would be declined.

Adams also remembered Russell's stating that Dayton had made a proposition on the same subject to the French government, which had led him to suppose that Paris might have become the focal point for the negotiation. No, Russell replied. Dayton had only repeated the Marcy proposal which was "inadmissible" to the British government. Adams nodded. That was his own understanding, he observed, and the reason why he had not pressed for the Marcy amendment — "undoubtedly the first wish of my government" — as a condition for American adherence to the Declaration of Paris. The United States had recently decided not to make the Marcy amendment a condition to accession.[29]

Russell seemed satisfied and promised to submit the American proposal of a convention to the British cabinet for consideration. Such a proposition involved a departure from past procedure. States had customarily adhered to the Declaration of Paris by dispatches or notes, not by conventions. Yet Russell deferred to Adams's observation that the structure of the American government rendered requisite some distinct form of agreement upon which the United States Senate could "exercise their legitimate authority of confirmation or rejection." Adams foresaw, however, that the peculiar American approach might complicate British relations with the other parties to the declaration. This complication might interfere with the negotiation, even if the British government followed through in good faith.

Worse still to Adams was the possibility of "gross inattention" or more "double-dealing" on the part of Russell. Adams warned Seward that both dangers "must hereafter be equally guarded against." Hence, Adams awaited the result of cabinet consideration of his proposal with little optimism — and with his opinion of Russell somewhat lowered by their latest encounter. Russell's attitude, however, was far less severe. He wrote his Paris representative on the same day: "I like Adams very much, though we did not understand one another at first."[30]

Early in July, Seward received Dayton's report that the French would consider no amendments to the Declaration of Paris until the American request had been submitted to all nations party to the declaration. An exasperated Seward then went to the British legation to obtain a list of those countries for Dayton's use. While the list was being compiled, Seward told Lyons that the purpose of his proposal for United States's accession to the Declaration of Paris was to provide England and France with as much maritime security as possible during the current emergency. The American government, he said, "recognized the principles that the flag covers the cargo, and that the goods of a friend are free under an enemy's flag. Washington would do all in its power to protect the commerce of friends from the attacks of the so-called privateers of the rebels." It would not insist that its accession imposed an obligation on the other parties to aid in suppressing privateers sent out by disloyal Americans. At the same time, however, it could not accept any statement by a European government "that it did not intend, by accepting the accession of the United States, to contract any engagement affecting the states in revolt." Seward thought it would be best that "nothing was said on either side concerning this particular point," for any implied recognition of Confederate belligerent rights would be unacceptable to the Lincoln administration.[31]

Seward returned to his office to send fresh instructions to Dayton. Recalling that his original orders "required you to tender to the French government, without delay, our adhesion to the declaration of the congress of Paris, pure and simple," Seward pointed out that Dayton had produced a serious complication "by reason of your departure from the instructions which had been given to you." These directives had been designed "to remove every cause that any foreign power could have for the recognition of the insurgents as a belligerent power." Then, having learned that the French government "would recognize and treat the insurgents as a distinct national power for belligerent purposes," Dayton had assumed that his instructions were no longer applicable and that he could alter them to fit the new situation. "Good faith and honor," Seward pointed out, "now require us to agree to that proposition and abide by it . . . . We confide in your discretion to make such explanations as will relieve yourself of embarrassments, and this government of any suspicion of inconsistency or indirection in its intercourse with the enlightened and friendly government of France."[32]

While Seward's missive was on its way to Dayton, the Declaration of Paris negotiation was beginning to take a more promising shape in London. Soon after Adams left the Foreign Office on July 13, Russell wrote his ambassador at Paris that the British government had "no objection to the signature of the proposed convention," provided that Dayton was furnished with powers to sign a similar agreement with the French government. Yet the French were wary. Auguste Billault, acting for Thouvenel, asserted that Dayton had made "no offer of the kind." Observing that "there must be some particular reason for the U.S. proposing the conclusion of a convention, when a simple notification of their adherence to the Declaration of Paris would be sufficient for all purposes," Billault suggested that "Great Britain would do well not to act alone in the matter." He was joined in this opinion by Lord Cowley, the British ambassador at Paris, and by the British prime minister as well. Worried that the proposed negotiation represented an attempt by Seward to separate the two European powers in their dealings with the United States, Palmerston declared that the British ought to sign a convention only if done simultaneously with France.

Despite the cautious attitude of the French and the suspicions of his own colleagues, Russell was now anxious to conclude the convention proposed by Adams. To have British neutral maritime rights publicly affirmed by the United States in a solemn convention would be of great advantage in dealing with incidents and settling claims growing out of the Northern blockade. Having acquiesced in the imposition of the blockade, the British foreign minister wished to obtain official American acknowledgement that it must be effectively maintained in order to remain binding on neutral nations. Furthermore, the United States's voluntary cessation of privateering would be most desirable. This was especially true because the strained relations between the two countries might at any time turn into an armed clash. American privateers would then be free to wreak havoc on British merchantmen. Realizing that none of these concessions on the part of the United States government could affect France as drastically as England, Russell took the lead in trying to further the dual negotiation. Assuring the French that Adams had "expressed his strong conviction" that Dayton's instructions on the matter were "precisely similar" to his, Russell suggested that Billault "interrogate Mr. Dayton as to the precise nature of his Instructions." He also transmitted to the French government Adams's explanation of why a convention was constitutionally necessary to allow an engagement by the executive branch of the United States government to receive the assent or disapproval of the Senate.

In view of previous conversations, Russell wrote, he "would be prepared to sign the convention proposed with Mr. Adams if Mr. Dayton is prepared to sign a similar convention with M. Billault, & M. Billault has no objection to that course." As for the danger of a misunderstanding in regard to Southern privateers, the foreign minister added, "this convention cannot in any way alter the Proclamation and other Instruments by which Great Britain and France have declared their intentions to treat the two Parties engaged in the Civil War in America as belligerents. This declaration may be made verbally both to Mr. Adams and to Mr. Dayton."[33]

The British and French foreign ministers engaged in several telegraphic consultations and discussed the proposed convention with members of their respective cabinets. Russell then informed Adams that Her Majesty's government would be willing to enter a written agreement with the United States for its adherence to the Declaration of Paris, provided that a similar convention with France be signed simultaneously in the French capital.[34]

In order to give Russell an affirmative answer, Adams first had to overcome vigorous objections that the United States was signing away its traditional right of privateering. These remonstrances came from Dayton and other American diplomats in Europe. Expressing his impatience with envoys like James S. Pike at The Hague and Henry S. Sanford at Brussels (who had made themselves "very busy in opposing the instructions of the Department"), Adams reinforced Seward's insistence that Dayton comply at once with his original orders. Dayton reluctantly sent Thouvenel a note offering American accession to the existing Declaration of Paris. Yet he was so determined to absolve himself of any responsibility for the long delay in bringing the negotiation to fruition that Dayton apparently failed to notice a sentence in Russell's note which Adams found peculiar.[35]

After agreeing to sign a convention simultaneously with the French for American accession to the Declaration of Paris, Russell had written: "I need scarcely add that on the part of Great Britain the engagement will be prospective, and will not invalidate anything already done." On reading this remark, Benjamin Moran, the suspicious assistant secretary at the American legation, concluded: "This is a trick. What dirty object is aimed at we don't exactly know," but it appeared that the British foreign minister was preparing "something favorable to Southern piracy." Adams, not as quick to venture snap judgments, wrote Dayton that he did "not quite comprehend the drift" of the passage, but that its meaning would probably be disclosed as the negotiation progressed.[36]

While the Americans were puzzling over the British foreign minister's intentions, the latter was taking steps to insure unity among the European powers. He sent telegrams to his representatives in the major European capitals, asking whether their American colleagues had proposed conventions for the accession of the United States to the Declaration of Paris agreement. The missives also inquired whether the annexation of the Marcy amendment had been stipulated. The British government's position, he asserted, was "that the Powers who signed the Declaration of Paris ought to pursue one and the same course—namely to agree to conventions embodying the four articles . . . and nothing beyond." From Austria, Prussia, Spain, Russia, France and Sweden came assurances that the Marcy amendment would not be accepted if and when a convention was signed with the United States.[37]

Thus fortified with virtual unanimity among the European powers in favor of the British position, Russell was ready to sign the convention. The French foreign minister, however, still hesitated. Thouvenel thought that Seward's offer concealed "a trap" likely "to make trouble for us." He fervently wished for some pretext to decline the proposal which he thought was "a scheme of the Washington government to bind Great Britain and France to a declaration which they hoped to turn to account afterwards against the Privateers of the Southern States." He did not believe that the United States Senate would ever accept the convention.[38]

Russell intended to provide for this latter contingency. He wrote Palmerston that he would let Adams know before the two men met to sign the convention that its provisions would not alter the British neutral position toward the war in America. In reply, the prime minister suggested that the statement to Adams be "given in writing," in order to have a "record of the precise words." Despite Seward's warnings that the United States would deeply resent being asked to take official notice of allusions to Confederate belligerent rights, Russell prepared to send Adams his written caveat. He also had a copy made for Thouvenel in case the French government desired to issue a similar statement.[39]

Russell's written reservation declared that "to prevent any miscon-

ception as to the nature of the engagement to be taken by Her Majesty,"
he had no choice but to accompany the proposed convention with the
declaration: "In affixing his signature to the convention of this day between her Majesty the Queen of Great Britain and Ireland and the
United States of America, the Earl Russell declares, by order of her
Majesty, that her Majesty does not intend thereby to undertake any engagement which shall have any bearing, direct or indirect, on the internal differences now prevailing in the United States."[40]

Adams soon learned from Dayton that Thouvenel planned to make
the same reservation in the proposed convention. The French foreign
minister had asserted that his government would prefer to abandon the
negotiation entirely rather than omit the exception. Dayton regarded
such a qualification of the proposed agreement with great aversion,
"very much in the same light" as Adams himself viewed it. The two
European governments, Adams wrote Seward, seemed to contemplate a
course of action "of so grave and novel a character as, in my opinion,
to render further action unadvisable until I obtain further instructions."[41]

Adams declined to proceed further with the negotiation because of
the foreign minister's desire "to attach an outside construction disavow-
ing all application to the insurgents of the doctrine of no privateering."
If the parties to the instrument could not sign it "upon terms of perfect
reciprocity . . . without equivocation or reservation of any kind," Adams
declared, then the engagement had better be postponed "until nations
can understand each other better." Adams continued that should Russell's qualification be accepted, it would imply that the United States
desired to participate in the Paris declaration for the sole purpose of
"securing some small temporary object in the unhappy struggle . . . at
home," instead of for the "high purpose" of upholding neutral maritime rights. Was Russell's qualification to be taken as part of the convention itself? If so, then Adams, whose instructions were to bind the
United States to the Declaration of Paris and nothing more, would be
exceeding his authority by agreeing to it. If not, how could it possibly be
construed to modify the convention in any way, when the United States
Senate had not been allowed to pass on it? Were Adams now to agree to
a qualification which could scarcely fail to be regarded in one way or
another as an insult to America, he would hazard difficulties that he
earnestly wished to avoid. Hence, he declined to proceed in the negotiations "under its present aspect" until he had submitted the question once
more to the judgment of the authorities at home.[42]

Not transmitted to Russell was Adams's further thought that "once admit the right of parties to declare their respective constructions of a joint act and it will soon cease to have any joint obligation." The British foreign minister's proposition was "extraordinary" and typical of "the miserable shuffling practiced throughout this negotiation." Yet Adams found it difficult to blame Russell who had seemed to regard the American offer as satisfactory. The foreign minister had apparently been influenced by others to formulate the troublesome exception. But perhaps all would be to the ultimate advantage of the United States. A possible future quarrel over the application of the privateering article to the Southern corsairs would be avoided, as would a struggle at home between the proponents and enemies of the proposed convention. Meanwhile, until Great Britain became "more reasonable" in her relations with the United States, "it would be as well to preserve the right of privateering as a protection."[43]

A few days later, Russell sent Adams a mild rejoinder. Asserting that in relation to past Anglo-American treaties "serious differences" had arisen over "the precise meaning of words," he declared that in framing the new agreement he had merely desired to avoid another dispute. Certainly he had not meant to precipitate one. The British government had already concluded that a civil war existed in America and had declared its neutrality in relation to that conflict. The American government, however, had characterized the situation as one of rebellion and Southern armed vessels at sea as pirates. Even so, Great Britain, having recognized the belligerency of the South, had to grant the so-called Confederate government the right to send out privateers. Yet, without some qualification of the proposed convention, the United States might be inclined to argue that a European power signing a convention with it in which privateering was abolished would be bound to treat Southern privateers as pirates. Such an engagement to interfere in the American war would be contrary to the previously announced British policy of neutrality. Therefore, members of the British cabinet had declined to be bound by a convention that might be so construed, "without a clear explanation on their part."[44]

Russell's "clear explanation" had been too clear. It had implied a formal British recognition of Southern separation from the United States. His specious statement that he did not ask Adams to agree to his extra declaration, "simply to receive it," did not alter the situation. As Seward put it, when he learned of the British foreign minister's proposed qualification: "To admit such an article would, for the first time in the history of the United States, be to permit a foreign power to take cognizance of and adjust its relations upon . . . purely domestic differences existing within our own country." No such implied recognition of Southern belligerent rights could be countenanced. Nor could Seward accept such a special provision improving Great Britain's position relative to the internal difficulties in the United States while American obligations were not affected at all by the measure. Indeed, such "a radical departure" from the terms of the Declaration of Paris itself, which had made no exceptions in favor of any of the parties to it, made it necessary for the United States government to refuse "to accede to this noble act otherwise than upon the same equal footing upon which all the other parties to it are standing."[45]

In Paris, Dayton had anticipated Seward's reaction. As early as August 5, Dayton had warned Adams that Russell's meaning in saying the engagement would "not invalidate anything already done" was either to secure an escape clause (so that the British could claim not to be bound by the privateering article in dealing with the Southerners) or to sabotage the negotiation. He should not be surprised, Dayton wrote, "if the meaning, which he has *purposely* wrapped up in that general language, should in the end break off all negotiations. He may not refer to this language again, but unless you ask its meaning before the treaty is negotiated, it will be used by them afterward as an excuse for not carrying it into effect as respects the insurrectionists of the South."

Dayton exchanged sharp words with the French foreign minister over the proposed declaration. According to Dayton, Thouvenel "insisted somewhat pointedly that I could take no just exception to this outside declaration, simultaneous with the execution of the convention, unless we intended they should be made parties to our controversy; and that the very fact of my hesitation was an additional reason why they should insist upon making such contemporaneous declaration." Dayton answered that it was proper for such a declaration to be made in advance, only "*if France and England did not mean to abide by the terms of the treaty.*"

Dayton declared that the United States obviously had no desire to embroil foreign powers in its own domestic controversies. Its motive was rather "that they should keep out of them." But what Thouvenel proposed was a form of intervention about which the French government knew the Americans were "peculiarly sensitive"; therefore he would have to refer to his government for additional instructions before proceeding further. When Thouvenel learned that Seward desired to sever negotiations if the British and French governments insisted upon the outside declaration, he observed that "this only proved how right the two governments had been in making this declaration."[46]

By September both sides understood that negotiations over the Declaration of Paris had ended. Russell was happy to abandon the subject. It had begun to look "as if a trap had been prepared" by Seward to trick the European powers into assisting the United States in suppressing Southern privateering. Yet Seward's real motive throughout the negotiation was to reduce, not increase, the possibility of foreign involvement in the Civil War by committing his country as much as possible to the protection of neutral maritime commerce. He was forced to reject the British and French qualifying declarations, which would have put the United States in the position of recognizing that a state of war, rather than a mere rebellion, existed within its borders. Had the Lincoln administration admitted this, the way would have been open for European recognition of Confederate independence. That might have led to foreign interference in the conflict.[47]

All parties to the negotiation tended to blame its failure on connivance and bad faith on the other side.[48] Russell and Lyons suspected Seward's motives, and Seward and Adams became equally suspicious of British intentions. This mistrust became magnified during successive misunderstandings that none of the statesmen could believe were accidental.[49] Shortly, the news that the British consul at Charleston had opened a "negotiation" with the Southern rebels leaked into the Northern press. An aroused public forced Seward to withdraw the exequatur of Consul Robert Bunch and to protest his action. Lyons then informed his London superiors that the secretary of state might use "the Bunch affair" as a pretext to provoke an Anglo-American war. Around the British Foreign Office, suspicions of Seward's intentions verged upon paranoia.

Then came the *Trent* affair, involving an unauthorized seizure from a British mail steamer of two Confederate "commissioners" to Europe. Assuming that Seward had arranged the incident, British leaders prepared for war. Only the strenuous efforts of the secretary of state, however, averted conflict. A puzzled Lord Russell was forced to declare that he could no longer believe the tales of Seward's animosity toward England. They were, indeed, "buncombe."

The story of the Declaration of Paris negotiation conflicts with the view of many modern historians that Secretary of State Seward's policy toward Great Britain during 1861 was based initially on a "foreign war panacea" scheme and was then carried out for the remainder of the year with officious belligerence, so that British suspicions of and hostility toward Seward appear to be natural consequences of Seward's own attitude and behavior.

Throughout the abortive Declaration of Paris negotiation, Seward's motivation was intensely pacific. His actions and expressions, though firm in defense of his nation's interests, were quite conciliatory. Indeed, if any belligerency was exhibited during the course of the negotiation, it was reflected in the behavior of British and French diplomatists, not in that of Seward.

It is time that American diplomatic historians reexamine the myth of Seward's bellicosity toward England. They should consider whether the precarious Anglo-American relations prevalent in the first year of the Civil War were not a natural result of the distorted and inaccurate reports transmitted to London by Lord Lyons and Henri Mercier. These reports greatly reinforce a long-standing disposition among leading European statesmen (one not without adequate justification in history) to question the motives and to be apprehensive of the future actions of American political leaders. Close scrutiny of the Declaration of Paris negotiation would be a major step in a new interpretation of Civil War diplomatic history.

NOTES

[1] Seward to Charles Francis Adams, April 24, 1861, RG59, State Department Records, National Archives. Hereafter cited as NA.

[2] Roy P. Basler (ed.), *The Collected Works of Abraham Lincoln* (New Brunswick, N.J., 1953), IV, 339; U.S. Navy Dept. (comp.), *Official Records of the Union and Confederate Navies in the War of the Rebellion* (Washington, 1894-1922), Ser. II, III, 96-97; William M. Robinson, *The Confederate Privateers* (New Haven, 1928), 25-26; George W. Dalzell, *The Flight from the Flag: The Continuing Effect of the Civil War upon the American Carrying Trade* (Chapel Hill, 1940).

[3] An authoritative summary of the Declaration of Paris is John B. Moore (ed.), *A Digest of International Law* (Washington, 1906), VII, 562-63. For extended and unbalanced treatments of the 1861 negotiations, see Ephraim D. Adams, *Great Britain and the American Civil War* (New York, 1958), I, 137-71; Henry Adams, *The Great Secession Winter of 1860-61 and Other Essays* (New York, 1958), 363-89; Charles F. Adams, Jr., "The Negotiation of 1861 Relating to the Declaration of Paris in 1856," *Proceedings of the Massachusetts Historical Society* XLVI (October 1912), 23-84; Lynn M. Case and Warren F. Spencer, *The United States and France: Civil War Diplomacy* (Philadelphia, 1970), Chap. 3.

[4] Seward to Adams, April 24, 1861, NA.

[5] Russell to Lyons, May 18, 1861, FO115/241/II-III, British Foreign Office Records, Public Record Office, London. Cited hereafter as PRO.

[6] Ibid. See also Edouard Thouvenel to Count de Flahault, May 14, 1861, and Flahault to Thouvenel, May 16, 1861, Vol. 719, Archives diplomatiques, Archives of the French Ministry of Foreign Affairs, Angleterre. Hereafter cited as FMAE, AD.

[7] See Lyons to Russell, April 27 and May 6, 1861, Russell Papers, PRO; Lyons to Russell, May 2, 1861, FO115/253, PRO; Henri Mercier to Thouvenel, April 26, 1861, Vol. 124, FMAE, AD; Thouvenel to Count de Flahault, May 14, 1861, Vol. 719, FMAE, AD.

[8] Adams to Seward, May 21, 1861, NA; Russell to Lyons, May 21, 1861, FO115/241/III, PRO.

[9] Adams to Seward, June 14, 1861, NA; Russell to Lyons, June 22, 1861, FO115/243/I, PRO. Dayton had gone against his instructions and insisted to Thouvenel that the Marcy amendment be adopted before the United States adhere to the Declaration of Paris and demanded that European governments treat Southern privateers as pirates. In so doing, Dayton had reinforced French and English suspicions of Seward's ulterior purposes and retarded any chance of a successful conclusion of negotiations in London. See *Correspondence concerning Claims against Great Britain, Transmitted to the Senate of the United States, in Answer to the Resolutions of December 4 and 10, 1867, and of May 27, 1868* (Washington, 1869), I, 58-59.

[10] Adams to Dayton, July 2, 1861, Adams Papers, Massachusetts Historical Society. Hereafter cited as AP.

[11] Lyons to Russell, June 4, 1861, FO115/254, PRO; Mercier to Thouvenel, June 2 and 10, 1861, Vol. 13, Papiers de Thouvenel, FMAE, AD.

[12] Lyons to Russell, June 6 and 8, 1861, FO115/254, PRO.

[13] Ibid. Nor was Mercier. See Mercier to Thouvenel, June 13, 1861, Vol. 124, FMAE, AD.

[14] Lyons to Russell, June 13, 1861, FO115/254, PRO. Mercier to Thouvenel, June 10 and 14, 1861, Vol. 124, FMAE, AD.

[15] Lyons to Russell, June 8 and 13, 1861, FO115/254; Mercier to Thouvenel, June 14, 1861, Vol. 124, FMAE, AD.

[16] Lyons to Russell, June 17, 1861, FO115/254, PRO. Mercier to Thouvenel, June 18, 1861, Vol. 124, FMAE, AD. The wording in these two dispatches is so similar that one almost certainly was copied from the other.

[17] Ibid.; Frederick W. Seward, *Seward at Washington, As Senator and Secretary of State: A Memoir of His Life, with Selections from His Letters* (New York, 1891), I, 580-82.

[18] Lyons to Russell, June 17, 1861, FO115/254, PRO.

[19] Ibid.

[20] Ibid., June 10, 1861, PRO30/22/35, PRO. Two weeks earlier, Lyons had written: "Much will depend upon the conduct of France. The hope of the anti-English party [in the United States] is that she will try and engage us in difficulties here, and then leave us in the lurch, and play her own game in Europe." Ibid., May 27, 1861, PRO30/22/35, PRO.

[21] Lyons to Bunch, July 5, 1861, FO115/254, PRO. Lyons to Russell, July 8, 1861, FO115/254, PRO. For example, see Lyons to Russell, Sept. 27 and Oct. 14, 1861, PRO30/22/35, PRO. Lyons persisted in using the word "negotiation" to describe the approach to the Confederate government.

[22] Ibid., June 17, 1861, FO115/254, PRO. Seward to Adams, June 19, 1861, NA. See also Russell to Lyons, July 6, 1861, PRO30/22/96, PRO.

[23] Ibid., June 22, 1861, FO115/243/I, PRO. Seward to Dayton, April 24, 1861, NA; Dayton to Seward, April 22, 27 and 30, May 7 and 12, 1861, NA.

[24] Russell to Palmerston, June 11, 1861, GC/RU/661, PP; Russell to Lyons, June 21, 1861, FO115/243/I, PRO.

[25] *Claims against Great Britain*, I, 60; Dayton to Seward, June 22, 1861, NA.

[26] Adams to Seward, July 12, 1861, NA; Adams diary, July 11, 1861, AP.

[27] Ibid., July 13, 1861, AP; Russell to Adams, July 13, 1861, NA; Adams to Seward, July 19, 1861, NA.

[28] Yet Lyons had informed Russell in at least two dispatches, both received by June 13, that the United States desired to adhere to all the articles of the Paris declaration. Lyons to Russell, May 23 and June 4, 1861, FO115/253 &254, PRO; *Illustrated London News*, June 8, 1861.

[29] Adams to Seward, July 19, 1861, NA; Adams diary, July 13, 1861, AP.

[30] Adams to Seward, May 21 and July 19, 1861, NA; Russell to Lyons, May 21, 1861, FO115/241/III, PRO; E. P. Gooch (ed.), *The Later Correspondence of Lord John Russell, 1840-1878* (London, 1925), II, 320.

[31] Lyons to Russell, July 8, 1861, FO115/254, PRO.

[32] Seward to Dayton, July 6, 1861, NA.

[33] Russell to Cowley, July 17, 1861, FO27/1378/729, PRO; Ibid., July 13 and 20, 1861, FO115/244/I, PRO. Billault stated that he was "perfectly satisfied" with Russell's explanation. If Dayton were empowered to enter into a convention similar to the one proposed by Adams, he added, "there could be no difficulty on his part to the signature of such an instrument." Cowley to Russell, July 19, 1861, FO519/11, PRO.

[34] Russell to Adams, July 18, 1861, NA.

[35] Adams diary, May 24, July 19, 24-25, Aug. 1, 1861, AP.

[36] Russell to Adams, July 31, 1861, NA; Adams to Dayton, Aug. 1, 1861, AP; Sarah A. Wallace and Frances E. Gillespie (eds.), *The Journal of Benjamin Moran, 1857-1865* (Chicago, 1949), I, 856. Lyons was the inspiration for Russell's enigmatic expression. See Lyons to Russell, July 8, 1861, FO115/254, PRO.

[37] Ibid. July 12, 1861; Russell to Lyons, Aug. 3, 10 and 16, 1861, FO115/245/I-III, PRO.

[38] Cowley to Russell, Aug. 8, 1861, FO519/11, PRO. Edouard A. Thouvenel, *Le Secret de l'empereur* (Paris, 1889), II, 156.

[39] Palmerston to Russell, August 13, 1861, PRO30/22/21, PRO. Russell to Lyons, August 20 and 24, 1861, PRO30/22/96, PRO.

[40] Adams to Seward, August 23, 1861, NA.

[41] Adams diary, August 23, 1861, AP; Dayton to Seward, August 22, 1861, NA; Adams to Seward, August 23 and 30, 1861, NA.

[42] Adams diary, August 23, 1861, AP; Worthington C. Ford (ed.), *A Cycle of Adams Letters, 1861-1865* (Boston, 1920), I, 41.

[43] Adams to Seward, August 23 and 30, 1861, NA; Adams diary, August 19 and 23, 1861, AP; Adams to Dayton, August 24, 1861, AP.

[44] Adams to Seward, September 7, 1861, NA.

[45] Seward to Adams, August 17 and September 7, 1861, NA.

[46] Dayton to Seward, August 22, 1861, NA; *Claims against Great Britain*, I, 110-11, 117-18. See also Cowley to Russell, Sept. 24, 1861, FO519/11, PRO.

[47] In September, Seward announced that the United States would nevertheless abide by the last three articles of the Declaration of Paris "according to our traditional principles." Seward to Adams, September 14, 1861, NA. See also Russell to Palmerston, August 26, 1861, GC/Ru/667/1-2, PP.

[48] Adams confessed to "great respect" for Russell's "character." Nevertheless, he was "strongly inclined to believe" that Russell had been influenced by colleagues "who had in view the defeat of the negotiations from the beginning." Thus did Russell adopt an "uncertain and indirect" style of proceeding. Lynn M. Case is far too strong in recent references to "the bumbling way" of the "befuddled and forgetful foreign secretary." Case and Spencer, *The United States and France*, 95-96, 100.

[49] Even worse was the climate of mutual distrust that arose in Paris between Dayton, who spoke no French, and Thouvenel, who spoke no English.

V

Colonel Cyrus B. Harkie:
A Troubled Military Career

By WILLARD E. WIGHT

The colonels commanding the regiments of the Provisional Army of the Confederate States were men of many different personalities and qualifications. For some, the demands of military service brought forward and developed characteristics that enabled them to advance to general officer rank. Patrick R. Cleburne of the Army of Tennessee and John B. Gordon of the Army of Northern Virginia are good examples. Others, unable to meet the challenges of regimental leadership, realized their shortcomings and either resigned or secured less demanding assignments that more nearly suited their talents. Those who lacked the necessary qualities and still persisted in occupying positions of command were frequently dismissed from the service.

The military career of Cyrus B. Harkie differs from all of the above. It is, in fact, a special case. To be sure, Harkie did not progress to general officer rank. On the other hand, even though he manifestly lacked the personal qualifications to command a regiment, Harkie began and ended his career in the Confederate army as colonel of the Fifty-fifth Regiment, Georgia Volunteer Infantry. This dubious accomplishment is the subject of this essay.

One historian has concluded that "the Southerner made an admirable fighting man but a poor soldier."[1] While nothing is known of Harkie's ability as a fighting man or as a leader of fighting men, he serves as a perfect example of the historian's estimate of the Southerner as a soldier.

The differentiation between the Confederate as a fighting man and as a soldier stems from his want of military discipline. He never accepted the fact that such restrictions were necessary for the effective functioning of an army. Indeed, one inspecting officer wrote the adjutant and inspector general that "the source of almost every evil existing in the army is due to the difficulty of having orders properly and promptly executed. There is not that spirit of respect for and obedience to general orders which should pervade a military organization of such size and upon whose perfection of discipline such great issues of life and liberty depend. In my opinion, officers of all grades and departments are more or less to blame."[2]

A direct source of this deficiency was the brief employment in the Confederate army of the old militia custom of electing regimental officers from among the men in the unit. This resulted in a condition that has been described as "almost unparalleled in any other major war," for "the Confederate common soldier was the master of his officers."[3]

a consequence, Southern men in the ranks displayed "a typical democratic disrespect for authority," especially toward immediate superior officers. Discipline in the Confederate army became largely an individual matter between an officer and his men. The military unit reflected the character and qualifications of its commander. Hence, the commander made the unit.[4] These several characteristics are tellingly underscored by Cyrus B. Harkie's service in the Civil War.

Little has been discovered concerning Harkie's early life. He was born in 1832 in North Carolina. By 1850 his family moved to Randall's District of Cobb County, Georgia,[5] but were not listed in the 1860 census of either Cobb County or Randolph County, where the younger Harkie's military record began. In 1856, he graduated fourth in a class of eleven from the Georgia Military Institute at Marietta. A letter of recommendation written in early 1862 by Francis W. Capers, professor and superintendent of the institute, stated that Harkie graduated "with the highest distinction in mathematics, engineering & tactics." What occupation he followed after leaving the institute, however, is not known. Nonetheless, by mid-1861, Harkie was a resident of Randolph County, Georgia.[6]

When it became apparent that Georgia would secede from the Union, the state legislature authorized Governor Joseph E. Brown to raise 20,000 troops for local protection. Numerous military companies promptly responded to the danger. At Coleman, in Randolph County, a volunteer company awesomely called the Jackson Avengers was organized. The name honored James T. Jackson of Alexandria, Virginia, who had killed Abraham Lincoln's friend, Col. Elmer Ellsworth, as the latter attempted to remove a Confederate flag from the Marshall House Tavern, and then had been killed by Federal troops. Harkie was elected captain of this company and on June 1, 1861, in the name of the company, he tendered its services to the governor.[7]

One of the rudiments of a military company is possession of arms, and the Jackson Avengers were anxious for this status. Accordingly, on June 15, Harkie asked Governor Brown for muskets for his men. He also requested that the company be called into the service of the state at an early date. The latter plea reflected the widely held belief that this civil war would be short and that if one did not get into it early, the fun would be missed.

To the probable consternation of the fledgling company, the governor replied with deep regret that he could not arm the men as "nearly all the arms in the arsenals of the state are already gone." Governor Brown urged Harkie to "continue your organization, maintain & perfect as far as practicable your drilling & if the war continues long you will at some future day have a chance to render your country the service so eagerly desired."[8]

Actually the volunteers did not have long to wait. Fears of an attack on Savannah led the governor to call the Jackson Avengers into state service. The company left home on August 26 under orders to proceed to Camp Stephens, near Griffin. On October 1, the men arrived at Camp Lee, near Savannah, where they became Company H, First Regiment, First Brigade, Georgia State Troops.[9] Eight days later, an election — in conformity with the laws of the state — was held for the field officers of the First Regiment. Harkie was chosen colonel; Robert C. Saxon, lieutenant colonel; and Richard Sims, major. All were duly commissioned by the governor.[10]

Within a month, Harkie was under arrest and facing possible court-martial.[11] His troubles began when his officers needed wall tents "to shield them from the inclement weather and keep safe and secure the books of the regiment." Requisitions to the regimental quartermaster for these items, however, were not filled. On October 28, Harkie learned that such tents would arrive by train from Savannah. He gave the unfilled requisitions to Adjutant Joseph T. McConnell, who went to the depot and met Brig. Gen. George P. Harrison, Sr., commanding the brigade. Harrison told McConnell that there was a quantity of tents on the train and that "you will have the requisition filled." Yet when Quartermaster John G. Clarke was informed that the general had ordered the requisitions filled, he replied, "I shan't do it."

Adjutant McConnell returned to Harkie, who then carried the requisitions to the quartermaster. When advised of the type of shelters required, Clarke replied, "To my certain knowledge there is not a wall tent in the cars." Harkie accepted Clarke's rejoinder and was about to leave when one of his captains remarked that he did not believe the quartermaster. Harkie, thereupon, delayed his departure. He then discovered the tents on the train but consigned to the quartermaster of the First Regiment. Again Harkie asked that the requisitions be filled, whereupon Clarke replied, "I will if I please and if I don't please I shan't." Harkie angrily thrust the requisitions into Clarke's hand, directed the bundles of tents be opened and then ordered those he needed "to be taken for the use of the officers of his regiment."

Subsequent events indicate that the quartermaster complained of Harkie's actions. On October 28, General Harrison ordered Harkie arrested and confined to regimental limits. On November 5, Harrison appointed a three-man Court of Enquiry to review the conduct of certain officers. Though the record of this court is not available, other documents suggest that its investigation served as the foundation for charges of mutiny and sedition against Colonel Harkie and other officers of the regiment. In a November 17 letter to the governor, thirty-three officers of the regiment — including the lieutenant colonel and major — protested against the tribunal. They asserted that Harrison's directive was not even published in their regiment. They further recited a long list of instances in which the First Regiment had been denied camp equipage and tents while other regiments had received their share. No record of the action of the Court of Enquiry has been found.

President Jefferson Davis's call for troops to serve in the Confederate army, together with the growing certainty that the troops already organized in the state would be transferred to the Confederacy, led Harkie to apply to the secretary of war "for post of brigadier general in one of the brigades soon to be organized" in Georgia. With his application, he enclosed a letter of recommendation from Gen. Francis W. Capers, commanding the Second Brigade, Georgia State Troops. Capers, noting that Harkie had "enjoyed advantages which few officers of volunteers possess," stated that he would be "gratified to see him in office in command of a brigade & would expect the best results in the character and conduct of his command." The application was laconically endorsed by the office of the secretary of war with one word: "File."[12]

General Caper's expectations for Harkie were not fulfilled. Less than a month after Caper's glowing testimonial, Maj. Gen. Henry R. Jackson, commanding the First Division, Georgia State Troops, appointed a general court-martial "for the trial of Col. C.B. Harkie" and such other prisoners as might be brought before it with General Capers as president of the court.[13] Harkie was charged with violating the Ninety-ninth Article of War by having failed to maintain proper military discipline in his camp. He had also "allowed the sutler of said regiment to sell and dispose of intoxicating liquors within the lines of Camp Lee, this being forbidden." Furthermore, he had granted twenty-four-hour passes contrary to general orders. Finally, Harkie was charged with violating the Forty-second Article of War by absenting himself without permission of the commanding general for twenty-four hours or longer in violation of general orders.[14]

The accused was found guilty of all charges and specifications and sentenced to be reprimanded in general orders and suspended from his command for the remainder of his service. On April 1, 1862, the commanding general approved the proceedings of the court but expressed himself as "somewhat at a loss how to discharge properly the peculiar duty devolving upon him under the sentence of the court." After reviewing the actions of which Harkie, "a colonel of a regiment, himself the senior colonel of the brigade and division," had been found guilty, General Jackson concluded: "It is difficult to conceive how a reprimand of any kind couched in any language whatsoever can respond to the magnitude & serious significance of the case. If the simple recapitulation of the facts of that case be not sufficient for the purpose in view it seems idle to resort to additional words & the Gen. Commg. can do no more than dismiss Col. Harkie to his own reflections."[15]

Not all of the state troops mustered out in April and May, 1862, enlisted in the Confederate service. Yet over 300 of the men who had formed the First Regiment, Georgia State Troops, together with other volunteers, were organized on May 16, 1862, as the Fifty-fifth Regiment, Georgia Volunteer Infantry, Provisional Army of the Confederate States. On the following day, Harkie was elected colonel, Alexander W. Persons became lieutenant colonel and Daniel S. Printup was appointed major.[16]

By early August, the Fifty-fifth Georgia was at Chattanooga as part of Lt. Gen. Kirby Smith's army. The regiment participated in the 1862 invasion of Kentucky but by October was back in East Tennessee as part of Brig. Gen. Archibald Gracie's brigade. On November 2, the regiment left Lenoir Station, Tennessee, for Cumberland Gap. It reached the defile eighteen days later and immediately commenced building winter quarters. The men bivouacked in these "temporary" shelters until September 9, 1863, when the entire unit was captured by Federal troops under Maj. Gen. William S. Rosecrans.[17]

Harkie's relations with his troops revealed many of his shortcomings as a military commander. At one time during the regiment's stay at Cumberland Gap, Colonel Harkie, "though armed at the time, permitted his men to drag him from a railroad car and march him up and down the platform of the depot." On another occasion, they took him from his tent, placed him on a stump and compelled him first to go through the manual of arms with a tent pole and then to forward his resignation to the War Department.[18]

Apparently, after that pathetic demonstration, twenty-nine officers of the regiment signed a petition on December 14, 1862, advising Harkie that "believing that your own interest and the good of the Regt. both require your vacating the office you hold—respectfully ask your immediate resignation." Harkie replied the same day that "always subject to the control of those who put me in office the request will be complied with at an early day." Two days later, he tendered his resignation to President Davis in consequence, as he stated, "of some dissatisfaction or misunderstanding of the staff department." With this he enclosed copies of the petition from his officers and his reply.

These documents were forwarded through military channels and bore the endorsements of his superior officers. The brigade commander, General Gracie, wrote that "Col. Harkie resigns under accompanying charges," and he recommended the acceptance of his resignation. General Heth, the division commander, stated that the acceptance "will be advantageous for the service."[19]

Harkie outwardly complied with the request of his subordinates. Yet he modified his letter of resignation by urging the secretary of war that very same day to withhold action until the colonel's "arrival in Richmond which will be sometime in February next—perhaps in January." Secretary James A. Seddon, however, endorsed the request with the opinion that "it is unreasonable to wait as is asked it may be till Feby or later while the officers of the regt are rightly under the impression that the resignation is a settled thing."

On December 18, Harkie asked Adjutant General Samuel Cooper to withhold any action. "If an interview upon the subject is offered," Harkie suggested, "I will give the cause of my resignation in more detail." Action was postponed through December and January. Under Seddon's earlier recommendation appeared another written on February 3, 1863: "Old endorsement held up, but now recommend to take effect."

Before this could be done, another factor entered the picture. Harkie had not been content with his requests to the secretary of war and the adjutant general. He then had sought the assistance of Georgia congressman, Lucius J. Gartrell. The congressman asked the secretary of war to delay any action, and he characterized Harkie as a "gallant and valuable officer." On February 4, Secretary Seddon noted on this letter that "if not actually accepted, let the resignation be held up a while longer." No further action was ever taken.[20]

Regimental returns and muster rolls of the Fifty-fifth Georgia show that from December, 1862, through August, 1863, Harkie was under arrest awaiting trial. Harkie's official file contains two undated sets of charges and specifications signed by General Gracie, but on which of these he was tried is unknown.

One document contained two charges. The first was for violation of the Thirty-sixth Article of War. Specifically, Harkie was alleged to have sold, embezzled, misapplied and converted to improper use without proper authority two mules, one yoke of oxen, two wagons and a large amount of leather, all of which were Confederate property. The second charge was embezzlement and misapplication of public property. It specified that during November, 1862, in Tennessee and Georgia, Harkie had embezzled, misapplied and sold jean cloth valued at $1,000 and soap and candles worth $100 without authority and with the design of defrauding the Confederate States.

The second set of charges and specifications consisted of four charges. The first was for conduct prejudicial to good order and military discipline. Specifically, Harkie had granted leave of absence to three officers of the regiment without proper authority and had permitted a wagon master of his regiment to transport certain cargoes of jeans and leather, brought from Kentucky to Knoxville, without permission from proper authority. The second charge of conduct unbecoming to an officer rested upon the fact that he had lied to Gracie about the leave he had illegally granted to one of his officers. The third charge of breach of arrest stemmed from Harkie's journeying to Clinton and Knoxville, when he had been granted leave to stay only twenty-five miles from the camp. They fourth specification charged habitual neglect of duty, indifference and carelessness in discharge of duty. Harkie's attitude had been so bad "as almost to demoralize the regiment."

As a footnote to the charges of embezzlement and conspiring to defraud the government, an Atlanta newspaper published an item entitled "Grand Army Stealing." The article recounted the arrest in Atlanta of men engaged in "one of the grandest and boldest stealing transactions that have yet come to light among the army thieves." It then stated: "For four or five days the police observed two military gentlemen covering rather more ground than became plain, honest soldiers . . . and as the parties had not reported at Headquarters, they were closely watched. They had established a big camp about two miles from the city, and were doing a driving business with such enterprising gentlemen as were seeking investments. They had at their headquarters five large government wagons, heavily loaded with that 'Bragg Jeans': fine mules and horses and all the paraphernalia of a big camp. The concern was accompanied by eight men — Mr. Fulton, wagon master of the Fifty-fifth Georgia Regiment and some subordinates. They were met here by Captain Westmoreland, A.Q.M., of the same regiment who states that he was cut off from the main army in the great retreat: that at Knoxville and Dalton he tried to ship the goods but that all was right, only he had been a little careless, though no wrong had been intended." The report concluded that a grand wholesale thieving expedition was operating under protection of Confederate uniforms and official commissions. Fulton was found to have $2,500 in his possession. The whole of the camp and its appurtenances was estimated to be worth between $60,000 and $75,000.[21]

On October 9, 1862, President Davis signed into law an act providing for the creation of special military courts. These were to be composed of three judges, each having a colonel's rank, and one judge advocate with a captain's rank. One court was assigned to each army corps and department.[22] In January, 1863, while under suspension from his command and awaiting court-martial, Harkie applied to President Davis for appointment to one of the newly authorized military courts! He told the president that he was "led to prefer a place on one of the courts because it runs in the channel of my talent and profession for life." The accompanying recommendation of Harkie by Lt. Col. Alexander W. Persons of the Fifty-fifth Georgia is of interest because of subsequent relations between the two men. Persons wrote: "Colonel C.B. Harkie as an officer of distinction, loyalty, and military ability and [I] doubt not his desires and capacity to grace the position to which he aspires."[23]

Despite Persons's laudatory testimonial, word of Harkie's conduct had reached Gov. Joseph Brown of Georgia. In a communication to the secretary of war requesting reinforcements for an expected attack on Savannah in February, 1863, the governor stated: "The Fifty-fifth Regiment Georgia Volunteers, now at Cumberland Gap, while its commanding officer has behaved very badly, is an excellent body of men . . . on account of the character of the regiment having suffered by the conduct of Colonel Harkie." The governor thought that the regiment should be given a chance at active duty so that, through bravery and valor, the men could wipe out any stain that rested upon them.[24]

Meanwhile, Harkie remained in arrest from December, 1862, to August, 1863. Exactly when he was tried is not known but probably in September or early October, 1863. Harkie was found guilty on all charges and ordered to be dismissed from service. The reviewing officer, Maj. Gen. Simon B. Buckner, approved the sentence and forwarded the trial record to Richmond.[25] Lieutenant Colonel Persons was officially notified that he had been promoted to the rank of colonel and assigned command of the Fifty-fifth Georgia. Following the capture of the regiment at Cumberland Gap in September, 1863, Persons (who had been on detached service and hence was not captured) was assigned to temporary duty in Richmond with Brig. Gen. John H. Winder, commander of Confederate prisons.[26]

In February, 1864, a military prison, officially called Camp Sumter, was established at Andersonville, Georgia, to handle some of the prisoners-of-war who had become a military hazard at Richmond as well as a drain on the local food supply. Those members of the Fifty-fifth Georgia who had been on detached service, sick in hospitals, or on leave when their comrades were captured were ordered to Andersonville as guards, with Colonel Persons as their commandant. There he organized the remanents of the Fifty-fifth Georgia into three detachments.[27]

On April 22, 1864, this initial organization was disrupted by the publication of Special Orders No. 94 by the adjutant and inspector general at Richmond. Paragraph Fourteen of that directive stated: "The sentence of dismissal pronounced by the Military Court attached to the Department of East Tennessee against Colonel C.B. Harkie, Fifty Fifth Regiment Georgia Volunteers, is remitted by direction of the President upon whose mind the evidence in the case made a different impression as to the charges against Colonel Harkie from that upon the court. Colonel Harkie will be restored to duty with his command." Accordingly, on June 20, Harkie was ordered "to report to Brigadier General Winder, Commanding post, Andersonville, Georgia, for duty."[28]

Meanwhile, Persons was wondering whether he was now a colonel or merely a lieutenant colonel. He wrote to the secretary of war for clarification of his position. The answer he received has not been found, but its contents can be surmised from the fact that he was relieved from duty at Andersonville in July, 1864, and a month later was granted leave as a lieutenant colonel.[29] Either the anomaly of Persons's position was widely known or he had written for assistance in securing a new assignment; for Maj. Gen. Howell Cobb, commanding the Georgia Reserves, wrote to the secretary of war that he was "induced by the peculiar position of Col. A.W. Persons of the 55th Ga. since the restoration of Col. Harkey [*sic*] to suggest his name for consideration as commandant of the Post at Macon which is vacant." However, because Persons was still fit for active duty, he was subsequently ordered to rejoin the Fifty-fifth Georgia at Andersonville.[30]

Unfortunately for all concerned, Andersonville Prison became a veritable hellhole that seriously reflected upon the Confederacy's treatment of prisoners-of-war. So great was the outcry concerning conditions that Col. Daniel T. Chandler was sent to investigate and report on the situation. On August 5, 1864, the inspecting officer reported the Fifty-fifth Georgia as "thoroughly demoralized, mutinous, and entirely without discipline" and hence "should be at once removed from this point and their places supplied by better troops."

Chandler then recounted the regiment's treatment of Harkie at Cumberland Gap as if it had taken place at Andersonville. His final note on the regiment indicated that relations between Harkie and his men had not improved. The manhandling of Harkie, whatever its nature, had been concluded by compelling him to sign and forward his resignation, which he immediately recalled by telegram from Fort Valley, Georgia. He had then returned to Andersonville, but, as Chandler noted, "dares not assume command of the regiment."[31]

It may be remarked parenthetically that Harkie's status remained in limbo for some time. A muster roll of the Fifty-fifth Georgia, dated October 31, 1864, contained the following statement opposite Harkie's name: "Dismissed the service by sentence of military court of Department of East Tennessee last year—Have been unofficially notified he had been restored to his rank—have no idea what he is doing now."[32]

One of Andersonville's chief problems was that a creek flowing through the prison camp had been dammed, creating a swampy, unhealthy morass. At Colonel Chandler's request, Harkie (whom he described as colonel of the Fifty-fifth Regiment and a civil engineer) had devised a plan for draining the area, which Chandler recommended be implemented. Yet the adjutant general, upon receipt of Chandler's report, ordered General Winder to prefer charges against Harkie. To this order, the old veteran of many years' military service replied: "Colonel Chandler's statement concerning Colonel Harkie is given as a transaction at this post, whereas the occurrence, if it took place, took place at or near Cumberland Gap, and more than a year ago. As Colonel Chandler gives neither time, place, nor witness, charges cannot be framed. The transaction which really did take place at this post, and upon which charges might have been framed, is not mentioned. I am glad to say that the discipline of the Fifty-fifth Georgia Regiment is very much improved."[33]

Apparently this explanation did not satisfy the adjutant general. Winder was ordered to prefer charges based on the incident at Andersonville. On March 4, 1865, Winder forwarded "papers explaining the disreputable transaction which took place &c in the ill treatment of Col. Harkie." The papers were "referred to General Joseph E. Johnston for action and report." Nothing further has been found on this matter.[34]

Still present, however, was the resignation that Harkie had recalled from Fort Valley. Persons had submitted his own resignation, probably reluctant to serve again under Harkie. While Harkie's resignation was withdrawn at his own request, Persons's was withdrawn at the request of the officers and men of the Fifty-fifth Georgia. Nonetheless, Persons exerted himself to block the withdrawal of Harkie's resignation. He stated to Congressman Clifford Anderson of Georgia that "the Regiment (both officers and men) are clamorous for the acceptance of Col. Harkie's [resignation] and they have petitioned him again to be relieved of him." He described Harkie as "being freighted with scandal" and predicted certain mutiny if he remained with the regiment.[35]

Not even the last official record of Harkie reflects honor upon him. During March 7-20, 1865, Cyrus B. Harkie, colonel, Fifty-fifth Regiment, Georgia Volunteer Infantry, was a patient at Ocmulgee Hospital in Macon, Georgia. He was suffering from venereal disease.[36] It has been impossible to follow Harkie's life after the Civil War. This is regrettable, for his record in that period would doubtless prove as interesting as his military career.

NOTES

[1] David Donald, "The Confederate as a Fighting Man," *Journal of Southern History*, XXV (1959), 193.

[2] U.S. War Dept. (comp.), *War of the Rebellion: A Compilation of the Official Records of the Union and Confederate Armies* (Washington, 1880-1901), Ser. I, XLII, Pt. 2, 1276-77. Hereafter cited as *Official Records*.

[3] Donald, "Fighting Man," 182-83.

[4] Ibid., 181; Bell I. Wiley, *The Life of Johnny Reb* (Indianapolis, 1943), 235, quoting an inspector in the Army of Northern Virginia.

[5] "Seventh Census of the United States, Cobb County, Georgia," microfilm, Georgia Department of Archives and History.

⁶ *Official Register of the Officers and Cadets of the Georgia Military Institute, Marietta, July, 1856* (Atlanta, 1856); F.W. Capers to Judah P. Benjamin, February 24, 1862, C.B. Harkie file, Fifty-fifth Georgia Infantry, National Archives (comp.), "Compiled Service Records of Confederate Soldiers Who Served in Organizations from the State of Georgia" (microfilm copy, Georgia Department of Archives and History). Hereafter cited as "Compiled Service Records."

⁷ C.B. Harkie to Joseph E. Brown, June 1, 1861, Correspondence Received by Governor Joseph E. Brown, 1861-1865, Georgia Department of Archives and History. On June 10, 1861, the state's adjutant general forwarded commissions to the officers of the company. Adjutant General Letters Sent, April 25-July 12, 1861, 537, Georgia Department of Archives and History.

⁸ Executive Department Letters Sent, June 14-November 4, 1861, Pt. 1, 69, Georgia Department of Archives and History.

⁹ C.B. Harkie to Henry C. Wayne, February 3, 1862, Correspondence Received by the Georgia Adjutant and Inspector General, Henry C. Wayne, 1861-1865, Georgia Department of Archives and History.

¹⁰ Adjutant General Letters Sent, July 12-October 26, 1861, 876, Georgia Department of Archives and History.

¹¹ The events leading to Harkie's arrest are outlined in a November 17, 1861, letter from the officers of his regiment to Governor Brown. See Correspondence Received by Gov. Joseph E. Brown, 1861-1865, Georgia Department of Archives and History.

¹² C.B. Harkie to Judah P. Benjamin, February 24, 1862, enclosing Francis W. Capers to Benjamin of the same date, Harkie file, "Compiled Service Records."

¹³ Special Orders No. 180, Headquarters, State Forces, Savannah, Georgia, March 23, 1862, Henry Rootes Jackson Collection, Georgia Department of Archives and History.

¹⁴ General Orders No. 47, April 1, 1862, Ibid.

¹⁵ Ibid.

¹⁶ A total of 326 members of the First Georgia State Troops became members of the Fifty-fifth Georgia Infantry. Lillian Henderson (comp.), *Roster of Confederate Soldiers of Georgia, 1861-1865* (Atlanta, 1960-1964), V, 731-836. See also Harkie and Printup files, "Compiled Service Records."

¹⁷ Record of events cards, Fifty-fifth Georgia, Ibid.

¹⁸ A report by Col. Daniel T. Chandler, an Andersonville Prison inspector is the basis for this account. General John W. Frazer, who commanded the Confederate troops at Cumberland Gap when they were captured, stated that Harkie was "in suspension when I reached the gap and did not join the regiment while under my command." Frazer also regarded the Fifty-fifth Georgia "as the best regiment for discipline and efficiency." *Official Records*, Ser. I, XXX, Pt. 2, 611-12; Ser. II, VII, 548. See also Wiley, *Life of Johnny Reb*, 242, which first aroused the author's interest in Harkie's career.

¹⁹ C.B. Harkie to Samuel Cooper, December 16, 1862, Harkie file, "Compiled Service Records."

[20] Ibid.

[21] *Atlanta Southern Confederacy*, November 18, 1862. In June, 1862, Harkie had appointed Westmoreland as acting assistant Quartermaster of the Fifty-fifth Georgia. Reduced to the ranks six months later, Westmoreland then furnished a substitute and was discharged on March 1, 1863, at Cumberland Gap. Fulton had been designated wagon master of the regiment in August, 1862. In December of that year he was listed as in arrest at Knoxville, Tennessee. He returned to duty the following month but was captured with the regiment at Cumberland Gap. Howard had reported to Harkie in June, 1862, but on January 3, 1863, he resigned his commission and left the service. Westmoreland, Fulton and Howard files, Ibid.

[22] Wiley, *Life of Johnny Reb*, 220; William M. Robinson, Jr., *Justice in Grey* (Cambridge, Mass., 1941), 367-69.

[23] Harkie file, "Compiled Service Records."

[24] *Official Records*, Ser. I, LIII, 279.

[25] The papers were returned to Buckner on October 21 because they were incomplete. On November 17, 1863, the trial record again reached Richmond and on February 27, 1864, was submitted to the president. Record of Courts-Martial, 1861-1865, Record Group 109, National Archives, CXCVI, 196.

[26] Special Orders No. 302, December 21, 1863, adjutant and inspector general's office, assigned Persons to Richmond. During the compilation and publication of the *Official Records*, special orders issued by the Confederate adjutant and inspector general were printed in five volumes, one for each year. No place or date of publication is given, yet it is assumed that they were printed by the War Department. Cited hereafter as *Special Orders*. The above directive is in Ibid., III, 588.

[27] Ibid., IV, 116; Record of events cards, Fifty-fifth Georgia, "Compiled Service Records."

[28] *Special Orders*, IV, 250, 376.

[29] Persons file, "Compiled Service Records"; *Special Orders*, IV, 475.

[30] Howell Cobb to secretary of war, June 20, 1864, Persons file, "Compiled Service Records."

[31] *Official Records*, Ser. II, VII, 548.

[32] Muster roll of Fifty-fifth Georgia Infantry, Record Group 109, National Archives, microfilm, Georgia Department of Archives and History.

[33] *Official Records*, Ser. II, VII, 548-49, 755, 757-58.

[34] Record of Courts-Martial, CXCIX, 32, shows the disposition of Winder's communique.

[35] Persons file, "Compiled Service Records."

[36] Harkie file, Ibid.

VI

For the Union As It Was and the
Constitution As It Is:
A Copperhead Views the Civil War

By ARNOLD SHANKMAN

Had George Washington Woodward given his support to the Union during the Civil War, he might be remembered today as one of the outstanding Pennsylvania statesmen and jurists of the nineteenth century. Woodward, however, was a peace Democrat whose political views differed little from those of Clement L. Vallandigham, the celebrated Ohio Copperhead leader. Like Vallandigham, Woodward was an unsuccessful gubernatorial candidate in 1863; had he been elected, he would have been a thorn in the side of Abraham Lincoln. Not only did the Pennsylvanian believe that the president was an arbitrary despot, but he also insisted that the federal Conscription Act of 1863 was unconstitutional and that the South could never be defeated by force. Woodward misjudged Lincoln and the outcome of the war. His name has become so obscure that few Civil War scholars would recognize it today. This is unfortunate; for until we know more about Lincoln's Northern opponents, we will be unable to appreciate fully the complexity of Civil War politics.

Woodward was born in Bethany, Wayne County, Pennsylvania, on March 26, 1809, forty-five days after the birth of Abraham Lincoln. Unlike Lincoln, Woodward was not a child of poverty. Both of his grandfathers had distinguished themselves in the Revolutionary War and were relatively wealthy men. His father, Abisha, served his community first as sheriff and later as judge. Thus, the Woodward family was a part of Wayne County's tiny aristocracy.

As a youth, Woodward displayed an intellectual curiosity that could not be satiated by attending the local school (which met only three months of the year), by studying with his older brother John, or by reading those books which constituted the family library. His parents therefore sent him to a school in Geneva, New York, for a first-class education. The private academy, which subsequently became Hobart College, had an excellent academic program. It was here that he met Sarah Elizabeth Trott, whom he was to marry in 1832, and Horatio Seymour, who later became governor of New York and the Democratic presidential nominee in 1868.[1]

At nineteen, Woodward left the school and began to study law. In August, 1830, he was admitted to the bar of Luzerne County, Pennsylvania, where he quickly acquired a lucrative practice. By 1837, the residents of the Wilkes-Barre area were so impressed with him that they elected him a delegate to the convention held to revise the 1790 state constitution.

Woodward was the youngest delegate at the convention. Few expected that the twenty-eight-year-old lawyer from Wilkes-Barre would play a major role in the deliberations. Woodward took his duties seriously. His frequent speeches were noted for their eloquence, clarity and persuasiveness. On November 17, 1837, according to the official record of the convention, he suggested amending the state constitution so that immigrants arriving in the commonwealth after July 4, 1841, would be ineligible to vote or to hold public office. Most foreigners, Woodward insisted, did not know how to value the political privileges of Americans. They were all too often accused of "brow-beat[ing]" Pennsylvanians at the polls. Property rights and nearly all civil rights should be extended to the newcomers, he declared, but it was a travesty to allow aliens to "control" Pennsylvania elections. Other delegates denounced this recommendation so strongly that Woodward quickly withdrew the proposal.[2]

Woodward was a Democrat, and nearly all Pennsylvania immigrants voted for the Democratic candidates. By 1845, when he was a candidate for U.S. senator, he had greatly modified his opinion of immigrants. Seven years later, as a candidate for the state supreme court, he tried to explain his previous activities. Woodward asserted that he had never tried to deprive the immigrants of their right to vote. He declared that the speech attributed to him was actually the oration of a Whig reporter but, because of a stenographer's error, the speech had never been submitted to him for revision before it was printed in the proceedings of the convention. Had he seen the transcript of the speech, he would have quickly told the stenographer that he was not the author of the antiforeigner oration. Woodward further noted that on January 10, 1838, he had made it clear to his fellow delegates that he was not hostile to newcomers.[3] Nearly all Democrats accepted this explanation; but as late as the 1860s and 1870s, prominent Republicans who had been delegates to that convention insisted that Woodward had in fact tried to deprive aliens of their right to vote and to hold office. It is likely that they were telling the truth.[4]

More popular were Woodward's efforts to keep the vote from the commonwealth's black voters. He based his argument on two premises. First, the overwhelming majority of Pennsylvania's citizens had never intended that Negroes should vote. To grant them such a right would, in his words, constitute an offense against nature. Secondly, the black himself wanted civil freedom rather than political equality. It was the abolitionist who sought Negro enfranchisement so that he could better wage war on the Southerner.[5] Woodward's views prevailed, for it was not until after the Civil War that Pennsylvania blacks became eligible to cast ballots.

By the time that the Harrisburg convention adjourned, Woodward was vitally interested in political affairs. A few sessions had been held in Philadelphia where he came into contact with Pierce Butler, George Miflin Wharton, Charles Jared Ingersoll and his sons, and others active in state politics. Many Luzerne County natives were proud that so much attention was being lavished on one of their lawyers, and Woodward quickly came to be one of the rising stars in the state Democratic party. His skill as an attorney was so highly regarded that a young Philadelphian visiting Wilkes-Barre in August, 1840, lamented that he could not remain in the city another day to watch Woodward address a jury on behalf of four men accused of murder.[6]

In 1841, Woodward was named president judge for the judicial district comprising Centre, Clearfield and Clinton Counties. His popularity was such that two townships in the district were named after him; and in 1845, when James Buchanan became John Polk's secretary of state, several Democrats suggested that he be elected to fill the vacancy in the U.S. Senate. The Democratic caucus for nominating a successor to Buchanan decided to back Woodward. Normally this would have meant certain election, but Simon Cameron also sought the position. Woodward's alleged nativist sympathies, plus his hostility to a protective tariff proved lethal weapons against him. Democrats produced a letter in which the judge confessed that he might favor amending the state's naturalization laws. Yet he insisted that he would deprive no enfranchised foreigner of his ballot and that he thought it wrong to exclude immigrants from public office. Using persuasion, promises of patronage and quite possibly liberal sums of money, Cameron wooed Whig, Democratic and even nativist legislators to support his candidacy. This strategy worked. After five ballots, enough Democrats had bolted the party to deny Woodward the prize he had courted.[7]

The election was not the judge's only disappointment that year. In December, Polk nominated him to succeed Henry Baldwin on the U.S. Supreme Court. Secretary of State Buchanan was angry because the president had not consulted him before making the nomination and, moreover, thought that the position should go to John Read. Therefore he did nothing to support Woodward's candidacy, and three of his friends voted against the nominee's confirmation. In addition, Cameron induced Whigs and Democrats to vote against Woodward. On January 22, 1846, the Senate rejected the nomination.[8]

Woodward probably wanted a seat on the Supreme Court more than any other government position. Unlike most men in similar circumstances, he did not publicly express his displeasure with the action of the Senate. He chose instead to devote full time to his law practice. Many, including Governor William Bigler, admired his ability to withstand adversity. In May, 1852, after the death of Justice Richard Coulter, Bigler appointed Woodward to the Pennsylvania Supreme Court. Because of an 1850 constitutional amendment that made the position an elective one, the appointment lasted only seven months. Later that year the Democratic party decided to nominate him for a full fifteen-year term on the bench. Woodward won the election easily, despite allegations that he was an enemy of foreigners. Soon he was recognized as perhaps the ablest member of the state's highest tribunal.[9]

Thus, by 1860, Woodward was a respected member of the bench and a leader of the Pennsylvania Democratic party. Although he rarely spoke out on political matters, he was a conservative Democrat. He believed in a literal interpretation of the state and national constitutions. He insisted that the Union was "the product of the States," and that it could be maintained only if the "just rights" of the states were preserved.[10]

Among these "just rights" of a state was the freedom to regulate domestic institutions. Woodward himself expressed no personal love of slavery until after the election of Lincoln, and he had discouraged his son, George, from settling in Arkansas or Kentucky because they were slave states. Nonetheless, even though he publicly praised the 1780 Pennsylvania statute which abolished human bondage as "a proud monument . . . [which] wiped out the stain of slavery" from the Keystone State, he vehemently insisted that the federal government had no right to tamper with the peculiar institution in the South.[11]

Like many others in the commonwealth, he was troubled by the presence of freed blacks in Pennsylvania. He feared that emancipation would flood the state with Negroes who would compete with whites for jobs. In his own mind he began to equate emancipation with strike-breaking, racial amalgamation and anarchy. Although Woodward was a racist, he did believe that properly educated blacks were capable of self-government. He proposed that emancipated slaves be colonized in Africa. There, if they were diligent, they could attain great prosperity and spend their lives in happiness. Yet, even though he hoped to live to see the day when all blacks were in Africa and slavery on American soil was extinct, Woodward strongly opposed any plan that would force the South to colonize its slaves.[12]

By 1860, with slavery dividing the country, Woodward viewed with alarm the growth of the Republican party and the division of the Democrats into pro- and anti-Buchanan factions. Shortly after the adjournment of his party's initial convention, Woodward discussed the future of the republic with Judge William Strong, one of his colleagues on the supreme court. Both agreed that if the Democrats split at their Baltimore convention, Stephen A. Douglas would likely emerge as the party's presidential nominee. Judge Strong thought that Douglas would carry most of the Southern states. Woodward disagreed and expressed his belief that "Judge D w[oul]d not carry a state in the Union—North or South."[13] When the Democrats did split, Woodward endorsed Vice-President John C. Breckinridge. On November 6, 1860, he doubtless cast his ballot for the Kentuckian.

Abraham Lincoln's election disturbed many Democrats in the North, but few reacted with as much shock as Judge Woodward. In a remarkable series of letters to U.S. Attorney General (and later Secretary of State) Jeremiah Black, he frankly expressed his sentiments on the future of the country. Lincoln's election and abolitionist agitation, he believed, were making a civil war "irrepressible." He continued:

As a Northern man I cannot in justice condemn the South for withdrawing from the Union. I believe they have been loyal to the Union formed by the Constitution — secession is not disloyalty to that, for that no longer exists. The North has extinguished it. And if they do go out, don't let a blow be struck out against them by the present administration. Dissuade them if you can, but if you can't let them go in peace. I wish Pennsylvania could go with them. They are our brethern . . . . They have been good & peaceable neighbors. We are the wrong doers. We have driven them off & if we raise an arm to strike, the "stones of Rome will move to mutiny."

Woodward recommended that Black burn this letter after reading it, but the attorney general refused. Instead, he presented it to Buchanan and his cabinet. Secretary of the Treasury Howell Cobb offered $100 for a copy and others asked that the note be published and the author be commended for his devotion to his country. Woodward wisely chose not to allow the letter to appear in print.[14]

In a final communication to Black, Woodward (who confessed that he had been influenced by John Calhoun) reiterated his conviction that the Union was based on consent and that it would be folly to use bayonets to keep the country together. A state had the right to secede from the United States if it so desired. If a South Carolina convention endorsed secession, he argued, the Palmetto State "is as effectively out as if she had never been in, and you have no more right to maintain forts and arsenals and custom[s] houses within her borders than if she had never belonged to the Union."[15] No record exists that Black answered this letter, yet his own views on the matter were less radical than Woodward's.

Sometime during the late 1850s, careful perusal of the Bible persuaded Woodward that "human bondage had received Divine sanction" and that "slavery was an Institution of civilized and Christianized society." In fact, he believed that "slavery was intended as a special blessing to the people of the United States" and to "the slaves."[16] Needless to say, such thoughts were becoming increasingly unpopular in most parts of the North.

In Philadelphia, a city with extensive commercial ties with the slave states, people were receptive to Woodward's views. Though usually reticent to address crowds because of his position on the bench and because strangers frequently found him coldhearted and calculating, he agreed to speak before a massive rally of Philadelphians at Independence Square on December 14, 1860, to devise a peaceful means to keep the Union together. Woodward's oration, the most radical delivered that day, was an eloquent — if somewhat misguided — defense of slavery.

Calling upon all good citizens to protect the slaveholder from the assaults of abolitionist fanatics, he described slavery as an "incalculable blessing" to the Northerners and the British. Yankees had profited selling blacks to Dixie and now reaped a fortune sending their manufactured goods to Southern customers. True, he declared, the North had abolished "slavery and so gratified their innate love of freedom — but they did so gradually and so did not wound their love of gain." In return for giving up slavery, the Yankees gained "manufacturing and commercial prosperity which grew up from the productions of slave labor." His most startling assertion was that slavery, which he insisted was divinely sanctioned, benefitted the Negro. The black was not mistreated; he was consigned not to heathens but rather to Christian masters, who civilized him. Since Woodward was convinced of the blacks' inferiority, he did not doubt that if they were freed and forced to work for a living in the United States, the ex-slaves would starve to death.[17]

This speech, which was to be the last Woodward made in public until after the Civil War, was well received in most parts of the state. A Harrisburg newspaper called it "a truthful exposition of the causes of the existing perils of the Union"; a Presbyterian organ praised the judge for convincingly proving that slavery was not "sinful"; and the *Philadelphia Evening Bulletin* thought that his argument was "masterly and able." A few editors, however, felt that Woodward had been intemperate. The *Philadelphia North American and United States Gazette*, for example, disassociated itself from his words, and the *Bellefonte Central Press* described the assembly as "the most cowardly, cringing, and degrading meeting which ever disgraced the name of 'Union demonstration.'"[18]

As disunion became a reality, Woodward grew despondent and made a number of rash statements. In 1861 (according to John M. Broomall of Delaware County), Woodward delivered an address on the secession crisis to a gathering of supreme court colleagues and several lawyers. Woodward declared that if the nation were split, he hoped that the dividing line would be north of Pennsylvania and that the Keystone State would join the South.[19] Although many Democrats denied Broomall's story, it is likely that Woodward did make the statements ascribed to him. They coincided with what he had written to Black several months earlier and differed little from ideas expressed by several other Democratic politicians in the state.

Subsequent to the firing on Fort Sumter, Woodward made few public statements about the war. Perhaps modifying his views on secession after two of his five sons joined the Union army, Woodward contributed money to help raise a Federal regiment. One likely explanation for the silence was that in 1861 in most areas of Pennsylvania it was dangerous to voice any sentiments that could be construed as sympathetic to the South. The Unionist party, a coalition of Republicans and some war Democrats, was quick to label as a traitor anyone whose patriotism was suspect. During the political campaign that fall, Woodward's nephew,

Warren J. Woodward, a candidate for a judgeship in Reading, was denounced in the *Philadelphia Press* for having supported Breckinridge.[20] Although the Reading lawyer won the election, the smear campaign held a lesson for his uncle: voice opposition to the war only to trusted friends. However, George Woodward did not always heed this admonition. He later had ample reason to wish that he had.

By 1862, peace sentiment was increasing in Pennsylvania. Many persons were tired of the conflict and the sacrifices it demanded. Woodward seemed to respond to this shift in public opinion. When speaking with Judge Thomas Cunningham of Beaver County, he declared that the best move Lincoln could make would be to withdraw the Union army north of the Mason-Dixon Line and to offer peace terms to the Confederacy. Cunningham, appalled by this recommendation, campaigned for Woodward's gubernatorial opponent in 1863.[21]

During the 1863 canvass, it was alleged that Woodward greeted his son, George, who had been wounded at Gettysburg, with "You were lucky only to have been wounded in both legs. You should have been shot in the heart for fighting for such a cause." The story was false, but it was true that George Washington Woodward and Major George Abisha Woodward of the Second Pennsylvania Infantry disagreed about the war. In June, 1862, Major Woodward was severely wounded in combat, captured and sent to Libby Prison in Richmond. Upon his release, he returned home to Philadelphia and the care of his father. According to the son, the judge freely criticized the war but never once uttered a word of sympathy for the rebellion. However, he did suggest that the North call for a six-month truce, during which efforts would be made to find a peaceful solution to the conflict. Major Woodward questioned whether the scheme was practical, since the South would never consent unless the Union blockade was lifted. If that were done, the soldier explained, the Confederates would have ample time to stockpile enough British arms to fight for several more years if the combat resumed. Judge Woodward pondered what his son had said and then declared, "If they wouldn't consent to a truce with the blockade maintained, *I would fight it out to the bitter end.*"[22]

Significant numbers of Pennsylvania Democrats agreed with Woodward on the desirability of a temporary truce. At an 1863 Democratic party assembly, a group of Westmoreland County residents endorsed the following resolution:

That in order to secure our government from the terrible war in which we are engaged, we are in favor of an armistice of a month between the two armies, that terms of peace may be offered. That we believe if the Federal Government would offer to make peace on constitutional terms, that . . . this bloody strife could be very soon settled and peaceably adjusted.[23]

Not only did Woodward believe that the war could not be won on the battlefield, he also began to fear that the conflict represented a threat to state rights. Instead of government by "constitution loving citizens whose hearts were large enough to embrace the whole country," the nation was under the rule of men who refused to realize "that a centralized despotism would be the death of popular liberty."[24] Whether or not he would admit it, Woodward was a Copperhead. He shared the peace Democrats' antipathy toward greenback currency, arbitrary arrests, the denial of the writ of habeas corpus, the suppression of antiadministration newspapers and a federal conscription act. He hoped that enough war critics would be elected to state and national offices to force the Lincoln administration to reevaluate its military position.

No evidence exists that Woodward himself sought any political office. Although he had once expressed a desire to be the reporter for the Supreme Court and make more money than he was then earning, he was reasonably content with his job.[25] Some had proposed that he succeed David Wilmot in the Senate in 1863. Yet Woodward did nothing to encourage his candidacy, and he seemed undisturbed when the post went to Charles R. Buckalew.

Of greater interest to Woodward was the gubernatorial contest waged in Pennsylvania that year. The ailing incumbent, Andrew G. Curtin, had expressed a desire to retire at the end of his term. Even if Curtin chose to seek reelection (as he later did), many doubted that he could defeat a strong Democratic contender because of his alienation of the Cameron faction of the Unionist party. In addition, some mistakenly believed that Curtin had mismanaged state funds allocated to feed and equip Pennsylvania soldiers.

Among those Democrats who sought their party's nomination were Hiester Clymer and William Witte. Both had made enemies among party leaders; hence, a few Democrats began to search for a less controversial candidate. Among those approached was Woodward. The judge insisted that he did not want the nomination and that his talents were "more judicial than executive." Yet he confessed that if he were governor, he would "stand by the few state rights that are left . . . [and do his] best to administer the constitution & laws as they are written." In short, he told his friends, "whilst I do not seek the nomination I will not decline it."[26]

Woodward did not bother to attend the Democratic nominating

convention in Harrisburg. In fact, while it was in session, he left his Philadelphia home and went fishing. For eight ballots, Witte and Clymer fought for the nomination. Then, seeing that the convention was dead-locked, Witte's forces threw their support to Woodward, who became the party candidate on the ninth ballot. The delegates seemed pleased with their choice. One confided in his diary: "Much enthusiasm at the nomination of Geo. W. Woodward for Governor — & [Walter] Lowrie for Supreme Court."[27]

While Democrats were happy with their new candidate, even a few Unionists conceded that Woodward was "a citizen of unimpeachable character, and able jurist" and "a man of decided ability." Many appar-ently were ignorant of his political beliefs. The June 19, 1863, issue of the prowar *Philadelphia Inquirer* hailed the judge as "a patriotic gentle-man"; a Pittsburgh Unionist organ maintained that he was "but little committed to the extreme doctrines of the [Democratic] Party"; and a Georgia paper was critical of the Keystone State's Democracy, recom-mending that its members "soon change their position and travel *Wood ward* — that is, to Fernando."[28]

The judge wisely decided not to stump the commonwealth and to allow his friends to address rallies in his behalf. This he justified by noting that since he was still a member of the Pennsylvania Supreme Court, it would be undignified for him to discuss issues that were pend-ing in the state courts. However, Woodward also had private reasons for not taking the stump. Although capable of writing an eloquent speech, he was not an accomplished orator. His words rarely electrified an audience. Hence, it was better for him to allow such persuasive speakers as J. Glancy Jones, Francis W. Hughes, William Bigler, Jeremiah S. Black and William B. Reed to woo the electorate. Woodward was also a man of integrity, and it would be difficult for him to talk about the war and disguise his peace sympathies. By saying nothing and pointing to two sons who had donned the blue, he could create the image of being a critic of Lincoln but not of the war. Yet he was at times forced to make public statements in favor of the conflict that contradicted his private utterances.[29]

Both Unionists and Democrats realized the significance of the cam-paign.[30] While it was sometimes overshadowed by the Clement Vallan-digham-John Brough contest in·Ohio, the Pennsylvania election was of great importance. Charles Mason of the New York-based Society for the Diffusion of Political Knowledge (a Copperhead propaganda organiza-tion) had good reason to write a prominent Philadelphia Democrat: "We consider the election in your state as more important than in N. York. We are working earnestly for it."[31]

Unionists energetically searched Woodward's record for any blemishes that might cost him favor with the voters. They first alleged that he was an enemy of foreigners and pointed to his effort in 1837 to deprive them of the suffrage. Woodward denied this allegation. To prove he was a friend of the immigrant, he quickly penned a note which opposed extending the time limit before which aliens could be naturalized even "one hour beyond the period now fixed by law." Moreover, Democrats declared that Andrew Curtin had been a "high priest" of the Pennsylvania Know-Nothing party. He had even stated on one occasion that the reason a Dutchman's head was so hard was because he had two skulls.[32]

Another mark against Woodward, or so the Unionists thought, was his 1862 concurrence in a verdict that deprived Pennsylvania soldiers stationed outside the commonwealth of the right to vote in state and federal elections. What Curtin's supporters failed to tell the electorate — and this the Democrats did for them — was that soldier-voting frauds had marred the 1861 election, that the Pennsylvania Constitution tolerated soldier-voting only within the boundaries of the state, and that the Unionist member of the state supreme court had agreed with Woodward that the volunteers were not entitled to vote.[33]

As the Unionists desperately searched for a proper election issue, they stumbled upon Woodward's December, 1860, Philadelphia speech. They began to ridicule the judge for implying that slavery was both biblically sanctioned and a blessing to the North. Once again Democrats discovered that they could turn this issue to their advantage. Certainly more Pennsylvanians were opposed to slavery in 1863 than had been in 1860, but emancipation was unpopular with key segments of the voting population — the Irish and the Germans, and the aristocracy of Philadelphia, many of whose members had social and familial ties with the South. Woodward's friends persuaded an ex-Pennsylvanian, Episcopal Bishop John Henry Hopkins, to write a biblical defense of slavery, which they used as a campaign document. Naturally Unionists castigated Hopkins for espousing doctrines they believed unworthy of a clergyman; but a significant number of Pennsylvanians (at least a third of the potential voters) agreed with the bishop.[34]

Racism was widespread in the commonwealth. Woodward's friends boasted that their candidate had worked to restrict the suffrage to whites. "White men of Pennsylvania," asked the Democrats, "are any of you so governed by your passions and prejudices as now to admit negroes in terms of political and social equality? If so, vote for Curtin; if not, vote for Judge Woodward."[35]

It was only when Unionists began to question Woodward's loyalty that they uncovered his Achilles heel. Antiwar sentiment began to decline after the Confederate defeats at Gettysburg and Vicksburg. For Woodward to win the election, not only would he need the votes of Copperheads, which he already had, but also those of war Democrats, not all of whom would support a man in favor of a compromise solution to the conflict. Ammunition for the Curtin forces often came from antiwar Democrats. When, on June 30, 1863, the *Meadville Crawford Democrat* proudly proclaimed that "Judge Woodward is every inch a Copperhead and will receive the full vote of his party," it was not only winning antiwar votes for Woodward but also prowar votes for Curtin. The same thing happened when Hiester Clymer addressed a rally at Canonsburg. He promised that if Woodward, Vallandigham and Seymour ran the statehouses at Harrisburg, Columbus and Albany, "they would unite in calling from the army troops from their respective States for the purposes of compelling the Administration to invite a convention of the States to adjust our difficulties."[36]

Capitalizing on the reluctance of some voters to cast ballots for a man of suspect loyalty, Unionists persuaded John Broomall and Thomas Cunningham to inform the electorate of Woodward's true feelings about the war. In addition, George Hart, who claimed to have ridden with Woodward in a stagecoach from Gettysburg to Wrightsville on July 7, 1863, alleged that the Democratic candidate had denounced the war as an unconstitutional, abolitionist conflict from which the North could gain neither credit nor honor.[37]

Occasionally the Curtin men went overboard in their claims. For example, Nathaniel B. Browne, ex-postmaster of Philadelphia, roundly denounced Woodward as a secessionist who would carry out the principles of John Calhoun better than Calhoun himself. Browne was later forced to admit that he did not know Woodward personally and that he had based his argument on a perusal of Woodward's 1860 speech in Philadelphia. Democrats wryly noted that Browne praised that speech when it had been delivered.[38]

At least once Woodward used trickery to answer his critics. A Unionist maintained that Woodward had told a Justice *Hale* that he favored recognition of the South. A peace Democrat asked whether the judge had ever made such a statement to a Judge *Hall*. Woodward replied that he knew no Judge Hall and that "so far as from ever avowing belief in secession or favoring recognition of the Southern Confederacy, I am and always have been opposed to both and am in favor of suppressing the rebellion by which both are supported . . . . Neither secession nor the malignant fanaticism that cause it will ever find an advocate in me."[39]

Woodward soon became disturbed at being the subject of so many allegations. He asked Jeremiah Black to "convince the people of Penna that no traitor blood lurks in my veins." He then added: "If I am a traitor, I pray you tell the people of Pennsylvania so, but tell them also to whom I would betray a people among whom I was born and have always lived with and with whom my all of earthly good & honor is embarked."[40] Black and others did their best to portray their candidate as a patriot desirous of suppressing the rebellion and of restoring the Union. Nonetheless, many voters continued to have doubts about Woodward's loyalty.

As the election approached, Gen. George B. McClellan was asked to endorse Woodward in a public letter. The general was reluctant; but after he was assured that Woodward would win with or without his help, and that such an endorsement would boost his chances to be the Democratic presidential nominee in 1864, McClellan finally consented. In his note, McClellan declared that if it were in his power, he would "give to Judge Woodward my voice and my vote."[41]

Such efforts proved futile to counteract Unionist claims that a vote for Woodward was a vote for treason. "If Judge Woodward shall be chosen Governor," declared the *Chambersburg Franklin Repository* on October 7, 1863, "it will send a thrill of joy throughout the desolated land of traitors. They hope and appeal for his success." Added the *Harrisburg Telegraph* of September 8, 1863: "Woodward made Governor would be equal to Pennsylvania admitted to the frail sisterhood of the Confederacy." As election day approached, a fair number of Pennsylvanians came to fear that Jefferson Davis would be more gratified by Woodward's victory than by a defeat of the Union armies.

On October 13, 1863, Andrew Curtin won reelection as governor, by a slender margin of less than 16,000 votes out of nearly 525,000 cast. It is impossible to determine precisely what factor was decisive in Woodward's defeat. Yet doubts as to the judge's patriotism were certainly extremely important. Peace Democrats quickly persuaded themselves that electoral frauds had cheated their candidate of victory.[42] To be sure, hundreds of soldiers were furloughed and scores of war clerks were sent home so that they could vote for Curtin. Edwin Stanton, a former friend of Woodward, claimed credit for the victory, but it is likely that the Unionists would have triumphed even without the help of Billy Yanks and the secretary of war.

After the election Woodward moved from Philadelphia back to Wilkes-Barre. He seriously considered suing some of his detractors for slander but later changed his mind.[43] Interestingly enough, the election made him chief justice of the Pennsylvania Supreme Court. The judge occupying that position had been defeated in his bid for reelection; Woodward, as the senior member of the court, assumed that spot.

In November, 1863, the old court ruled that the federal Conscription Act of 1863 was unconstitutional. Outgoing Chief Justice Walter Lowrie delivered the opinion of the court, but Woodward filed his own concurring opinion in which he argued that the Conscription Act unconstitutionally subjected state militia to federal drafting. Woodward further maintained that a national volunteer army could suppress any foreign or domestic enemy. The court issued a temporary injunction which forbade further conscription in the state.[44]

The ruling caused a sensation in Pennsylvania. The *Johnstown Democrat* of November 18, 1863, hailed the verdict by exulting: "Our Supreme Court has honestly met the issue and faithfully discharged a duty." The *Tunkhannock North Branch Democrat* of December 2, 1863, singled out Woodward's opinion as "able and convincing." According to the *Philadelphia Age*, the ruling meant that the enrollment act "ceases to be a law, and it becomes the duty of every good citizen to resist its enforcement." Should the federal government continue to draft Pennsylvanians, it added, "to resist them [the federal officials] would be everyone's right and duty." After reading the verdicts of Lowrie and Woodward, Congressman Philip Johnson unsuccessfully tried to persuade his colleagues in Washington to adopt a resolution requesting President Lincoln to submit the question of the constitutionality of the draft law to the Supreme Court.[45]

Unionists, of course, denounced Woodward and his colleagues as traitors and bided their time until December, when David Agnew replaced Lowrie on the court. Federal officials ignored the verdict and continued to conscript Pennsylvanians. On December 12, 1863, a motion was filed to dissolve the court's injunction; and on January 16, 1864, by a 3-2 verdict, the court reversed itself. Woodward's belief was now the minority opinion. Peace Democrats condemned the new verdict as a base surrender to federal despotism.[46]

Woodward was disappointed with the new ruling. Although friends proposed that he be the Democratic 1864 presidential candidate, he avoided political issues for the remainder of the war. In fact, he announced in 1864 that he would not seek reelection to the supreme court when his term expired in three years. Naturally he endorsed George B.

McClellan for president, and he advised his friends to vote for the general "as the last hope and refuge for our suffering country."[47] Yet he made no political speeches in behalf of the Democratic party. From 1864 to the expiration of his term on the court, Woodward busied himself with official duties and avoided the political limelight.

He celebrated his retirement by taking a trip to Europe, and he fondly contemplated resuming his law practice in Wilkes-Barre. Fate, however, postponed his return to private life. While Woodward was abroad, Congressman John Denison suddenly died. The former supreme court justice was elected to fill out the vacancy. In 1868, the voters of Pennsylvania's twelfth district again sent him to Congress. During his brief stay in Washington, he joined with the small group of representatives opposed to both harsh reconstruction and political equality for blacks.

To his own surprise, and as early as the end of 1865, Woodward had discovered that he approved of Andrew Johnson's lenient reconstruction policy. Like the president, he believed that once the Confederates had laid down their arms, the overwhelming majority of Southerners would again become loyal citizens entitled to govern themselves. In addition, both the new congressman and Johnson were convinced that blacks were not the civil and political equals of whites. "If Negroes ever acquire the right to vote in the States," Woodward declared, "they must obtain it from the States themselves. The Federal Government cannot confer it, for it has no suffrage to bestow outside the District of Columbia and the territories."[48]

Ostensibly, his was a state rights opinion, but Woodward knew that the South was not likely to grant the right to vote to ex-slaves. Consistently he voted against all bills to improve the lot of the blacks. He steadfastly argued that the "ignorant" Negroes should be colonized in Africa.[49]

Because Johnson and Woodward were both sympathetic to the plight of the white Southerner and indifferent to the suffering of blacks, it is not surprising that when the Radicals sought to impeach the president, the Pennsylvanian soundly denounced the 1867 tenure of office act as "a gross violation of the Constitution and . . . [a] usurpation of executive power by the legislative department." His opinions, Woodward alleged, were not based on partisanship or friendship (since he had never voted for Johnson). Rather, he was supporting the president because he truly believed that Johnson was "trying to restore the Union, to pacificate the country, [and] to administer his high office with a faithful regard to the obligations of the Constitution and the best interest of the people."[50]

When his wife died in 1869, Woodward announced that he wanted to return to Pennsylvania and hence would not seek reelection to Congress.

In 1870, friends persuaded him to run for the office of president judge of Pennsylvania's eleventh judicial district, but he was defeated in the October elections.

Before long, however, his services were again in demand. In 1872, he became a delegate to the convention assembled to amend the state constitution. Taking a leading part in the deliberations of the assembly, he served as chairman of the committee on private corporations. Although then a resident of Philadelphia, he actively championed the rights of rural counties and defended limiting the representation of large cities in the legislature.[51] This was his last public service. In the spring of 1875, while travelling in Europe, George Washington Woodward died of complications resulting from pneumonia.

Both Republicans and Democrats offered eulogies. If Woodward had been controversial in his lifetime, all was forgiven by the time of his death. Lawyers, judges, politicians and friends remembered Woodward's exemplary moral character, his devotion to his family and the Episcopal Church, and his fine legal mind. Few had agreed with him all the time, but nearly everyone believed him to be one of the most serious, selfless and conscientious jurists in the history of the commonwealth. Had he composed his own epitaph, he might well have chosen his response to a voter who solicited a bribe from him for his influence with the electorate. Woodward, then a candidate for a judgeship, responded: "I will not pay one cent of money to secure my election, nor do I desire the votes of any persons who can be influenced by money."[52]

To some of his contemporaries, Woodward was a traitor deserving a halter about his neck. Yet no evidence exists that he ever engaged in treason as defined by the Constitution. He was a man who loved the Union of his fathers; but, hampered by a rigid mind, he was unable to adjust fully to the political realities of the 1860s. A tender family man who was never guilty of cruelty to his neighbors, he defended unequal treatment of blacks, whom, like so many other white Americans, he could never accept as political or social equals. To the Lincoln administration he was a dangerous troublemaker more interested in maintaining state rights than in winning the war. But to Woodward a Union in which the states were but pawns of a centralized government was not worth defending. If he misjudged the motives of President Lincoln and his supporters, so too did the Unionists misinterpret his political philosophy and loyalty to the United States.

No one today would claim that Woodward was either a politician of the first magnitude or the most important Copperhead in the North. Nonetheless, he was a noteworthy figure as deserving of scholarly study as several secondary Union and Confederate generals about whom impressive biographies have already been published.

NOTES

[1] George A. Woodward, *Biography of George Washington Woodward* (n. p., 1924), 14-15.

[2] *Proceedings and Debates of the Convention of the Commonwealth of Pennsylvania to Propose Amendments to the Constitution* . . . (Harrisburg, 1838), V, 445-48, 450. Hereafter cited as *Constitutional Convention Proceedings.*

[3] *Niles' National Register,* LXVIII (June 28, 1845), 263; George B. Kulp, *Sketch of the Life and Character of George W. Woodward* (Wilkes-Barre, 1875), 7.

[4] *Woodward on Foreigners* (n. p., 1863); *Muncy Luminary,* October 6, 1863. Unless otherwise indicated, all journals cited are Pennsylvania newspapers.

[5] *Constitutional Convention Proceedings,* X, 16-24.

[6] Oscar Harvey and Ernest Smith, *A History of Wilkes-Barre* (Wilkes-Barre, 1930), V, 19.

[7] *Niles' National Register,* LXVIII (June 28, 1845), 262-65; Frederick Godcharles, *Chronicles of Central Pennsylvania* (New York, 1953), III, 300, 402.

[8] Milo Quaife (ed.), *The Diary of James K. Polk during His Presidency, 1845-1849* (Chicago, 1910), I, 138-39, 145, 183-85, 187, 194-96; James G. Blaine, *Twenty Years of Congress, from Lincoln to Garfield* (Norwich, Conn., 1884-1886), I, 196.

[9] *The Old Guard,* I (1863), 227-28; David Brown, *The Forum* (Philadelphia, 1856), II, 138.

[10] Kulp, *Woodward,* 10; *Address of the Hon. George W. Woodward, Delivered on the Occasion of the Erection of a Monument to the Memory of Francis R. Shunk* (Philadelphia, 1851).

[11] *Constitutional Convention Proceedings,* X, 20; Woodward, *Woodward,* 30-31.

[12] *Constitutional Convention Proceedings,* X, 24; *Chambersburg Franklin Repository,* September 30, 1863.

[13] Undated entry in George W. Woodward legal notebook, 1859-1860, Pennsylvania Historical and Museum Commission.

[14] George W. Woodward to Jeremiah Black, November 18 and 28, 1860; Black to Woodward, November 24, 1860, Jeremiah Black Papers, Library of Congress. Hereafter cited as Black MSS.

[15] George W. Woodward to Jeremiah Black, December 10, 1860, Ibid.

[16] George W. Woodward to Jeremiah Black, November 18, 1860, Ibid.

[17] *Speech of the Hon. George W. Woodward, Delivered at the Great Union Meeting in Independence Square, Philadelphia, December 13, 1860* (Philadelphia, 1863).

[18] *Harrisburg Patriot and Union*, December 15, 1860; *Christian Observer and Presbyterian Witness*, December 20, 1869; *Philadelphia Evening Bulletin*, December 13, 1860; *Philadelphia North American and United States Gazette*, December 14 and 15, 1860; *Bellefonte Central Press*, December 20, 1860.

[19] *Lancaster Evening Express*, September 26, 1863; *Congressional Globe*, Thirty-eighth Congress, First Session, March 24. 1864, 1121-22.

[20] Warren J. Woodward to Charles Buckalew, September 6, 1861, Buckalew Papers, Wilkes College.

[21] *Lancaster Evening Express*, September 28, 1863; *Lancaster Examiner and Herald*, September 30, 1863; *Harrisburg Telegraph*, October 1, 1863.

[22] Woodward, *Woodward*, 32; *Philadelphia Age*, September 25, 1863.

[23] *Harrisburg Patriot and Union*, February 2, 1863. Similar resolutions were adopted throughout Pennsylvania.

[24] George W. Woodward to Lewis Coryell, June 1, 1863, Coryell Papers, Historical Society of Pennsylvania. Hereafter cited as Coryell MSS.

[25] Ibid.; George W. Woodward to Jeremiah Black, November 28, 1860, Black MSS.

[26] Thomas Morris to Lewis Coryell, April 15, 1863; George W. Woodward to Lewis Coryell, June 1, 1863, Coryell MSS.

[27] *Harrisburg Telegraph*, June 18, 1863; Christopher Ward diary, June 18, 1863, Historical Society of Pennsylvania.

[28] Fernando Wood, who was mayor of New York City during the secession crisis, once declared that his city should secede from the Union and join the Confederacy. *Turnwold* (Ga.) *Countryman*, July 14, 1863; *Pittsburgh Dispatch*, July 28, 1863; *Philadelphia Evening Bulletin*, July 31, 1863.

[29] *Wellsboro Tioga Agitator*, June 24, 1863.

[30] William Kelley to Anna Dickinson, August 2, 1863; Evan Randolph to Anna Dickinson, December 7, 1863, Anna Dickinson Papers, Library of Congress; Erwin Bradley, *The Triumph of Militant Republicanism* (Philadelphia, 1964), 175-77.

[31] Woodward was every bit as much a war critic as the more celebrated Vallandigham. Charles Mason to Peter McCall, August 31, 1863, Cadwalader Collection, Historical Society of Pennsylvania; Arnold Shankman, "Candidate in Exile: Clement Vallandigham and the 1863 Ohio Gubernatorial Election" (Master's thesis, Emory University, 1969).

[32] *York Gazette*, September 22 and October 13, 1863; *Harrisburg Patriot and Union*, August 15, 1863.

[33] *Wilkes-Barre Luzerne Union*, December 25, 1861; May 28, 1862; *Harrisburg Patriot and Union*, August 15, 1863.

[34] *The Views of Judge Woodward and Bishop Hopkins on Negro Slavery at the South, Illustrated from the Journal of a Residence on a Georgia Plantation by Mrs. Frances Kemble* (n. p., 1863); John Henry Hopkins, *A Scriptural, Ecclesiastical and Historical View of Slavery* (New York, 1864).

[35] *Easton Argus*, quoted in *Meadville Crawford Democrat*, September 15, 1863.

[36] *Clearfield Raftman's Journal*, September 9, 1863; *Washington Reporter and Examiner*, October 7, 1863.

[37] *Pittsburgh Gazette*, October 5, 1863; *Muncy Luminary*, October 13, 1863.

[38] *Philadelphia Inquirer*, August 27, 1863; *Philadelphia Age*, August 28 and September 19, 1863; *Harrisburg Telegraph*, September 11, 1863.

[39] *Montrose Democrat*, October 1, 1863; *Johnstown Democrat*, October 7, 1863; *Philadelphia Daily Ledger*, October 10, 1863.

[40] George W. Woodward to Jeremiah Black, September 10, 1863, Black MSS.

[41] George B. McClellan to Charles J. Biddle, October 12, 1863, George B. McClellan Papers, Illinois State Historical Society; *Chambersburg Franklin Repository*, quoted in *Harrisburg Telegraph*, October 31, 1863.

[42] *Philadelphia Age*, October 16, 1863; John Bell Robinson, *An Address to the "People" of the Several Sovereign States of the United States on the Frauds Committed on Their Elective Franchise* (Philadelphia [?], 1864).

[43] *Philadelphia Evening Bulletin*, October 19, 1863; George W. Woodward to Peter McCall, October 23, 1863, Cadwalader Collection; Nicholas Wainwright, "The Loyal Opposition in Civil War Philadelphia," *Pennsylvania Magazine of History and Biography*, LXXXVIII (1964), 160.

[44] *Pittsburgh Post*, November 10 and 11, 1863; Jack Leach, *Conscription in America* (Rutland, Vt., 1952), 378-79.

[45] Henry Lea, *The Record of the Democratic Party, 1860-65* (Philadelphia, 1866[?]), 25-26.

[46] *Philadelphia Evening Bulletin*, January 16, 1864; *Philadelphia Inquirer*, January 18, 1864; Charles Ingersoll to Jeremiah Black, January 20, 1864, Black MSS.

[47] *Erie Observer*, July 9, 1864; George W. Woodward to George B. McClellan, August 31 and November 6, 1864, McClellan Papers, Library of Congress.

[48] George W. Woodward, *Speech on Negro Suffrage — The Reconstruction Laws, March 21, 1868* (Washington, 1868), 10.

[49] Ibid., 7-11; *George W. Woodward, S. S. Cox, and C. A. Eldrich on the Reconstruction of Georgia* (Washington, 1869), 6.

[50] George W. Woodward, *Speech on the Impeachment of the President* (Washington, 1868), 5; Woodward, *Woodward*, 36; George W. Woodward to Hugh McCulloch, October 17, 1865, McCulloch Papers, Library of Congress.

[51] Kulp, *Woodward*, 12.

[52] Ibid., 23.

VII

Chaplain William E. Wiatt:
Soldier of the Cloth

By JAMES I. ROBERTSON, JR.

Bell I. Wiley, the foremost authority on life within the ranks of Union and Confederate armies, has observed that "generally speaking the quality of Civil War chaplains was poor." However, Wiley hastened to add, "many chaplaincies throughout the war were held by good men impelled by lofty motives and thoroughly devoted to the cause of righteousness."[1] The recent discovery of a remarkable diary compiled by a middle-aged Virginia chaplain not only substantiates that conclusion but also depicts Rev. William E. Wiatt as one of the most faithful clerics on either side of that embattled generation.

This Confederate chaplain came from a long-established and highly respected family in Gloucester County, a tidewater area on Virginia's Middle Peninsula. He was the third of three sons of Dr. William Graham and Louisa Stubbs Wiatt. Born July 31, 1826, at the Gloucester residence of M.V. Kerns, William Edward Wiatt spent the bulk of his early youth in local academies. Strong religious convictions were a constant supplement to his education. Wiatt had barely turned sixteen when he made a "profession of religion"; and on August 7, 1842, he was baptized as a member of Ebenezer Church in Gloucester County.[2] An active and abiding association with the Baptist faith continued for the next seventy-five years.

At eighteen, this young man of large eyes, prominent nose, medium height and build embarked on a teaching career.[3] His first post was a primary school in the Little Plymouth community of Gloucester County. Wiatt's interests expanded and matured during his five years in that position. He became enamored of the Masonic Order, joined a local chapter and rapidly developed into one of the more active Masons of his day. On December 10, 1846, he married Catherine Rebecca Spencer of neighboring King and Queen County.[4] Early the following year, he received a lay license to preach at Olivet Church in his wife's county. Yet tragedy abruptly intervened. In October, 1849, Rebecca Wiatt died. The loss of his young wife was a primary factor prompting Wiatt to accept a new teaching position in the Covington, Kentucky, school of James Dabney.

The Kentucky sojourn was generally unpleasant and unrewarding. Plagued throughout his life by minor ailments,[5] Wiatt found the new environment discomforting. "I never spent such a disagreeable time scarcely in my life," he wrote of his first months in Kentucky. He was unhappy with the hot and humid climate, with the "free school" where he taught, and with the people in the community. Of the Covington residents he stated: "You will not hear them converse on any book subject. All their knowledge nearly consists in plain matter-of-fact things. They seem to think more of making money than anything else."

Wiatt found some solace in a local Masonic chapter. Yet his thoughts dwelled repeatedly on religion and Gloucester County. In a letter to a friend, he inquired about the ministerial status of a Baptist church in Gloucester and added: "I feel more for Gloucester than any other place. I try to pray frequently that God would look upon her favorably and make His cause to flourish greatly [there]."[6]

He steadfastly attended all Baptist services in Covington. On at least two occasions he delivered guest sermons to congregations that "seemed to be attentive and respectful." Such responses made Wiatt increasingly anxious to enter the ministry. Unfortunately, no such opportunities appeared.[7]

In 1851, Wiatt left Kentucky for a teaching post in Lowndes County, Alabama. A young widower far from home and friends, he badly needed companionship. This void played a large part in his September 29, 1852, marriage to Charlotte Laura Coleman. This second union lasted twelve years, produced five children and was for Wiatt a very settling experience. By his own admission, however, the most profound event in his life occurred in April, 1854, when, at the request of the Hickory Grove Church in Lowndes County, he was ordained a Baptist minister.[8] Wiatt assumed his new clerical duties with such zeal that teaching quickly became of secondary importance.

Early in 1856, what Wiatt had sought for so long became a reality. He received a call to become pastor of Providence and Union Baptist churches in his native Gloucester County. Wiatt eagerly moved his family to Virginia and entered his new duties with complete devotion. He preached at each church twice a month. He also proved to be a conscientious and hardworking pastor. The Providence congregation trebled in five years and was one of the first white churches in Virginia to number Negroes among its members. Wiatt's overall accomplishments were so progressive that his initial salary of $70 annually increased fivefold in the 1856-1861 period.[9]

The tranquility of success suddenly burst with the explosions of civil war. Wiatt promptly resigned both pastorates in the spring of 1861 and enlisted in the Confederate army as a private in the Twenty-sixth Virginia Infantry Regiment. His stay in the ranks was brief. On October 4, 1861, the thirty-five-year-old Wiatt was appointed chaplain of his regiment. His chaplaincy was unique in that he was the only "Holy Joe" the Twenty-sixth Virginia ever had—one of the few Civil War chaplains who served with the same unit for the duration of the war.[10]

The length of Wiatt's army ministry, on the other hand, was no more singular than the war record of the Twenty-sixth Virginia Infantry. Organized and mustered into service in May, 1861, the unit was the principal regiment from the Middle Peninsula. The counties of King and Queen, Gloucester and Mathews supplied nine of the first ten companies.[11] From the outset the regiment experienced a high incidence of sickness, attributable in great part to the fact that most of its members were farm boys who had had little previous contact with "city diseases" normally associated with childhood. Hence, during the Twenty-sixth Virginia's first service in the fortifications at Gloucester Point, it suffered epidemics of measles and mumps as well as outbreaks of malaria and typhoid fever. By August, 1861, only about 250 of 1,200 men in the oversized regiment were fit for duty. Not until the end of the year was the regiment back to reasonably full strength.[12]

Equally shattering to the regiment's potential and morale was a subsequent high desertion rate. In the spring of 1862, the Twenty-sixth Virginia was manning part of the peninsular defenses when Federal Gen. George B. McClellan disembarked his Army of the Potomac around Yorktown and began a massive advance on Richmond. Confederate authorities saw no alternative but to consolidate their outnumbered forces. This meant the abandonment of the Gloucester area. To many men in the Twenty-sixth Virginia, the idea of defending Richmond while their own homes and families were at the mercy of the enemy was too much to bear. Moreover, the one-year enlistment of the troops was then about to expire; and even if the Confederacy carried out a proposed plan of conscription, it would be unenforceable in the Union-held Middle Peninsula. Thus, mass desertions occurred that spring as men simply walked home. The absenteeism reached such a proportion that at the July 1, 1862, battle of Malvern Hill (at which the Twenty-sixth Virginia was but a spectator), the 1200-man regiment numbered only thirty-one officers and 424 men present for duty.[13]

More incredible than these statistics was the battle record of the Twenty-sixth Virginia. For the first two years of the war, while opposing armies grappled throughout Virginia, the regiment performed monotonous garrison duty on the outer fringes of the Richmond defenses. It was involved in no fighting larger than a skirmish. The third year of the war found the regiment on defense duty in South Carolina and Florida, still without any coveted battle scars. Not until July, 1864, did the Twenty-sixth Virginia taste real combat; but in the remaining nine months of the war it participated in more bloody actions than did most regiments in four years of campaigning.

The Twenty-sixth Virginia was stationed in the Gloucester defenses when Wiatt assumed the duties of chaplain. Few guidelines existed as to the nature of his job. The Confederate government did not provide anything akin to a full set of rules and regulations for army chaplains. The precise rank of chaplains was never determined, and the salary was pathetic. As a result, the individual merit of each chaplain played the dominant role in how well—or how poorly—he was accepted by those whom he presumably served.[14] The Twenty-sixth Virginia at the outset was not known for any pious spirit, so Wiatt had a large and barren vineyard in which to labor.

His early efforts produced at best mixed results. Lieutenant Josiah Ryland attended a prayer meeting in January, 1862, and wrote of Wiatt: "I cannot enjoy his sermons, he is so lifeless." A few weeks later, Ryland commented that Wiatt's sermons would be much more interesting "if he would only let go." Yet by the summer of that year Wiatt had obviously learned from experience, for the critical Ryland then stated: "[I] went over to hear Wiatt, who stirred up my dull, cold heart. I think him one of our best Chaplains."[15] Indeed, Wiatt soon established himself as "one of the most laborious and useful Chaplains in the army." The Rev. George F. Bagby, a colporter who worked closely with Wiatt through much of the Civil War, termed him "one of the most faithful men I ever knew."[16]

In April, 1862, the Twenty-sixth Virginia was reassigned to a newly formed brigade under controversial Gen. Henry A. Wise. A prominent

Virginian who had served as both governor and U.S. congressman, Wise was then elderly, erratic and glaringly lacking in military experience. His initial Civil War campaigns in western Virginia and on Roanoke Island had ended in disaster. Nevertheless, because of his status as a senior brigadier, he was given command of a brigade consisting of the Twenty-sixth, Thirty-fourth, Forty-sixth and Fifty-ninth Virginia.

Wise's inabilities, however, relegated the unit to oblivion for much of the war. One writer has summarized his problems by stating: "He showed fatherly kindness toward the officers and men under his command, but was fiercely critical and provocative in his relations with officers of equal and superior rank . . . . Every commander he ever had soon found it expedient to shunt him off on some detached service where, hopefully, he would be out of the action."[17] This explains why Wise's huge brigade spent the sixteen most critical months of the war (April, 1862-September, 1863) performing unimportant post duty in the Chaffin's Farm area downriver from Richmond.

It was during the Twenty-sixth Virginia's long period of military inactivity that Chaplain Wiatt began keeping a diary. His initial entry was made October 1, 1862; and for the remainder of the war, the 8" x 5" leather notebook was his most constant companion. Wiatt let no day pass without making a lengthy notation. Quite often he made several entries during a single day. For example, he would describe a soldier's suffering in the morning and then report the soldier's death that afternoon. Except for semicolons used in lieu of periods, plus occasional errors in capitalization, Wiatt's prose was a reflection of himself: intelligent and straightforward.

The journal is a highly spiritual and personal document. Wiatt, displaying little interest in military matters, was far more concerned with baptisms than with battles. He occasionally repeated rumors of engagements in other military theaters, and he penned good descriptions of the marches of the Twenty-sixth Virginia. Yet the diary is almost entirely a personal account of the religious activity in a single regiment.

Therein lies its great historical value. The entries provide perhaps the most detailed, day-by-day account in existence of "Christ in the Camp." Wiatt noted the nature of church services and prayer meetings, biblical sources for every sermon preached, summaries of confessionals held with individual soldiers, the names of both converts and "backsliders," the volume of tracts, testaments and newspapers distributed, visitations, collections and a host of other subjects pertinent to his duties as chaplain. Wiatt surely prided himself on being a Christian soldier; but, as his journal shows, he was totally a Christian and only incidentally a soldier.

He was ill at the time he began the diary. When his health did not improve, he obtained sick leave and went home to Gloucester until mid-November. He returned to the regiment still unwell, yet he quickly immersed himself in a multitude of pastoral duties. To him it was "a blessed comfort" to feel that he was "instrumental in any way in honouring God."[18] So Wiatt sought every imaginable way to attain that goal.

He would usually visit two or more companies each day and then hold a prayer meeting, Bible class or counseling session in the evening. In May, 1863, he even began conducting a reading class for the illiterate in the regiment. Wiatt was a veritable lending library in the Twenty-sixth Virginia for religious materials—Bibles, pamphlets, tracts, hymnals and such Baptist newspapers as the influential *Religious Herald*. He constantly replenished his reading supplies by oral and written pleas to church groups in Richmond, Gloucester and elsewhere. Ever active in Masonic endeavors, Wiatt personally established two lodges in Wise's brigade. He never failed to promote the virtues of the Masons to all potentially interested soldiers, and lodge brothers came to regard him "as a father."[19]

Wiatt was also an indefatigable fund-raiser. From the ranks of the Twenty-sixth Virginia in the winter of 1862-1863, he solicited $219.50 "for the relief of the bereaved and suffering of [the battle of] Fredericksburg," as well as $191.55 "for sufferers in Richmond." In February, 1863, he also collected $65 to purchase materials for the construction of a chapel at the regimental encampment at Burton's Farm.

Other duties kept him busy. Wiatt wrote a host of letters for uneducated and incapacitated soldiers. Whenever he journeyed behind the lines, he performed countless errands for the men and then returned to camp laden with mail, food and religious supplies. He visited other chaplains in search of advice and other regiments in search of sinners. He made regular calls to army hospitals and jails. He habitually sought areas where spiritual work was needed, and he was ever ready to preach a sermon to anyone at any time. His busiest day, naturally, was Sunday. A diary entry for one Sabbath illustrated the wide range of Wiatt's activities:

Distributed 30 odd 'Heralds' and 'Advocates' among the camp for Sab [bath] reading; also among the prisoners & guards; one of the prisoners told me he was trying to be Christian; visited Holt[20] (Poindexter's company); very ill; he seems in a great deal of trouble; he was once a professor of religion but has backslidden; I read to him and talked with him endeavouring to comfort him; visited hospital and left papers and Tracts; commenced the Bible Class at 9 1/2 o'clock; was much gratified at seeing so many officers and men present (about 20) the first day; we took the 1st and 2d Chs. of Matthew; had a very pleasant interchange of views &c.; I hope that this B[ible] Class will be the means of doing much good; at about 11 o'clock preached to a house pretty well filled and attentive from Heb. VIII:3; distributed 11 Texts (all I had left); in the evening held p[rayer] m[eeting]; a large crowd present; Bro. Pollard[21] conducted it and spoke on the 'Good Fight'; I followed; distributed a large number of Tracts; recd. and gave out books.

Wiatt's intimate knowledge of the Bible is best reflected in the multitude of scriptural texts he used for sermon topics. A tabulation of biblical references (which Wiatt was always careful to note in his diary) reveals that he had a strong preference for New Testament sources. The Gospel of John was his favorite book. He also made repeated use of the other gospels, The Acts and Hebrews. His principal Old Testament sources were Psalms and Isaiah. Rarely did Wiatt preach more than once from the same biblical verse. The major exception was John 19:30 — "When Jesus therefore received the vinegar, he said, 'It is finished': and he bowed his head, and gave up the ghost." The first sermon cited in the diary was based on this quotation, and Wiatt used the same text on three other occasions during the course of the war. He also broke custom by preaching twice from Isaiah 49:15 — "Can a woman forget her sucking child, that she should not have compassion on the son of her womb? Yea, they may forget, yet I will not forget thee."

The latest biblical text utilized by Wiatt was for an evangelical sermon and came from Revelations 3:15- 16 — "I know thy works, that thou are neither cold nor hot: I would thou were cold or hot. So then, because thou art lukewarm, and neither cold nor hot, I will spue thee out of my mouth." One of the earliest biblical references for a sermon (and one that was obviously aimed at the North) was Deuteronomy 32:28-29 — "For they are a nation void of counsel, neither is there any understanding in them. O that they were wise, that they understood this, that they would consider their latter end!"

A sampling of other biblical texts will illustrate how Wiatt applied religious tenets to the environment of civil war. One Sunday morning service revolved around Matthew 6:33 — "But seek ye first the kingdom of God, and his righteousness; and all these things shall be added unto you." Another evolved from John 3:3 — "Jesus answered and said unto him, 'Verily, verily, I say unto thee, Except a man be born again, he cannot see the kingdom of God.'" An 1863 revival meeting had as a theme Ezekiel 33:11 — "Say unto them, As I live, saith the Lord God, I have no pleasure in the death of the wicked; but that the wicked turn from his way and live; turn ye, turn ye from your evil ways . . . "

On the eve before a long and potentially dangerous march, Wiatt exhorted the soldiers with Hebrews 13:5-6—"Let your conversation be without convetousness; and be content with such things as ye have: for he hath said, 'I will never leave thee, nor forsake thee.' So that we may boldly say, 'The Lord is my helper, and I will not fear what man shall do unto me.'" When Wise's brigade laid siege to the Federal garrison at Williamsburg, Wiatt resorted to the familiar words of Psalms 121:1 — "I will lift up mine eyes unto the hills, from whence cometh my help." The Confederate success in that expedition prompted from Wiatt a "well-received" sermon from I John 4:16—"And we have known and believed that love that God hath to us. God is love; and he that dwelleth in love dwelleth in God, and God in him."

Defeat in the Christmas, 1863, operations in South Carolina induced Wiatt to give a message of consolation based on John 12:46—"I am come a light into the world, that whosoever believeth in me should not abide in darkness." For soldier funerals, Wiatt used the biblical quotations now standard with such services. He was also particularly fond of James 4:14—"Whereas ye know not what shall be on the morrow. For what is your life? It is even a vapour, that appeareth for a little time, and then vanisheth away."

After each sermon mentioned in the diary would usually appear the simple entry: "Had a good crowd and one, seemingly, attentive and interested."

Individual counseling with soldiers occupied a large portion of Wiatt's time. The chaplain generally ended such meetings by giving the man a Bible or religious tract as a future bracer. Soldiers with spiritual problems called on Wiatt at all hours. At 2 A.M. on October 8, 1862, Lt. Robert R. Berry of Company E roused Wiatt from bed. "His mind is evidently very much disturbed," the chaplain noted. "He seems to think that the Devil has possession of him and that he must perish; he can't read the Bible, can't pray, and can't see any way of peace for himself." On the following day, however, Berry returned to Wiatt's tent "to tell me of the goodness of God to him; . . . all is light and love; Jesus appears to him in His true character and Satan has fled from him."[22]

More typical of Wiatt's quiet efforts to instill evangelical spirit in soldiers was this diary entry: "Had an interesting conversation with Cooper (W. K. Perrin's company), who has been so long disturbed on account of his sins; he has come to the determination at last to trust Jesus and publickly acknowledge Him in Baptism."[23]

Giving spiritual comfort to the sick and critically ill was of paramount importance to Wiatt. As he once observed: "I find nearly all of our men, when sick, admit their need of religion, and acknowledge that they think about it." Consequently, the Baptist cleric visited army hospitals at every opportunity. The most moving case that Wiatt witnessed was Pvt. Alexander Davis of Company C. In January, 1863, Davis received a vaccination for smallpox. Massive infection followed the innoculation. On January 29, Wiatt wrote: "Assisted in dressing Davis's arm; poor fellow! He is an object of sympathy, indeed; I have seldom seen one more dreadfully afflicted; his left arm is deprived of flesh nearly to the bone from the wrist nearly to the shoulder, and his right arm from the shoulder to the elbow; he cries; he feels himself a sinner and asked me to pray for him . . . . I visited him again in the evening, but he seemed too drowsy to listen to reading or prayer; may God give him pardon and peace." Davis died two days later.[24]

Wiatt either did not know or would not accept the fact that terminal comas often prevented soldiers from responding to the chaplain's ministrations. Three times in December, 1862, Wiatt visited an ill soldier named Washington Tarr. Although Wiatt implored the man "to look to Jesus," Tarr was "so near gone I fear he was not able to appreciate the advice." On the morning that Tarr succumbed, Wiatt commented: "He died a patriot, but alas! I fear not a Christian."[25] The diary entry for June 10, 1863, reveals a similar case: "Visited hospital; Blackstock (Poindexter's company) very ill; not much hope of his recovery; he is in a drowsy state constantly, and I cannot hold religious conversation with him as I desire."[26]

The monotony of brigade picket duty momentarily ceased in April, 1863, when Wise received orders to stage a demonstration against the Federal garrison at Williamsburg.[27] The subsequent campaign lasted twelve days. Wise's men flanked the town and destroyed the military depot at Whittaker's Mill. Wiatt was anything but elated over the action. Referring to the Fifty-ninth Virginia, a sister unit, he grumbled: "Col. [William B.] Tabb had not a man killed, but I understand that some 15 or 20 men were made drunk on Yankee liquor . . . . What a curse ardent spirits are to the world!"[28]

Wiatt never forgot the return march to Burton's Farm, the regimental encampment near Chaffin's Farm. Driving rain and "waist-deep" mud turned the fifty-mile journey into a nightmare. General Wise found the ordeal amusing. "Ah, you lazy boogers!" he once shouted to the struggling column. "I guess I have washed the lice off of you!"[29] Yet for Wiatt the march was a taxing experience. "I walked all the way and carried the guns of several of our men who were unwell or barefooted." For a week thereafter, the chaplain was confined to his bed with chills and fever.

During the long sixteen months of garrison duty below Richmond, Wiatt's opinion of the enemy changed noticeably. He had felt little animosity at the outset toward Federals. On December 18, 1862, he wrote: "Heard today of great depradations commited by the Yankees upon citizens of Gloucester, driving off sheep & hogs and cattle & horses; a great many in my neighbourhood robbed; don't know whether they visited my home or not; I leave all in God's hands." Nevertheless, continued Federal raids on the defenseless citizens of Gloucester angered the chaplain. In March, 1863, Wiatt obtained a seven-day furlough in order to remove his family from the county. He hastened home and then noted in his journal: "Went by my place and beheld a truly desolate sight; nobody at home; the dwelling house closed up; the out homes a good deal injured; a heap of blackened coals and ashes and bricks where the barn and carriage house stood; no hogs nor cattle nor sheep."

Two days later, Federal cavalry struck again. Wiatt was outraged. "Is not this the spirit of the Devil working in them? And can such perpetrations of wanton and brutal crimes prosper? I am an exile from my home and from my native County, but I had rather be away than to be there, subjected to the insults and outrages of a people who seem neither to fear God nor regard man." Only after his wife and children had been safely transferred to Alabama (so as not to expose them further "to Yankee insults or indignities") did Wiatt's resentment subside.[30]

The Southern patriotism that Wiatt felt was expressed largely in terms of Christian faith. In a passing reference to Confederate losses at Fort Donelson, Tennessee, he observed: "Some of the best blood of Virginia was spilt, but tis glorious to die the death of such a Christian patriot and soldier." New Year's Eve, 1862, found Wiatt in an exhorting mood. "Oh! how good God has been to me in the midst of so many and so great dangers! . . . How God has preserved and blessed our Confederacy! . . . Again, how He interposed most manifestly and most wonderfully for our deliverance & gives us the most signal victories over our enemies!" In March, 1863, Wiatt prayed that "if it be His will, may our independence be secured and peace established before summer. Oh! Lord, we are in thy hands." Then, early in May of that year, news reached the Twenty-sixth Virginia that a great battle had erupted in the tangled wilderness west of Fredericksburg. "Oh! Lord of Hosts," Wiatt pleaded, "be with our generals and with our men; fight for us and give us the victory, victory for Thy honour, and for our good."

Although Wiatt was on congenial terms with all officers in the brigade — which was no mean achievement for a chaplain — he rarely made mention of generals in his diary. Yet the untimely death at Chancellorsville of Gen. Thomas J. "Stonewall" Jackson moved him deeply. On May 11, he wrote: "Recd. intelligence today of the death of our beloved Gen. Jackson; a great general; a noble patriot; a brave hero and a pious Christian has fallen; . . . the whole Confederacy has suffered a great loss in his death and the whole Confederacy is deeply afflicted; but we have a good God to bear us on to victory and to peace, and, while we lament the gallant dead [of Chancellorsville], we will trust in the loving God and go forward."

Shortly thereafter, a full-scale revival likened to "a religious phenomenon unique in the history of warfare" swept through the Confederate ranks.[31] It had begun early in 1863 inside Robert E. Lee's army. The victory at Chancellorsville, followed by Lee's ill-fated invasion of the North, sent the revival spirit surging through other military units stationed in Virginia. Lieutenant Fred Fleet of the Twenty-sixth Virginia wrote home in late June: "I wish very much that we could have a great outpouring of God's Grace with us as I see there has been in the noble army of Northern Virginia."[32]

Fleet did not know that Wiatt had already reacted with characteristic fervor. As the lieutenant was writing his parents, army missionary Andrew Broaddus, Sr., arrived at the camp of the Twenty-sixth Virginia. Broaddus quickly discovered "that through the labors of Brother Wiatt there were evident indications of an approaching revival of religion."[33]

Wiatt formed an evangelical team with Broaddus and colporter George F. Bagby. The Baptist trio promptly embarked on a thirty-eight-day series of church services, soldier counseling, prayer meetings and baptisms. Broaddus informed his headquarters: "The chapel has been well filled with attentive hearers of the word. Already some . . . who had forsaken their first love have returned with weeping and rejoicing to the Lord's vineyard."[34] Wiatt was equally happy. "The good work of the good Lord seems to be progressing," he announced early in July. "A great deal of seriousness prevails. . . . The Lord be praised in the conversion and salvation of souls."

Indeed, Wiatt became so totally immersed in the army revival that he made no mention in his diary of the three-day holocaust at Gettysburg. Even when his wife informed him of the death of their infant son William, the chaplain wrote simply: "Oh! Lord, give me grace to enable me to bear my afflictions" — and then he returned in his diary to particulars of the revival.

Evangelist Broaddus summarized part of Wiatt's labors in a letter written at that time. "The meeting held with the Twenty-sixth Regiment, Wise's Brigade, which commenced more than four weeks ago, is still in progress. About 175 have professed religion, among whom are a number of what are called *backsliders* . . . . Brother Wiatt has baptized sixty-four, and about an equal number have united with a Methodist class."[35] Wiatt himself radiated pleasure that so many men "had come to the Lord." However, he added, "many are yet in their sins; Oh! Lord, bring all unto thee." He described the mental agony of one soldier in that category. "Bristow seemed overwhelmed with trouble on account of backsliding; he came in my tent and after conversation and prayer seemed to feel better; I scarcely ever saw a man come to suffer more and to confess more fully."[36]

The success of Wiatt's efforts during the six-week religious resurgence is evident in a report that he sent to a church newspaper in Richmond. Wiatt forwarded $186.98 contributed by the Twenty-sixth Virginia for the purchase of Bibles and tracts. He then stated: "We have been holding prayer-meeting constantly . . . and we scarcely ever fail, how tired soever the men may be, to have a large congregation. It is a glorious sight to behold a hundred or two young Christians mingling their voices in praise to their Saviour . . . . I have already baptized 71 in this regiment . . . I have baptized 36 in the Thirty-fourth and Forty-sixth [Regiments]."[37]

Two days later, the regiment's long sojourn at Burton's Farm ended. By then, thanks to sixteen months of almost uninterrupted maneuvers on the parade ground, the Twenty-sixth Virginia had become (in the opinion of General Wise) the best-drilled unit in the Confederate army. Hence, it was widely regarded as Wise's "pet regiment."[38] Yet the brigade as a whole had acquired an unwanted nickname. To fill the time and to supplement army rations, Wise had ordered the men to cultivate vegetable patches. The results were digestively rewarding, but the soldiers winced at being called Wise's Gardeners.[39]

Anxious to remove this slur and long desirous of battle, the ranks were elated when the brigade was directed to reinforce the besieged defenses at Charleston, South Carolina. Wiatt himself commented: "Our Regt. has done very little besides camp service since it has been a Regt. (more than two years now) and it seems right that we should do something in the field; . . . Oh! Lord, go with us and abide with us; help us to do our full duty towards Thee and towards our Country."

The six-day train trip was fatiguing but boisterous. On the day after the brigade's arrival at the upriver defenses of Charleston, Wiatt attempted to hold church services. It was futile—and a blow to his morale, coming as it did on the heels of the recent revival. "Am sorry to say that there was a great deal of noise and confusion around us; a great deal of Drinking among the men; and some of them who have lately professed religion; Oh! how distressing." Wiatt thereupon went over to the next camp and delivered several exhortations to the soldiers in Colquitt's Georgia brigade.

In fact, the chaplain rarely missed an opportunity to spread the faith in the new South Carolina surroundings. He baptized fifteen soldiers during his first two months outside Charleston. Nightly prayer meetings were held; and, wrote Reverend Bagby, "after the meeting is over, singing and other devotional exercises are continued in the different messes until bedtime."[40] Wiatt seemed to regard every Confederate soldier as a spiritual challenge. Following his first visit to Charleston (whose people and prices pleased him), he caught a river packet back to camp. Of the return trip he wrote: "Came up in a boat with four Irishmen; they were Catholics and quite irreligious; I gave them a lecture on temperance and preached Jesus to them." A somewhat similar incident occurred later when Wiatt was travelling to Charleston in a wagon. The driver gave a ride to two walking soldiers. "One was a Lutheran," Wiatt stated. "I exhorted him to faithfulness as a Christian; the other was a backslider, had been a Baptist; I exhorted him to return from his wanderings."

Meanwhile, Wiatt was hard at work restoring a Christian atmosphere to the Twenty-sixth Virginia. He superintended the construction of a pine arbor that served as a makeshift chapel. He played the leading role in the formation of a Regimental Christian Association. Within a month it had 171 members. He continued to make hospital calls, which were always productive, and jail visits, which were not. Twice he counselled with Pvt. Harrison Ball, a deserter awaiting trial. Wiatt "read the Scriptures to him and conversed with him on the subject of religion." Ball remained an unmoved agnostic.[41]

On October 30, 1863, Gen. P.G.T. Beauregard and Louisiana statesman Pierre Soulé reviewed Wise's brigade. The Virginia unit, Wiatt proudly noted, "made a very fine appearance and was highly complimented by the Gen.; he said it was the finest looking body of men he had seen; . . . Gen. B. complimented the 26th Va. especially, saying it was a '*very fine Regiment.*'" The chaplain then penned unusually vivid pictures of the two dignitaries:

Gen. B[eauregard] is about 40 years old or a little upwards, has a grey head, dark moustache (rather short) & small imperial, balance of his face clean shaven; he has a very swarthy complexion; he is very quick in his movements, particularly in turning his head, and seems to see everything about him; I suppose he is about 5 ft. 7 or 8 in. in height and weighs 145 or 150 lbs.; he was dressed rather plainly, rode a splendid dark mare, and sat elegantly on horseback; his face indicated, to me, mainly silence and modesty, but a good degree of sprightliness; he was accompanied by Hon. Pierre Soulé of Louisiana, who instead of being a thin, tall man, as I had pictured to my own mind, is a low, fat, sleepy and dull looking personage; he sits very awkwardly on horseback and rides badly, is quite hump-shouldered; how different he appears from the brilliant orator I have always heard that he was; he is clean shaven and dressed in a suit of light 'pepper & salt' cloth.[42]

Shortly thereafter, Wiatt received a twenty-five-day furlough to visit his family in Montgomery, Alabama. The chaplain was waiting for a westbound train in the Charleston depot when, to his surprise, President Jefferson Davis entered the station.[43] Wiatt "had the pleasure of seeing" the Confederate leader. He described Davis as "about 6 ft., spare, weighs, I judge, about 135 or 140; was dressed plainly; wore a little beard under his chin; had a very pleasant but determined look."[44]

Wiatt returned to the regiment in time for its second engagement — and first defeat. Early in December, Federal forces occupied Legareville on James Island. This move posed a threat to the major portion of the Confederate defenses of Charleston. Beauregard thereupon ordered a counterthrust: a battalion of artillery, with the Twenty-sixth Virginia in support, attacked Legareville on Christmas Day. The assault was a complete failure because the Confederate cannon were no match for the heavier guns of Federal ironclads anchored in the river. The Virginians were angered by the whole affair. They had endured a hard march, spent all of Christmas Day digging redoubts for the guns and then found themselves under severe bombardment from the formidable USS *Marblehead*. Lieutenant Mills of the Twenty-sixth Virginia wrote his brother after the campaign: "I never heard Infantry abuse Artillery as ours did. [Our] Artillery ought to have sunk the boat in 15 minutes."[45]

Chaplain Wiatt was an injured bystander in this action. On the march to Legareville, one of the brigade wagons ran over his left foot. He was confined to an ambulance thereafter. Yet Wiatt recovered sufficiently by December 27 to conduct a prayer meeting of thanksgiving. "Several exhortations by [the] Brethren," he stated, "all expressing their gratitude to God for His merciful deliverance on Christmas day; Oh! that God may bring good out of this matter."

Early in January, 1864, Wiatt proudly announced how widespread "the work of the Lord" was in the Twenty-sixth Virginia. "During the three months and a half of our campaign here, about twenty-five of our officers and men have professed Christ. I have already baptized fifteen, and several more will follow . . . . A great deal of zeal and love for Christ are exhibited . . . . We have a flourishing Christian Association, composed of some two hundred or more members . . . . We don't cease to remember our churches in prayer. Do they remember us?"[46]

Duty at Charleston ended on February 23, when Wise's brigade embarked by train for Savannah, Georgia. Wiatt very quickly came to dislike the new locale. "At night," he wrote on February 24, "a good many of our officers and men (some professors of religion among them) attended the theatre, where they witnessed a very indecent performance, I understand; too great a spirit of worldly mindedness prevails among us, and I fear that our proximity to the city will have a very bad influence over the Regt." Wiatt was surely relieved when, three days later, the Twenty-sixth Virginia was ordered to entrain for coastal defense duty at Lake City, Florida.

There, on March 3, Wiatt fumed at the sight of eight captured Negro soldiers. "Cowardly wretches!" he stated of Federal authorities. "They cannot subdue us themselves and they force the ignorant and timid negroes to help them." He was certain that Union army commanders were using threats and bayonets to make the blacks "a breastwork for their cowardly carcasses."

Wiatt customarily began several evangelical movements in the new regiments he encountered at Lake City. He found the Eleventh South Carolina particularly in need of spiritual guidance. Late in March, however, the deteriorating health of his wife sent him rushing to her bedside in Alabama. On April 19, Charlotte Wiatt died. "I am sure Heaven gained a saint," Wiatt wrote that day. "May her pious example & peaceful end stimulate me to more faithfulness & may I meet her in Heaven and share with her the saints' everlasting rest." He then entrusted his two young daughters to the care of in-laws and returned to the Twenty-sixth Virginia.

"I fear the religious condition is not as good as when I left it," he noted. "The Regt. has been moving about a good deal and that seems to distract the minds of the men." One of the company commanders attested to the renewed zeal of Wiatt's labors. In a letter home that spring, Capt. Abram W. Poindexter stated: "Our chaplain, Rev. William E. Wiatt, is untiring in his efforts among us, and is constantly working for the spiritual welfare of the men. He is greatly beloved by all, and may his labors among us be blessed more abundantly."[47]

A fellow officer writing during the same period reflected (for the first time in his correspondence) a deep sense of piety that was obviously the outgrowth of Wiatt's activities. "I know that it may be the Will of God that I should offer up my life upon my Country's Altar," he stated, "yet God's Grace will be sufficient for me in that hour of trouble."[48]

For Wise's brigade, the hour of trouble began that spring. When Federal Gen. Benjamin F. Butler led his Army of the James westward from Norfolk in a new thrust at Richmond, Jefferson Davis recalled all Virginia troops to the capital's defenses. "Going back to our native state!" Wiatt exclaimed on May 4. "How glad our men seem to be!" Four days later, the Twenty-sixth Virginia was constructing fortifications near Petersburg. The regiment experienced real action for the first time and suffered heavy casualties in the May 16 battle of Drewry's Bluff (or Fort Darling).[49] A month later, the Twenty-sixth Virginia lost its battle flag in the fighting around Petersburg. However, it was at the July 30 Battle of the Crater that Wise's brigade proved it was not composed "of a parcel of renegade Virginians and cowards."[50] For five hours, Wise's men maintained their position against repeated Federal assaults. Their steadfastness enabled Lee to regroup his forces and to deliver a successful counterattack that preserved the Richmond-Petersburg defenses.[51]

Such a victory may well have been a curse in disguise. In the long months that followed, Lee's besieged army suffered severely. Wiatt did not detect this at first. On September 1, 1864, he noted in his diary: "The summer has passed and the fall has come; how grateful should we be to God for His many & great blessings to us! He has not permitted our enemies to overcome us yet; He has given us many victories and our enemies some defeats during the past summer; Oh! His mercies have been many and very great towards us and we have abundant reason not only to be grateful but to trust Him."

By early October, Wiatt was beginning to sense a bleak future. "Very cold last night," he wrote. "I fear there will be much suffering if we are compelled to remain in the trenches this winter." His prophecy all too quickly came true. On November 26, Lieutenant Mills of Wiatt's regiment commented that "many of the men were entirely destitute of blankets and overcoats and it was really distressing to see them shivering over a little fire made of green pine wood. . . . We have to carry some men to [the] hospital for frostbite &c. Some have come in off picket crying from cold like children." Mills added: "I have never seen our army so *completely whipped*."[52]

In these trying times, Wiatt exerted himself to carry the gospel into the trenches. He was in the earthworks almost daily, distributing tracts, preaching and offering prayers to the soldiers. Occasionally he assisted the surgeons in treating men wounded in the continual exchange of fire between the two entrenched armies. Yet because Wiatt felt his presence to be of more value to the men at the front, he remained with them and quietly faced their dangers. Except for a minor wound from an exploding mortar shell, the chaplain escaped injury.

In the autumn of 1864, Wiatt had a brief respite during a review of Gen. Robert F. Hoke's division by Lee and some of the Army of Northern Virginia's principal generals. The chaplain was able to gain a place near the reviewing officers. For the first time he beheld Lee and his lieutenants at close range. That night Wiatt penned interesting descriptions of the individuals:

> Gen. Lee is a fine looking man, looks to be about 55 or 60, has a heavy grey beard (wears it in full) and he weighs, I judge, 190 or 200 lbs., is about 5 ft. 11 in. high and well proportioned; had on a plain suit of bluish grey and three stars *with no wreath* on his coat collar; he seemed quite affable; . . . he seemed to be in excellent health, and by no means jaded by the severe campaigns through which he had passed and is passing; may the good Lord continue to him life & health & wisdom, and, above all, His own fear.

Wiatt described Gen. A.P. Hill as "a small man, can be scarcely more than 5 ft. 8 in. high, nor weigh more than 125 or 130 lbs.; . . . he wears a heavy, long, sandy beard; he looks rather weather beaten; he was dressed very plainly, rode a splendid grey horse and seemed to have perfect control of himself & of his horse in the saddle; he seemed to be very lively and talkative."

Gen. Henry Heth was "a small man, wears only a mustache, dresses plainly (or rather was this evening); has dark hair and quite a brilliant eye, when excited; he seems to be quite social and humorous; I fear he is too fond of ardent spirits, though I do not know anything about his habits."

Robert F. Hoke, Wiatt noted, "has one of the most benignant, pleasant faces I ever saw; he is tall & straight, has very black hair & beard." In contrast, Gen. William W. Kirkland "is rather small, looks downward, and did not exhibit a great deal of expression."

Wiatt regarded Gen. Hagood Johnson as "quite young and very handsome, of medium size [with] light hair and whiskers." Gen. Alfred H. Colquitt was "quite round shouldered," with "very black hair & beard" and possessed of "a haggard look" plus "a great deal of determination in his countenance." Gen. William N. Pendleton was "a large man, somewhat like Gen. Lee in size, looks & beard."

This review was but a momentary diversion from the horrors of war. Wiatt's efforts to strengthen Christian faith as a shield against tribulation did nothing to stem the tide of events. Yet his pastoral influence inside his regiment was such that Pvt. Younger Longest reassured his home folks with a simply written poem:

> So let our lips and us express
> The holy gospel we profess.
> So let our works and virtues shine
> To prove thy Doctrine divine.
> Thus shall we best proclaim abroad
> The honors of our saviour God.
> When the salvation reigns within
> And grace subdues the power of sin.[53]

Toil as faithfully as he did, however, Chaplain Wiatt could not deter Northern might and divine providence. On Sunday morning, April 2, 1865, he conducted church service for a large congregation that included General Wise and other brigade officers. The sermon text was Psalms 4:6 — "There may be many that say, Who will shew us the way? Lord, lift thou up the light of thy countenance upon us." Wise later recalled that the men "were kneeling to God, under the prayers of Chaplain W.E. Wiatt of the 26th, when an order announced the defeat of Pickett at Five Forks and that we must fall back to the Appomattox [River]."[54]

Wiatt endured the painful week of retreat with a mixture of loyalty, sadness and disbelief. At the April 6 battle of Sayler's Creek, the Twenty-sixth Virginia saved Wise's brigade from entrapment "by its regular and orderly and steady rally." Nevertheless, the Virginians lost both their spirit and their second battle flag in the fighting.[55] Three days later, the Confederate retreat ended in surrender. Wise wrote of his men that Palm Sunday: "Oftentimes in marches, on picket, in the trenches, in camps and in charges I have seen them sad and almost sink, but I never saw their *tears* until their beloved commander-in-chief ordered them to surrender their arms. Then they wept." Very few were left to weep. The Twenty-sixth Virginia, which had numbered 1,200 men at the outset of the war, contained ninety-five soldiers at Appomattox. William E. Wiatt was one of them.[56]

The chaplain was stunned that day when news of Lee's surrender first trickled down through the ranks. "Has God forsaken us? Is our Confederacy ruined?" he wondered. "I, for one, can't believe it; . . . Can all the prayers, & faith, & hope, & anxiety, and blood, and sacrifices, in the name of the Lord . . . be in vain?" In a few hours, no further doubts existed. Wiatt then wrote: "A touching incident occurred in the afternoon; Gen. Lee rode along from the enemy's lines, and hundreds of officers & men thronged each side of the road and waved hats and sent up cheers; The old hero rode in solemn silence, with head uncovered, his countenance indicating deep sorrow; I could not refrain from shedding tears again; It has been a sad day to us; May God's grace be sufficient for us."

Wiatt's postwar career was long, varied and fruitful. Yet it did not begin auspiciously. The horse that he was allowed to take home from Appomattox was his major asset.[57] His Gloucester County home was in ruins. What remained had to be sold to meet debts incurred by the war. Penniless and unemployed, Wiatt nevertheless wasted no time in beginning life anew. He promptly resumed the pastorate of Union Baptist Church,[58] brought his motherless children home from Alabama and supplemented his meager church stipend by teaching school. In 1866 he began an eleven-year stint as county surveyor, a post that required little time but further enhanced his income. In 1870 Wiatt became the first superintendent of schools for Gloucester County. His seven-year tenure in that position was eminently successful, as both school facilities and faculty salaries doubled in spite of the hardships of Reconstruction. Wiatt also found time to take a third wife. His July 18, 1871, marriage to Nannie B. Heywood ultimately produced four children.

He eventually resigned the school superintendency to devote full time to the ministry. He was pastor of a number of churches in his home county until 1887, when he accepted the position of state missionary in the mountains of Virginia. Wiatt moved his family to Giles County and for sixteen months "enjoyed good health and did the hardest work of his life, preaching at sixteen places and walking over the mountains to his appointments."[59]

Pleas from Gloucester congregations led to Wiatt's return home. There he labored faithfully until his 1909 retirement. "I do not expect to live in idleness," he wrote at the age of eighty-three.[60] Yet the death of his wife in 1911, plus advancing years, took their toll. Wiatt lived with his children and delivered guest sermons until February 14, 1918, when he died quietly in his ninety-first year. The local Masonic lodge had charge of the funeral. The scriptural texts used at the service were a fitting benediction: "Know ye not that a prince and a great man in Israel is fallen this day? . . . Servant of God, well done."[61]

As a comparison with other Confederate army chaplains reveals, Wiatt had below average experiences and above average talents. He did not possess Nicholas Davis's military eye or prowess; he did not fraternize with generals to the extent of Charles Quintard; his religious activities never reached army or corps levels, as was the case with J. William Jones and Beverly Lacy; he was not a carping and outspoken observer as is reflected in the diary of James Sheeran; nor did he have a lust for battle such as characterized Andrew Potter and Randolph McKim. Rather, Wiatt's army ministry was on a local, in-the-ranks scale. It was an unostentatious chaplaincy, ever solicitous of the common soldiers, and thus quite similar to the labors of such Union army clerics as Arthur Fuller and William Corby.[62]

The three most recent studies on Confederate chaplains have each sought to stereotype the ideal army minister of that era. Frank Hieronymus, the leading writer on the subject, has stated of Southern chaplains: "They had a doubly difficult task — to bolster the morale of a losing army. Some way in the midst of it all they found the grace to give, to serve, to keep primary the eternal verities of life . . . [and to] divert men's attention to the straight and narrow gate that leads to life eternal, paradoxically through the valley of the shadow of death." Another historian observed of the successful chaplain: "No matter how well he might preach in the chapel, he must prove his devotion to the men who were forced to undergo suffering in the campaign. His mere presence was a boost to morale. His good example under hardship rendered his influence a much more potent force." The best chaplain was self-denying, a third writer has asserted, "and those who measured up were more self-denying than not. They were the brave and faithful companions — comforting their men and pointing them toward eternal things — while walking on the road to Appomattox."[63]

Unknowingly, each of these writers was describing Chaplain William E. Wiatt.

NOTES

[1] Bell I. Wiley, " 'Holy Joes' of the Sixties: A Study of Civil War Chaplains," *Huntington Library Quarterly*, XVI (1953), 290, 297.

[2] The basic source for information on Wiatt's life is a eulogistic and somewhat exaggerated obituary in the *Gloucester* (Va.) *News Reporter*, February 28, 1918. Shorter sketches are in *Confederate Veteran*, XXVII (1919), 348; George B. Taylor, *Virginia Baptist Ministers* (Lynchburg, Va., 1935), 65-66.

[3] For pictures of Wiatt, see J. William Jones, *Christ in the Camp; or, Religion in Lee's Army* (Richmond, 1904), facing p. 327; *Confederate Veteran*, XXVII (1919), 348.

⁴ Two children, one of whom died in infancy, came from this marriage.

⁵ William E. Wiatt to Thomas B. Montague, January 7, 1850, Montague Family Papers, Virginia Historial Society.

⁶ William E. Wiatt to Thomas B. Montague, May 31, 1850, Ibid.

⁷ William E. Wiatt to Thomas B. Montague, January 7 and July 15, 1850, Ibid.

⁸ *Gloucester News Reporter*, February 28, 1918.

⁹ Ibid.

¹⁰ Jones, *Christ in the Camp*, 524; U.S. National Archives (comp.), "Compiled Service Records of Confederate Soldiers Who Served in Organizations from the State of Virginia" (Washington, 1961), Microfilm Roll 722. Hereafter cited as "Compiled Service Records." The average length of service of Confederate chaplains was about eighteen months. Frank L. Hieronymus, "For Now and Forever: The Chaplains of the Confederate States Army" (Dissertation, University of California at Los Angeles, 1964), 139.

¹¹ A Mississippi company was initially assigned to the Twenty-sixth Virginia in order to give it a full complement. In October, 1861, a company from Halifax County replaced the Mississippians. The regiment was an all-Virginia unit thereafter. Lee A. Wallace, Jr., *A Guide to Virginia Military Organizations, 1861-1865* (Richmond, 1964), 142.

¹² Ludwell Lee Montague, *Gloucester County in the Civil War* (Gloucester, Va., 1965), 10. An officer in the regiment later stated that the Twenty-sixth Virginia lost twenty percent of its complement through illness before it fought its first major battle. George D. Harmon (ed.), "Letters of Luther Rice Mills, A Confederate Soldier," *North Carolina Historical Review*, IV (1927), 300. Hereafter cited as "Mills Letters."

¹³ U.S. War Dept. (comp.), *War of the Rebellion, A Compilation of the Official Records of the Union and Confederate Armies* (Washington, 1880-1901), Ser. I, Vol. XI, Pt. 2, 916-18, 928. Hereafter cited as *Official Records*, with all references being to Ser. I. See also Ibid., XL, Pt. 2, 119; Betsy Fleet and John D.P. Fuller (eds.), *Green Mount: A Virginia Plantation Family during the Civil War* (Lexington, Ky., 1962), 237, 267, for statements on desertion in the regiment.

¹⁴ For discussions of the snarled governmental red tape that hampered army chaplains in the Confederacy, see Hieronymus, "For Now and Forever," 101-25; *Religious Herald*, September 26, 1861; June 25, 1863.

¹⁵ Sidney J. Romero, "The Confederate Chaplain," *Civil War History*, I (1955), 137.

¹⁶ Jones, *Christ in the Camp*, 493, 504.

¹⁷ Montague, *Gloucester County*, 21. See also *Southern Historical Society Papers*, XXV (1897), 3. Hereafter cited as *SHSP*. In April, 1863, Lieutenant Mills of the Twenty-sixth Virginia wrote his brother: "I do hope that it will never fall to my lot to go into a fight under Gen. Wise. If it does, I will have to 'stare fate in the face & trust to luck.'" "Mills Letters," 291. See also Fleet and Fuller, *Green Mount*, 185, 302n.

¹⁸ Unless otherwise noted, all quotations given are from the Wiatt diary. The

original journal is now in the possession of J. Streeter Wiatt of Montgomery, Alabama. The writer is deeply indebted to Mr. Wiatt and other members of the family for assistance and encouragement in the preparation of this article.

[19] *Confederate Veteran*, XXVII (1919), 348.

[20] Pvt. Henry T. Holt of Company K, Twenty-sixth Virginia, enlisted September 30, 1861, and succumbed to "Typhoid Pneumonia" on May 26, 1863. "Compiled Service Records," Roll 713.

[21] A Gloucester County farmer, Joseph L. Pollard was thirty-two at his June 13, 1861, enlistment. He became a sergeant in Company I of the Twenty-sixth Virginia and surrendered with the remnant of his regiment at Appomattox. Ibid., Roll 717.

[22] From a patriotic standpoint, Satan did not flee entirely. Berry, a waterman at his May 28, 1861, enlistment, resigned from service October 18, 1862, because of "ill health." Ibid., Roll 707.

[23] John J. Cooper was a twenty-year-old farmer at his 1861 enlistment. In the July 30, 1864, battle of the Crater, he received a gunshot wound in the back and was discharged from service soon thereafter. Ibid., Roll 710.

[24] Davis, a native of Gloucester County, enlisted on the day that First Manassas was fought. He was sick for much of the 1861-1862 period. Detailed to work in the brigade hospital in November, 1862, he died February 1, 1863, of erysipelas. Ibid. An officer wrote at this time that at least four men in the Twenty-sixth Virginia had perished from smallpox vaccinations. "Mills Letters," 292.

[25] Tarr enlisted October 15, 1861, at Richmond. A native of Pennsylvania, he was on the regimental sick list during February-August, 1862. In November he was discharged from service, yet Tarr was too ill from dysentery to leave the hospital. Hence, he was a civilian in a military hospital during the last two months of his life. "Compiled Service Records," Roll 720.

[26] John T. Blackstock, a Halifax County farmer before the war, was also sick during most of his time in service. On August 2, 1863, he died at the brigade hospital of "inflammation of the Bowels." Ibid., Roll 708.

[27] Lieutenant Fred Fleet of the Twenty-sixth Virginia wrote of the beginning of the campaign: "We were up and ready to start by 3 o'clock, and after our Chaplain had made a few remarks and prayed with the regiment, we started off." Fleet and Fuller, *Green Mount*, 219.

[28] On this occasion the Confederates did indeed confiscate and consume some whiskey. Lieutenant Mills of the Twenty-sixth Virginia wrote home: "Col. Singler, Col. of Cavalry of the Holcombe Legion, was so much under the influence of liquor that he had to make three attempts before he could mount his horse — the horse standing as still as a horse could stand." "Mills Letters," 291. For details of the Williamsburg operation, see *Official Records*, XVIII, 206-09, 994-95.

[29] "Mills Letters," 289.

[30] Wiatt's diary is amazingly barren of references to his family. However, in mid-February, 1863, he did express his feelings pointedly. "My wife's troubles are very many & very great, but I trust God is with her, and that her religion

comforts her . . . . What a blessed privilege it is to be with one's family! How many thousands of our poor soldiers are denied this privilege, and how many will never see their families again in this world! Oh Lord! put a stop to this dreadful war."

[31] John Shepard, Jr., "Religion in the Army of Northern Virginia," *North Carolina Historical Review*, XXV (1948), 365. The factors behind the revival are summarized in Bell I. Wiley, *The Life of Johnny Reb* (Indianapolis, 1943), 183-84.

[32] Fleet and Fuller, *Green Mount*, 244.

[33] *Religious Herald*, July 9, 1863.

[34] Ibid.

[35] Ibid., July 30, 1863. A brief report by Bagby of initial efforts to bring the soldiers "from darkness to light" is in Ibid., September 3, 1863.

[36] Llewellyn M. Bristow enlisted May 4, 1862, in Company H of the Twenty-sixth Virginia. He was reported "sick in quarters" at the time of the revival. In April, 1864, Bristow transferred to the Thirty-fourth Virginia. "Compiled Service Records," Rolls 708, 801.

[37] *Religious Herald*, September 17, 1863.

[38] *SHSP*, XXV (1897), 5; Aristides Monteiro, *War Reminiscences by the Surgeon of Mosby's Command* (Richmond, 1890), 29.

[39] Fleet and Fuller, *Green Mount*, 207, 213, 231.

[40] Jones, *Christ in the Camp*, 351-52.

[41] Ball may have been the hardest case Wiatt ever encountered in the army. He was a forty-year-old laborer at his June 13, 1861, enlistment. When Wiatt visited him in the Charleston jail, Ball was in his third arrest for desertion. A court-martial somehow spared him from a firing squad and returned him to the ranks. In mid-October, 1864, Ball deserted the regiment at Petersburg and was never seen again. "Compiled Service Records," Roll 707. See also Fleet and Fuller, *Green Mount*, 186-87, 207.

[42] Wiatt's depiction of Beauregard parallels the usual descriptions, but his summation of Soulé stands in contrast to those normally found. See T. Harry Williams, *P.G.T. Beauregard: Napoleon in Gray* (Baton Rouge, 1954), 51-53; Mrs. Burton Harrison, *Recollections Grave and Gay* (New York, 1911), 160; Gerald M. Capers, *Occupied City: New Orleans under the Federals, 1862-1865* (Lexington, Ky., 1965), 62-63.

[43] Davis was en route to Richmond after a stormy conference with dissatisfied generals in the Army of Tennessee. The officers were demanding the removal of Gen. Braxton Bragg for incompetent leadership in the bloody and barren victory of Chickamauga.

[44] More detailed descriptions of Davis's appearance are in Arthur J.L. Fremantle, *Three Months in the Southern States, April-June, 1863* (London, 1863), 214-17; Bell I. Wiley, *The Road to Appomattox* (Memphis, 1956), 9-10.

[45] "Mills Letters," 295. For specifics of the Legareville engagement, see *Official Records*, XXVIII, Pt. 1, 747-49; LIII, 16-23; Fleet and Fuller, *Green Mount* 293-95.

46 *Religious Herald*, January 21, 1864. Colporter Bagby's reports of religious life in the Twenty-sixth Virginia at this time are in Ibid., January 28 and February, 1864.

47 Ibid., April 21, 1864.

48 "Mills Letters," 299-300.

49 In the Drewry's Bluff fighting, the Twenty-sixth Virginia lost two killed and forty-eight wounded. *Official Records*, XXXVI, Pt. 2, 261.

50 Ibid., LI, Pt. 1, 1247; "Mills Letters," 301.

51 For the gallant conduct of Wise's brigade at the Crater, see *Official Records*, XL, Pt. 1, 791; *Confederate Veteran* XXVII (1919), 456.

52 "Mills Letters," 303-4. See also Fleet and Fuller, *Green Mount*, 347-48.

53 Younger Longest to his brother, October 23, 1864, Virginia Historical Society.

54 *SHSP*, XXV (1897), 16.

55 Ibid., 5; *Official Records*, XLVI, Pt. 1, 1258.

56 *SHSP*, X (1882), 420; XV (1887), 431, 433-34.

57 "Compiled Service Records," Roll 722. Wiatt's own file contains only bi-monthly notations that he was present on duty plus a number of receipts for payment of his $80 monthly salary.

58 *Religious Herald*, February 1, 1866.

59 *Gloucester News Reporter*, February 18, 1918.

60 Taylor, *Virginia Baptist Ministers*, 65.

61 *Gloucester News Reporter*, February 18, 1918.

62 See Nicholas A. Davis, *Chaplain Davis and Hood's Texas Brigade* (San Antonio, 1962); Arthur H. Noll (ed.), *Doctor Quintard, Chaplain, C.S.A.* (Sewanee, Tenn., 1905); Jones, *Christ in the Camp*; Beverly T. Lacy, "An Address of the Chaplains of the Second Corps ('Stonewall' Jackson's), Army of Northern Virginia, to the Churches of the Confederate States," SHSP, XIV (1886), 348-56; James B. Sheeran, *Confederate Chaplain: A War Journal* (Milwaukee, 1960); H.A. Graves, *Andrew Jackson Potter: The Fighting Parson of the Texas Frontier* (Nashville, 1881); Randolph H. McKim, *A Soldier's Recollections* (New York, 1910); Richard F. Fuller, *Chaplain Fuller: Being a Life Sketch of a New England Clergyman and Army Chaplain* (Boston, 1863); William Corby, *Memoirs of Chaplain Life* (Notre Dame, Ind., 1894). More pious accounts of the chaplaincy service are William W. Lyle, *Lights and Shadows of Army Life* (Cincinnati, 1865), and Henry Clay Trumbull, *War Memories of an Army Chaplain* (New York, 1898).

63 Hieronymus, "For Now and Forever," 165, 313; Charles F. Pitts, *Chaplains in Gray* (Nashville, 1957), 93; Herman Norton, *Rebel Religion* (St. Louis, 1961), 114.

VIII

The Boys Who Stayed Behind:
Northern Industrialists
and the Civil War

By MAURY KLEIN

Not all the young men who lived during the Civil War era rushed to arms. In our obsession with war, its every twist and nuance, we sometimes forget that only a part of that generation bothered to fight the war or even to tender it active support. While the war undoubtedly touched the lives of everyone, its influence upon individual Americans varied as widely as their responses to its effects. Like other great conflicts, it separated the generation into two broad groups: those whose lives were "touched with fire," as Oliver Wendell Holmes, Jr., put it, and those whose lives continued to revolve around more immediate personal concerns.

Our understanding of the 1860s could gain a new dimension from a closer study of this distinction. Historians have overwhelmingly concentrated their efforts upon those Americans engaged in or engulfed by the war effort. The result has been a badly skewed historiography. The war has distorted American history as much as it disrupted the 1860s. It has become the crossroads at which every major issue, event or trend of the nineteenth century seems to begin or end its journey. The abnormalities of the war experience hinder efforts to find and define continuity in our national development.

It may be a useful corrective to inquire into that other generation which did not march off to the front but instead stayed home to look after personal interests. By "other generation" we do not mean people who lacked patriotism but rather those who simply gave the war effort a low priority in their personal scheme of things. Some did indeed lack any real interest in the crisis and either ignored the uproar as best they could or resented it as an intrusion into their private affairs. Others simply had what to them were more important things to do.

Among this generation were men who found the wartime situation a golden opportunity for self-advancement. Many young Americans used these years to establish themselves in business, thereby stealing a march on their peers caught up in the clash of arms. Some of these "go-getters," to use Daniel J. Boorstin's term, made themselves a fortune before the war ended, while others merely planted the seeds of long and prosperous careers. For them war was not an interruption but a positive boost to their ambitions.

To the historian this group of go-getters should be no less important than the generation absent at the battlefield. Their ranks included many who became the architects of industrial America and set the tone for the postwar era. Collectively they were to dominate the economy and therefore much of American life during the half century between the Civil War and World War I. In this great work they would, of course, be joined by others either returning from the armies or growing up after them. But their profitable wartime experience gave these go-getters a significant head start in the scramble for success. Even before the Gilded Age began, they were well into the gilding.

So little has been done in studying these men that even a brief survey seems useful as a guide for further exploration. The following does not purport to be systematic, scientific or complete; it is rather a set of impressions garnered from a random sample of sixty individuals (listed in Appendix I) who did not see military service during the war. Information on these men has been culled from standard biographical sources supplemented when possible by biographies, autobiographies and general historical accounts.

The sample consists of men between seventeen and thirty years old in 1861. Their average age was slightly under twenty-four, a figure which coincides with the best contemporary estimates on the average age of Union soldiers.[1] Of the sixty, only six were completing their education during some part of the war years. Four of these earned law degrees; in 1863, Charles A. Pillsbury left Dartmouth for Montreal, where he became a clerk in a produce commission firm; and Eckley B. Coxe went to Europe to study mining. The remaining fifty-four were all engaged in business.

Every one of these men achieved great success in business during the postwar years, nearly all becoming millionaires.[2] Most were entrepreneurs who either started their own enterprises or gave new direction to old ones. Their primary fields of endeavor were:

FIELD[5]	NUMBER
Banking and Finance	12
Construction	2
Insurance	1
Manufacturing[a]	7
Mercantile Enterprises	8
Mining	4
Law	3
Processing Raw Materials[b]	8
Transportation[c]	13
Utilities (Gas)	2
TOTAL	60

a. Includes brewing and meat packing.
b. This odd category lumps together such activities as iron and steel production, oil refining, lumber production and flour-milling.
c. Includes railroads, shipping and traction enterprises.

The sample includes not only a wide variety of fields but also a sizable diversity in the scale of success. Some of the men were national business leaders, while others were either outstanding local successes (e.g., James B. Farwell, Anthony J. Frame and Herman Kountze) or simply prominent in their field (e.g., Eckley B. Coxe, Harris C. Fahnestock, Edward T. Lauterbach and Alexander E. Orr). Social origins appear no less diverse. The sample divides almost evenly between men from well-to-do families and those from modest origins.

Despite this diversity, the most striking fact about the sample is the large number of business titans found in it. The list resembles a roll call of the richest and most powerful American businessmen of the late nineteenth century. The presence of men like Andrew Carnegie, J.P. Morgan, John D. Rockefeller, George F. Baker, Jay Gould, James J. Hill, Gustavus Swift, Charles A. Pillsbury, George M. Pullman and Marcus A. Hanna tempts one to conclude that the sample contains a preponderance of those entrepreneurs who dominated the process of American industrialization.[3] Many of the more familiar figures not on the list are absent because they were either too young or too old for military service during the Civil War.[4]

While this correlation does not prove that the war accelerated the careers of the men in the sample, it does suggest the possibility of an important connection. The concentration of titans on the list cannot easily be explained by other factors. Conversely, it is hard to think of many outstanding business leaders who did serve in the military. The war produced few heroes who later excelled at business beyond the local level.[5] Hordes of ex-soldiers achieved success in politics, for late nineteenth-century office seekers generally traded heavily on their war records. However, as virtually all historians emphasize, the era belonged to the businessman, not the politician.

How did the war years accelerate the careers of those men in the sample? Historians have already suggested several ways in which the conflict set the stage for the rapid, almost explosive growth of the American economy between 1865 and 1900. This stage-setting function of the war looms as the heart of the matter.[6] The first shots came when the American economy was overwhelmingly agricultural; when most markets were local or regional; when business enterprises were of modest size; when sources of capital were primarily domestic and relatively small; when labor was exceedingly scarce; when the federal government wavered over what role it should play in economic affairs; when the political process was strained by savage clashes among conflicting interest groups (some of which were hostile to industrial growth); and when federal, state and common law remained obstacles to the organization of enterprises on a large scale.

The historical setting of the war is also important. It discourages comparison of the Civil War with other wars, especially World Wars I and II. By its nature, a civil war has a different impact upon a nation's economy than a foreign war. Moreover, the world wars, unlike the Civil War, were fought by a United States already industrialized. As the only major American war during the nascent period of American industrialization (1820-1900), the Civil War played a unique stage-setting role.

In general terms, the war helped create an ideal environment for rapid industrialization. It swept away most of the political embroilments that had absorbed so much attention and energy (and incidentally left the federal government virtually paralyzed) during the antebellum years. As one historian wrote, "the war freed men of the obsessive involvement in politics; the war, in fact, cleared the air everywhere."[7] Above all, it destroyed the power of the Southern planters in national politics and elevated the Republican party to undisputed control of the federal government. Charles and Mary Beard stressed this point nearly half a century ago:

Viewed in the large, the supreme outcome of the civil strife was the destruction of the planting aristocracy which, with the aid of northern farmers and mechanics, had practically ruled the United States for a generation. A corollary to that result was the undisputed triumph of a new combination of power: northern capitalists and free farmers who emerged from the conflict richer and more numerous than ever. It was these irreducible facts . . . that made the Civil War a social revolution.[8]

The rapidity of the change was impressive. Between 1865 and 1900 the nation was virtually bereft of outstanding political figures. The men who dominated the age made their mark in business and commerce. Most of them were indifferent to, if not contemptuous of, politics. The age of Calhoun, Clay and Webster gave way to the age of Carnegie, Gould and Rockefeller.

Once in power, the Republican party pursued policies conducive to rapid industrialization. For the most part, Northern Democrats acquiesced in these policies, and the leadership of both parties shared the same assumptions on many economic matters. This had not been true before the war, when the Southern Democrats opposed most probusiness legislation. During the war, Congress passed a wide range of legislation favoring industrial development. In each case the new laws marked a significant departure from prewar policy.

The tariff exemplified the new trend. Since the Walker Tariff of 1846, the trend of protection had been steadily downward until the Morrill Tariff of 1861, a measure passed before hostilities erupted. During the war, the ratio of duties to dutiable imports was raised from about 20 percent in 1860 to 47.6 percent in 1865.[9] Several major industries, notably iron and steel, cotton, wool, paper, glass and leather, benefited from this protectionist policy. In little more than a decade, iron and steel mushroomed into a giant industry capable of competing without protection. Yet the wartime duties remained unchanged for nearly twenty years, allowing firms more funds for profit, expansion and technological innovation at the consumer's expense. Frank W. Taussig summarized this point:

> The identical duties fixed in 1864 were left in force for a long series of years. When a general revision came to be made in 1883, they had ceased to be thought of as the results of war legislation . . . . Hence the war tariff, though from time to time patched, amended, revised, not only remained in force . . . for nearly twenty years, but became in time the basis for an even more stringent provision.[10]

The war also radically transformed American banking and finance. The pressing need to provide huge outlays of funds compelled new methods of government finance and generated a reorganization of banking which benefited both investment and commercial banking operations. As Henrietta Larson has observed: "Banking, like our economic organization in general, had for some time been changing in the direction of greater specialization and large scale activity, with its center in New York. The Civil War accelerated that development. The war necessitated the speeding up and the enlargement of our financial machinery in order to carry the heavy burdens of war finance. The result was a great change in both commercial and investment banking."

The pivotal legislation was the National Bank Act of 1863, which replaced the Independent Treasury System with a national bank system. Originally adopted to provide a market for government war bonds, the system proved a boon to private finance and helped fashion a monetary policy favorable to commercial and industrial growth.[11]

The sources of federal income also underwent a profound change. Prior to the war the federal government derived virtually all its revenue from customs and land sales. Wartime expenses necessitated new sources of income. These included excise taxes, an income tax, an inheritance tax, a special manufacturers' tax and a license tax. The Internal Revenue Act of 1864 was so sweeping that it reminded economist David A. Wells of the Irishman at Donnybrook Fair: "Whenever you see a head, hit it; whenever you see a commodity, tax it."[12] This revenue program, coupled with other wartime economic legislation, also marked a radical extension of federal authority.[13]

After the war the income, inheritance and most manufacturing taxes were quickly repealed. Thereafter the government obtained its revenue primarily from the tariff and various excise taxes. In effect the tax burden had been lifted almost entirely from industrialists and placed upon consumers. Government policy thus helped create optimal conditions for obtaining the large amount of capital needed to finance industrial growth. Freed of any significant tax burden, businessmen and corporations tended to plow much of their earnings back into expansion.

The Homestead Act of 1862 also gave indirect aid to industrial growth. This opening of the public domain, which had long been resisted by Southern representatives, spurred the rapid postwar settlement of the West. Despite the act's many shortcomings, Fred A. Shannon estimated that about 400,000 families or some 2,000,000 people obtained free land under its provisions.[14] The tremendous growth in agricultural production that ensued created large surpluses, most of which were sold abroad. These farm surpluses, in turn, helped give the United

States a favorable enough balance of trade to induce foreign capital into American industry.

The West also became an important market for industrial and manufactured goods, but its prosperity depended upon reliable transportation. Here too the wartime government played a pivotal role. Antebellum plans for transcontinental railroads got deeply enmeshed in sectional politics, but after 1861 Republican congresses pushed them along with little opposition. To insure completion of these gigantic projects, the federal government donated land and provided other kinds of aid. In all, the railroads received a total of about 156,000,000 acres of public domain, much of which was later sold to settlers. Completion of the first transcontinental railroad in 1869 was the first fruit of transportation policy after the sectional deadlock had been broken.[15]

Another vital area, labor supply, also received governmental support. In 1864 Congress passed "An Act to Encourage Immigration" which established a federal commissioner of immigration and created a contract labor law for the importation of working people. Although the law did not long survive the war, it evidenced a growing support among businessmen for a liberal immigration policy. For half a century the industrial and business communities would remain the staunchest supporters of an open door for immigrants. The war also dealt nativism a crippling, if temporary, blow as foreigners of every stripe rallied to the Union cause.[16]

The effect of all this wartime legislation was to create a climate more favorable for economic expansion than existed in any previous period of American history. In the decades after Appomattox, political, social, religious and legal institutions added their sanctions to the prevailing laissez-faire system. Especially, the law lent its impressive weight to the protection of private enterprise. Led by the Supreme Court, American jurists relentlessly narrowed the sphere of governmental interference in business affairs.[17]

Nowhere did the war affect industrial development more strikingly than in the South. Throughout the remainder of the century, the prostrate Confederate states never approached the scale of economic growth in the North. They nonetheless made giant strides in industrialization that would scarcely have been possible without the war. The abolition of slavery, the devastation of war, the downfall of the planter aristocracy, and the widespread poverty all compelled the region to diversify its economy. By 1870, the South was ripe for industrial development, and ambitious Southerners hurried north in search of capital to do the job.[18]

Before 1860, planter-dominated state governments resisted most efforts to diversify the economy. During Reconstruction, however, the Southern states were controlled by a coalition of native and "foreign" interests eager to promote industrial development. Even after the restoration of "home rule," the new leadership proved sympathetic to business enterprises and not averse to luring Northern money southward for that purpose. For the remainder of the century, Northern capital became the lifeblood for Southern industrial development.

The spirit of the New South was primarily an economic one, a receptivity to industrialization as a consequence of defeat. The war did not create significant new industries in the South, but it did bring about an environment suitable for their development. The result was a South radically different from that which existed prior to 1860.

Finally, the war created conditions which proved an ideal spawning ground for a rising generation of entrepreneurs. Many of the business leaders of the late nineteenth century established their careers during the war years. By ignoring the call to arms and devoting their energies to business, these men profited from the unusual opportunities generated by the wartime demand for goods and services. When the fighting ceased, they possessed an advantage of both capital and experience over their peers returning from the battlefield. In that way they enjoyed a significant edge during the frenzy of postwar industrial development that would not have been possible without the war.

By all these criteria, the war accelerated American industrialization in crucial, if unmeasurable, ways. It destroyed the influence of the agrarian and strongly antiindustrial South upon the federal government. It brought the probusiness Republican party to power and thereby paved the way for a host of national policies essential for rapid industrial expansion on a large scale. It rendered the defeated South ripe for industrialization and speeded the settlement of the West.

On a less tangible level, the war eliminated much of the political strife that had debilitated national policy before 1861. It produced a generation of entrepreneurs hungry for opportunity and bent on exploiting the resources of a rich continent. The reaction of a war-weary people to four years of brutal combat, capped by an inconclusive peace, helped fashion an ideal climate for this exploitation. As the importance and interference of the national government receded steadily after 1865, the major restraints to individual and corporate activity disappeared.

Perhaps all of these things would have happened had the war not occurred. That question is best left to devotees of counterfactual propositions. It is doubtful that all of them would have taken place or that the process would have occurred as swiftly as it did. Whatever importance one attaches to the prewar decades as a period of nascent industrialization, it must be remembered that this development was taking place in a social, political and economic environment that was badly out of joint. After 1865, the men, the means and the spirit of the age marched in nearly perfect unison.

How were the careers of the sixty men in the sample accelerated during the war years? The war gave the boys who stayed behind four years to advance their interests while many other young men were involved in the war effort. This point cannot be emphasized too strongly, for these were no ordinary years. Opportunities for profit and advancement abounded in the turbulent atmosphere of a society at war. Bright, intelligent and ambitious young men found more openings than usual and less competition. The abnormal demands of war gave some a chance to cement future careers and others the chance to reap windfall profits as a nest egg for later ventures.

Opportunities for great profits beckoned on all sides. A son of banker Thomas Mellon begged his father for money to speculate in wheat. Writing from Wisconsin, he declared that people "continue growing richer and don't care when the war closes."[19] Mindful of the educational value afforded by the prevailing climate, Mellon bluntly forbade another son from enlisting:

> I had hoped my boy was going to make a smart intelligent businessman and was not such a goose as to be *seduced from duty* by the declamations of buncombed speeches. It is only greenhorns who enlist. *You can learn nothing in the army* . . . . In time you will come to understand and believe that a man may be a patriot without risking his own life or sacrificing his health. There are plenty of other lives less valuable or ready to serve for the love of serving.[20]

Most of those in the sample apparently came to a similar conclusion. Few even tried to enlist, fewer still stayed home because of disability, and several hired substitutes.[21] Some grew defensive about their failure to enter the service. "I was represented in the army," John D. Rockefeller insisted. "I sent more than twenty men, yes, nearly thirty. That is, I made such arrangements for them that they were able to go."[22]

Whatever their attitudes toward military service, the sample individuals all made good use of the war years and often effective use of the conditions spawned by the war. In broad terms they turned the era to their advantage in four ways. First, a few profited from business coups which directly utilized wartime conditions. Second, several men improved their fortunes through government contracts and the swollen demand for goods and services generated by wartime needs. Third, the bankers in particular benefited greatly from the abnormal financial climate created by the conflict and by the unique circumstances involved in financing the war. Finally, everyone in the sample gained invaluable business experience simply by operating in the strained and unusual environment of a society at war. The conflict, in effect, telescoped their learning years and left them prepared to tackle more ambitious enterprises.

Although it is impossible to determine exactly how many of the sample made personal coups during the war, a few notable cases have surfaced. Philip D. Armour pulled off a lucrative speculation in pork during the closing days of the conflict.[23] Jim Fisk played a dangerous but rewarding game running contraband cotton out of the occupied South for a Boston firm.[24] On Wall Street, young Jay Gould was laying the foundation for his meteoric career through market speculation. To reduce the uncertainties inherent in a wartime market, the ingenius Gould managed to rig a telegraphic connection to some unknown accomplice in the War Department. Through this arrangement he obtained military news well ahead of his rivals.[25] Finally, the worst taint attached to the reputation of J. P. Morgan arose from his reputed profits on a sale of rifles to the Federal government.[26]

Other men were content to reap the profits of contracts for provisions of every kind. Andrew Carnegie, serving his apprenticeship on the Pennsylvania Railroad under the tutelage of Thomas A. Scott, benefited from the road's heavy wartime traffic and also made nearly a million dollars from outside investments of his own.[27] The Ames brothers, entering their father's shovel works in 1863, earned a fortune selling tools to the government.[28] John D. Rockefeller did equally well as a commission merchant in Cleveland. In 1863, he built his first refinery and two years later, joined by brother William, plunged completely into the oil business.[29]

Peter Widener, hustling in his brother's Philadelphia meatshop and active in the local Republican party, obtained a contract to supply nearby troops with meat. The $50,000 he made from this business provided the resources for later investments in meat stores and street railways. In the same city, John Wanamaker, who had opened a clothing business with Nathan Brown in 1861, found himself deluged with lucrative orders for uniforms.[30] William Elkins, another Philadelphian, did nearly as well selling produce and in 1862 invested in oil. And in South Bend,

Indiana, Clement Studebaker used war orders to help build what later became the world's largest wagon works.[31]

Bankers and financiers thrived on the challenges of a wartime economy. The profound changes in American banking wrought by the financial demands of the conflict accelerated the careers of those young bankers who were privileged to participate in that difficult work. Harris C. Fahnestock was one such young man. In 1862, at the age of twenty-two, he became a partner in Jay Cooke's newly opened Washington house. His impressive performance with Cooke's firm, which did more business in government securities than any other banking house in the country, insured Fahnestock a bright future in the profession.[32]

Much of Fahnestock's later career was spent with the powerful First National Bank of New York. George F. Baker, the major figure in the growth of First National and a longtime associate of J.P. Morgan, began his connection with that institution during the Civil War. Prior to 1863, Baker had worked as a clerk at the state banking department in Albany. His industry and intelligence caught the eye of John Thompson, the leading light among the founders of the First National, soon after passage of the National Bank Act. He joined the founding group in 1863 and rose to the position of cashier by 1865. In time both Baker and the First National would emerge as titans within a strong industry.[33]

Charles Yerkes, the traction magnate immortalized in fiction by Theodore Dreiser, used these years to advance his brokerage business in Philadelphia. Like Gould and others, Yerkes profited handsomely from speculating on the uncertainties bred by the war. He had joined the Philadelphia exchange in 1859 and opened his own banking firm three years later.[34] Meanwhile, in distant Omaha, Herman Kountze and his brothers were establishing a powerful regional banking house which culminated in 1864 with the organization of the First National Bank of Omaha. During these same years, the Kountze brothers were also organizing banks in Denver.[35] Joseph W. Drexel, who was to become Morgan's partner in Drexel, Morgan & Company, spent the war years banking, first in Chicago and then, upon his father's death in 1863, in the latter's Philadelphia house.[36] William A. Nash was busy working his way to the presidency of New York's Corn Exchange Bank, while a prominent local banker, Anthony J. Frame, was doing the same with Waukesha County Bank in Wisconsin.[37]

Other men in the sample used the war years to advance themselves either in the fields with which they would later become identified or in some related line of business. Six of the remaining individuals gained experience (and usually rapid advancement) in family firms. Charles Deere, William E. Dodge, Mark Hanna, Victor Newcomb, Frederic P. Olcott and Arthur Sewall all emerged from the war era with their careers well launched. In each case, the family did a thriving business during the conflict.[38]

Those not blessed with family connections hustled on their own. In 1862, Gustavus Swift opened a retail butcher shop in Barnstable, Massachusetts, and soon extended his efforts to a slaughterhouse and shops in neighboring towns. Michael Cudahy was learning the meat trade from a Milwaukee packer. Marshall Field rose with lightning speed in the mercantile business, going from general manager of Cooley, Farwell & Co. in 1861 to a partnership in Field, Palmer & Leiter four years later. By 1863, Clement Griscom, later a dominant figure in International Mercantile Marine, had worked his way up to a partnership in Peter Wright & Sons, a Philadelphia importing firm.[39]

Already intrigued by the possibilities of the sleeping car, George M. Pullman went to the Colorado mining region in 1862 to run a general store while he worked on his designs. In 1863, he returned to Chicago and obtained his first patent the following year. In 1860, John W. Mackey left San Francisco to scour the mines of Nevada. He did well during the war years, but his fabulous windfall, the Comstock Lode, did not come until 1872. Another hustler involved in the Comstock, James Keene, remained in San Francisco where he worked at mining, milling, freighting and even teaching to earn himself a stake for bigger things.[40]

A few men had already found their place and passed the war working steadily upward. In 1861, H.H. Rogers went to the Oil City district of Pennsylvania with a friend and built a refinery. Frederick Weyerhauser was organizing a logging and lumbering enterprise in Illinois and Wisconsin. Richard McCurdy served as counsel to Mutual Life Insurance Company throughout the war years and achieved a vice-presidency in 1865. A.J. Cassatt left a railroad project in Georgia when the fighting began and returned north to work for the Pennsylvania Railroad, with which he spent his entire business career. Another brilliant railroad president-to-be, Charles E. Perkins, started his career as a clerk on the Burlington & Missouri Railroad in 1859 and rose to acting superintendent by 1865. In Louisville and Bucyrus, Ohio, an energetic merchant named August Juilliard was busy laying the foundations of a prosperous career.[41]

Of course, some men did not reach their goals in so straight a line. Yet even for them, the war years were invaluable. James J. Hill acquired a solid business and transportation education working for a Mississippi River packet steamboat firm. In 1865, he embarked on his first independent venture. Frederick Pabst served as a steamer captain on the Great Lakes before turning to brewing in 1865. One scion of a wealthy family, Cornelius Vanderbilt III, apprenticed with two New York banking houses during the war before receiving in 1865 a position as assistant treasurer of the New York & Harlem Railroad on the family-owned New York Central System. Anthony Brady, an indefatigable promoter, was cutting his business teeth in a variety of enterprises including granite quarries and a tea store operation in Albany.[42]

Such a brief survey cannot demonstrate, let alone measure, in what ways the war accelerated the careers of these sixty men. Nor can it prove the men to be representative of some type. But it does point to the striking and apparently significant fact that a remarkable roster of late nineteenth-century American business leaders chose not to participate actively in the Civil War but spent those years pursuing private interests. Since wars breed abnormal conditions in any society, and since the Civil War came just when America was on the threshold of rapid industrialization, it seems plausible that these factors are related.

Specifically, it appears that the war years bred an unusually hardy generation of entrepreneurs. The men in this sample may well have become successful without the edge given them by the war years, but probably they would not have gone so far so fast. One must keep in mind the peculiar moral and social climate bred by four exhausting years of bloodletting. War can bring personal priorities sharply into focus in a manner unmatched by the routine of peacetime. Another trait shared by the men in the sample was ambition—their fierce determination to succeed, their dogged pursuit of objectives.

When the war ended, these representatives of the "other" generation had come a long way in four years. The peculiar conditions of wartime society had much to do with their progress. Most businessmen liked to think that their devotion to personal affairs also aided the North's cause. Most preferred to view themselves as doing what was best for country as well as self. Thus banker Henry Clews proclaimed in retrospect that "Wall Street came to the rescue of the country when the war broke out." Clews later added: "It is true that they were well paid for it."[43]

More likely, it was not Clews but that coarse and crafty speculator Daniel Drew who touched the heart of the matter. "Along with ordinary happenings, we fellows in Wall Street had the fortunes of war to speculate about," he recalled. "It's good fishing in troubled waters."[44] The generation of the 1860s contained more than its share of extraordinary anglers. For those among them who were ambitious and alert to opportunities, the years from 1861 to 1865 proved a propitious time to be casting out their lines.

APPENDIX I

Sample of 60 Business Leaders, Age 17-30 in 1861, Who Did not See Military Service Service During the War

Name	Age in 1861	Primary Business Activity after 1865
Frederick L. Ames	26	manufacturing
Oliver Ames	30	manufacturing
Philip D. Armour	29	meat packing
George F. Baker	21	banking
Anthony M. Brady	18	construction, utilities
Andrew Carnegie	26	iron and steel
A. J. Cassatt	22	railroad executive
William A. Clark	22	banking, mining
Thomas J. Coolidge	30	banking, mercantile
Eckley B. Coxe	22	mining engineer
Michael Cudahy	20	meat packing
Charles Deere	24	manufacturer of farm implements
Chauncey M. Depew	27	law, railroad executive
Samuel C. T. Dodd	25	corporation law
William E. Dodge	29	mercantile, mining
Joseph W. Drexel	28	banking
William L. Elkins	29	traction, oil, gas
Harris C. Fahnestock	26	banking
James B. Farwell	19	contractor
Marshall Field	26	mercantile
James Fisk	27	financier
Roswell P. Flower	26	banking
Anthony J. Frame	17	banking
Jay Gould	25	railroads, telegraph
Clement A. Griscom	20	shipping
Marcus A. Hanna	24	mercantile
James J. Hill	23	railroads
Melville E. Ingalls	19	law, railroad executive
August Juilliard	25	mercantile
James R. Keene	23	mining, financier
Herman Kountze	28	banking
Edward T. Lauterbach	17	corporation law
John W. Mackay	30	mining, real estate
Richard A. McCurdy	26	insurance
Franklin McVeagh	24	mercantile
J. P. Morgan	24	banking

Appendix I (continued)

Name	Age in 1861	Primary Business Activity after 1865
H. Victor Newcomb	17	banking, railroads
Frederic P. Olcott	20	banking
Alexander E. Orr	30	mercantile
Frederick Pabst	25	brewing
Henry C. Payne	18	railroads, utilities
Charles E. Perkins	21	railroad executive
Charles A. Pillsbury	19	flour milling, grain trade
George M. Pullman	30	manufacturer of sleeping cars
John D. Rockefeller	22	oil
William Rockefeller	20	oil, copper, gas
H. H. Rogers	21	oil
Arthur Sewall	26	shipbuilding
Anson P. Stokes	23	mercantile, banking
Clement Studebaker	30	wagon manufacturing
Gustavus Swift	22	meat packing
Cornelius Vanderbilt III	18	railroads
John Wanamaker	23	mercantile
Frederick Weyerhauser	27	lumber and timber
Henry Whitney	22	coal, gas, interurban railroads
William C. Whitney	20	corporation law
Peter Widener	27	traction, utilities
James T. Woodward	24	banking
Charles T. Yerkes	24	traction, banking

APPENDIX II

Prominent Business Leaders Beyond the Sample Age Parameters of 17-30 in 1861

Name	Age in 1861	Name	Age in 1861
William H. Aspinwall	54	Andrew Mellon	6
John J. Astor	39	John G. Moore	14
Alexander Graham Bell	14	Levi P. Morton	37
Edward W. Clark	33	Charles Pratt	31
Charles Crocker	39	Joseph Pulitzer	14
Daniel Drew	64	Thomas F. Ryan	10
James B. Duke	5	Russell Sage	45
Henry DuPont	49	Jacob Schiff	14
George Eastman	7	Thomas A. Scott	38
John Murray Forbes	48	Jessee Seligman	34
Henry Clay Frick	12	Joseph Seligman	42
Elbert Gary	15	Leland Stanford	37
John W. Gates	6	A. T. Steward	58
Meyer Guggenheim	43	James Stillman	11
Henry O. Havemeyer	14	Isador Straus	16
Abram S. Hewitt	39	Nathan Straus	13
Collis P. Huntington	40	Theodore Vail	16
Emanuel Lehman	34	Cornelius Vanderbilt	67
Cyrus W. McCormick	52	William H. Vanderbilt	40
Thomas Mellon	48	George Westinghouse	15

(Those born shortly after 1861 include Henry Ford, Amadeo P. Giannini, William Randolph Hearst, George W. Perkins, Charles M. Schwab and Richard W. Sears.)

NOTES

[1] Benjamin A. Gould, *Investigation in the Military and Anthropological Statistics of American Soldiers* (New York, 1869), 86-88.

[2] Some might object to categorizing the lawyers in the sample as businessmen. In fact, all of them either abandoned the law for business careers or practiced corporation law which involved them deeply in business activities.

[3] There is, of course, no way of showing that this sample is representative of the men who did not serve in the military or of anything else. A major problem in extending this study lies in defining a target sample and formulating criteria for inclusion within it. In determining the effect of wartime conditions upon individual careers, one needs both some techniques to determine those effects and some working measures for evaluating relative success or failure. In this limited sample, the definitions are mostly impressionistic and the evidence circumstantial. Even so, the conclusions drawn here, especially as they pertain to the large number of business titans, would probably still hold true if the sample were enlarged.

[4] For a sample of some of these individuals, see Appendix II.

[5] Among those who did succeed in business after serving in the war were George F. Baer, Calvin S. Brice, John C. Calhoun, William P. Clyde, Grenville M. Dodge, Henry DuPont, Henry L. Higginson, John H. Inman, Oliver H. Payne and Samuel M. Thomas.

[6] Thomas C. Cochran, in "Did the Civil War Retard Industrialization?" *Mississippi Valley Historical Review* XLVIII (1961-1962), 197-210, has argued that the war led to a relative slowdown in economic growth. Since the publication of Cochran's article, historians have debated the accuracy of his thesis, expending most of their effort on prolonged disagreements over the statistical evidence. Too often the dispute has ignored the larger issue raised by Cochran. Industrialization was a complex process that involved far more than the rate of industrial growth. It should be viewed as a gradual, long-term process in which basic economic, social and political factors interacted to create not only new means of production but also sweeping changes in the whole structure of society. Profound transformations in social and political organizations and institutions accompanied the creation of that new economic order we call the industrial system. The extent to which the war affected the rate of industrial growth during the 1860s is irrelevant to the broader question of whether the conflict produced changes that affected industrialization. For a discussion of the Cochran thesis, see the excellent review article by Harry N. Scheiber, "Economic Change in the Civil War Era: An Analysis of Recent Studies," *Civil War History* XI (1965), 396-411.

[7] Louis M. Hacker, *The World of Andrew Carnegie: 1865-1901* (Philadelphia, 1968), 5. Hacker declared that "the real leap forward . . . began with the end of the Civil War. Not only does the statistical evidence demonstrate this; the structural changes, political and economic, to make unimpeded progress possi-

ble, occurred only in that era . . . . I am not saying that during the Civil War itself large-scale industrial growth began; I am saying that the Union's defeat of the slave South cleared the way for industrialization. The mores of the nation, for good or for ill, had radically changed." Ibid., xxvii, xxix.

[8] Charles A. Beard and Mary Beard, *The Rise of American Civilization* (New York, 1927), II, 99.

[9] U.S. Bureau of the Census, *Historical Statistics of the United States: Colonial Times to 1957* (Washington, 1960), 539. The ratio of duties to total imports rose from about 16 percent to 38.5 percent.

[10] Taussig concluded that "it would be untrue to say that protection did not exist before the great struggle began — the tariff of 1861 was a distinctly protectionist measure; but it is clear that the extreme protectionist character of our tariff is an indirect and unexpected result of the Civil War." Frank W. Taussig, *The Tariff History of the United States* (New York, 1931), 155-229.

[11] Henrietta Larson, *Jay Cooke: Private Banker* (Cambridge, 1936), 96. See also Fritz Redlich, *The Molding of American Banking: Men and Ideas* (New York, 1951), 85-95; 355-96; Bray Hammond, *Sovereignty and an Empty Purse: Banks and Politics in the Civil War* (Princeton, 1970).

[12] Taussig, *Tariff History*, 164. See also the table in Scheiber, "Economic Changes in the Civil War Era," 407. Scheiber also stressed that the major fiscal innovation of the war lay not merely in increased federal expenditures but in a dramatic shift in the composition of federal revenues.

[13] Hammond is quite insistent on this point: "The legal tender and revenue acts of February and June 1862, and the national currency act of February 1863, had already pushed the exercise of federal power beyond precedent in any field . . . . But other measures of the 37th Congress which impinged similarly on federal and state powers and prestige were the Morrill land grant act for colleges, the act incorporating the Pacific railway, the homestead act, and the national bankruptcy act. In these measures, basic and lasting federal powers were realized. Though war-time enactments they were permanent measures whose purposes and powers were undiminished by peace." *Sovereignty and an Empty Purse*, 359-60.

[14] Fred A. Shannon, *The Farmer's Last Frontier: Agriculture, 1860-1897* (New York, 1945), 51-58.

[15] For general accounts, see Julius Grodinsky, *Transcontinental Railway Strategy, 1869-1893* (Philadelphia, 1962); Arthur M. Johnson and Barry E. Supple, *Boston Capitalists and Western Railroads* (Cambridge, 1967); Robert W. Fogel, *The Union Pacific Railroad: A Case in Premature Enterprise* (Baltimore, 1964); Richard C. Overton, *Burlington West: A Colonization History of the Burlington Railroad* (Cambridge, 1941); John F. Stover, *American Railroads* (Chicago, 1961).

[16] Emerson D. Fite, *Social and Industrial Conditions in the North During the Civil War* (New York, 1910), 188-94; John Higham, *Strangers in the Land* (New York, 1963), Chap. 2.

[17] The literature on these subjects is voluminous. The most comprehensive account is Sidney Fine, *Laissez-Faire and the General Welfare State* (Ann Arbor, 1956). See also J. Willard Hurst, *Law and the Conditions of Freedom in the Nineteenth Century United States* (Evanston, 1956).

[18] The literature on postwar Southern industrial development is scant except for a few studies of particular industries, especially textiles. See Maury Klein, *The Great Richmond Terminal* (Charlottesville, 1970). For general histories with bibliographies, see C. Vann Woodward, *Origins of the New South 1877-1913* (Baton Rouge, 1951) and Monroe Lee Billington, *The American South* (New York, 1971).

[19] Matthew Josephson, *The Robber Barons* (New York, 1934), 59.

[20] Ibid., 50. The italics are mine.

[21] Hill tried to enlist but was rejected because he had one blind eye. Hanna served briefly in a hastily recruited regiment to defend Washington in 1864. Weyerhauser left Germany in the early 1850s to escape military service there. Those who hired substitutes included Oliver Ames, Armour, Carnegie, Gould, Morgan and Rockefeller.

[22] Allan Nevins, *John D. Rockefeller: The Heroic Age of American Enterprise* (New York, 1940), I, 139-40. "I wanted to go in the army and do my part," Rockefeller said later, "but it was simply out of the question. There was no one to take my place. We were in a new business, and if I had not stayed it must have stopped — and with so many dependent on it."

[23] *Dictionary of American Biography*, I, 347-49. Cited hereafter as *DAB*.

[24] W. A. Swanberg, *Jim Fisk: The Career of an Improbable Rascal* (New York, 1959), 17-21.

[25] Murat Halstead and J. Frank Beale, *The Life of Jay Gould* (New York, 1892), 73-74. Halstead estimated that Gould was a millionaire by the end of the war, but so little is known about his career during this period that the claim cannot be verified.

[26] For differing interpretations of this episode, see Josephson, *Robber Barons*, 60-63; Herbert L. Satterlee, *J. Pierpont Morgan: An Intimate Portrait, 1837-1913* (New York, 1939), 110-15.

[27] Joseph F. Wall, *Andrew Carnegie* (New York, 1970), Chap. 7.

[28] *DAB*, 246-47, 254-56.

[29] Ibid., XVI, 65-66; XXII, 568-76; *National Cyclopedia of American Biography* (New York, 1898-1963), XI, 63-64 (hereafter cited as *CAB*); Nevins, *Rockefeller*, I, 129-91.

[30] *DAB*, XX, 185-86, XIX, 407-9.

[31] *DAB*, VI, 84-85, XVIII, 180-81; *CAB*, IX, 324, XI, 109.

[32] Larson, *Cooke*, 92, 107, 113, 184-85. Of Fahnestock, Cooke wrote: "As my brother [also a partner in the Washington house] knew little of financial matters I looked round to find one I could rely upon and whom I believed to be fully capable of managing the office . . . . I found such a partner in my young friend at Harrisburg, Mr. H.C. Fahnestock." Ibid., 114.

[33] Ibid., 418-21; *DAB*, XXI, 44-45. When Jay Cooke & Co. failed in 1873, the First National Bank took in most of its New York office staff, including Fahnestock, who had moved there from Washington.

[34] *DAB*, XX, 609-11. For the two classic novels based upon Yerkes's career, see Theodore Dreiser, *The Financier* (New York, 1912) and *The Titan* (New York, 1914).

[35] *CAB*, XVIII, 159-60.

[36] *DAB*, V, 457. Drexel, Morgan was established in 1871.

[37] Redlich, *Molding of American Banking*, 184, 196, 218-20.

[38] John Deere produced farm implements; Phelps, Dodge & Co. was a prominent commission house, as were Hanna, Garretson & Co. and H.D. Newcomb Co.; Olcott's father ran a bank in Albany; E. and A. Sewall Company of Bath, Maine, were leading shipbuilders.

[39] *DAB*, IV, 584-85, VI, 366-67, VIII, 6-7, XVIII, 245-46; *CAB*, IV, 186.

[40] *DAB*, X, 283, XII, 75-76, XV, 263-64; *CAB*, IV, 287, XV, 238-39; Stanley Buder, *Pullman: An Experiment in Industrial Order and Community Planning 1880-1930* (New York, 1967), Chap. 1.

[41] *DAB*, III, 564-67, X, 244, XIV, 465-66, XVI, 95-96; *CAB*, XIV, 52.

[42] *DAB*, II, 581-82, IX, 36-41, XIX, 173-74; *CAB*, III, 342, XXXIV, 227-28; J.G. Pyle, *The Life of James J. Hill* (New York, 1917), I, 29-82.

[43] Henry Clews, *Fifty Years in Wall Street* (New York, 1908), 39-40.

[44] Josephson, *Robber Barons*, 59.

IX

Bibliography of Bell Irvin Wiley

Compiled by JOHN PORTER BLOOM

BOOKS

Southern Negroes, 1861-1865. Yale University Press, 1938. Reprinted: 1953, 2d edition, Rinehart Co.; 1965, with a new foreword by C. Vann Woodward, Yale University Press; 1974, paper, The Louisiana State University Press.

* *The Life of Johnny Reb, the Common Soldier of the Confederacy*. The Bobbs-Merrill Co., 1943.

The Plain People of the Confederacy. The Louisiana State University Press, 1943. Reprinted: 1963, Quadrangle Books; 1971, Peter Smith.

(With Kent Roberts Greenfield and Robert R. Palmer) *The Organization of Ground Combat Troops*. Historical Division, Department of the Army, Washington, 1947.

(With Robert R. Palmer and William R. Keast) *The Procurement and Training of Ground Combat Troops*. Historical Division, Department of the Army, Washington, 1948.

* *The Life of Billy Yank, the Common Soldier of the Union*. The Bobbs-Merrill Co., 1952.

(Editor) *"Co. Aytch," Maury Grays, First Tennessee Regiment; or, A Side Show of the Big Show*, by Sam R. Watkins. McCowat-Mercer Press, 1953.

(Editor) *Fourteen Hundred and 91 Days in the Confederate Army. A Journal Kept by W[illiam] W[illiston] Heartsill for Four Years, One*

Month, and One Day. Or, Camp Life, Day by Day, of the W.P. Lane Rangers from April 19, 1861, to May 20, 1865. McCowat-Mercer Press, 1953.

(Editor) *Rebel Private Front and Rear*, by William A. Fletcher. New edition. The University of Texas Press, 1954.

(Editor) *The Confederate Letters of John W. Hagan.* The University of Georgia Press, 1954.

(Editor) *The Reminiscences of Big I*, by William Nathaniel Wood. McCowat-Mercer Press, 1956.

The Road to Appomattox. Memphis State College Press, 1956. Reprinted: 1968, college edition (paper), Atheneum Co.

(Editor) *Kentucky Cavaliers in Dixie: the Reminiscences of a Confederate Cavalryman*, by George Dallas Mosgrove. McCowat-Mercer Press, 1957.

(Editor) *Recollections of a Confederate Staff Officer*, by Gilbert Moxley Sorrel. McCowat-Mercer Press, 1958.

(Editor, with the assistance of Lucy E. Fay) *This Infernal War: the Confederate Letters of Sgt. Edwin H. Fay.* The University of Texas Press, 1958.

They Who Fought Here. Text by Bell I. Wiley, illustrations selected by Hirst D. Milhollen. Macmillan Co., 1959.

(Editor) *The Letters of Warren Akin, Confederate Congressman.* The University of Georgia Press, 1959.

(Editor) *A Southern Woman's Story: Life in Confederate Richmond*, by Phoebe Yates Pember. McCowat-Mercer Press, 1959.

Lincoln, Simples Homem de Povo. Preface and translation by Pinto de Aguiar. Universidade da Bahia, Brazil, 1959.

(Editor, with Joseph Rogers Hollingsworth) *American Democracy: a Documentary Record.* 2 volumes. Thomas Y. Crowell Co., 1961, 1962.

(Editor) *Four Years on the Firing Line*, by James Cooper Nisbet. McCowat-Mercer Press, 1963.

Embattled Confederates, an Illustrated History of Southerners at War. Illustrations compiled by Hirst D. Milhollen. Harper and Row Co., 1964.

Lincoln and Lee. The Clarendon Press, 1966.

(Editor, with Allan Nevins and James I. Robertson, Jr.) *Civil War Books, a Critical Bibliography.* 2 volumes. The Louisiana State University Press, 1967, 1969.

The Common Soldier of the Civil War. Illustrations selected by Frederic Ray, design by Krone Art Service. Historical Times, Inc., 1973.

Confederate Women. Greenwood Press, 1975.

* *The Life of Johnny Reb* and *The Life of Billy Yank* were published in full in a single volume under the title, *The Common Soldier in the Civil War*, Grosset and Dunlap, 1958. They were issued separately in paper covers, Charter Book series, Bobbs-Merrill Co., 1962. In 1971 they were reissued, with new introductions by Wiley, by Doubleday and Company.

ARTICLES AND SPECIAL STUDIES

"Splitting the [Debating] Teams Has Advantages," *The Gavel*, Delta Sigma Rho XII (January 1930), 9-10.

"Bridging the Gap between Decision and No-Decision Types of Debate," *Journal of Expression* IV (June 1930), 75-77.

"Vicissitudes of Early Reconstruction Farming in the Lower Mississippi Valley," *Journal of Southern History* III (November 1937), 441-52.

"Salient Changes in Southern Agriculture since the Civil War," *Agricultural History* XIII (April 1939), 65-76.

"Sitting in the Other Person's Place," *The Lamp*, Delta Zeta (May 1939), 257-59.

"Fundamentals of a College Education," *The Eleusis*, Chi Omega XLI (November 1939), 564-68.

"Camp Newspapers of the Confederacy," *North Carolina Historical Review* XX (October 1943), 327-35.

"Civil War Letters of Warren G. Magee," *Journal Of Mississippi History* V (October 1943), 204-13.

"The Building and Training of Infantry Divisions," *Army Ground Forces Historical Studies*, Number 12. Lithoprinted, October 1946. Also published in *Infantry Journal* LXII (1948), 6-10, 26-30, 30-36, 41-45.

"Problems in Nondivisional Training in the Army Ground Forces," *Army Ground Forces Historical Studies*, Number 14. Lithoprinted, October 1946.

(With Thomas P. Govan) "History of the Second Army," *Army Ground Forces Historical Studies*, Number 16. Lithoprinted, November 1946.

"Preparation of Units for Overseas Movement," *Army Ground Forces Historical Studies*, Number 21. Lithoprinted, November 1946.

"The Training of Negro Troops," *Army Ground Forces Historical Studies*, Number 36. Lithoprinted, November 1946.

"The Role of Army Ground Forces in Redeployment," *Army Ground Forces Historical Studies*, Number 37. Lithoprinted, November 1946.

"Redeployment Training," *Army Ground Forces Historical Studies*, Number 38. Lithoprinted, December 1946.

"The South and the Nation," *Louisiana Library Association Bulletin* XI (November 1947), 2-7.

"Training in the Ground Army, 1942-1945," *Army Ground Forces Historical Studies*, Number 2. Lithoprinted, April 1948.

"Activation and Early Training of 'D' Division," *Army Ground Forces Historical Studies*, Number 13. Lithoprinted, June 1948.

"The Movement to Humanize the Institution of Slavery during the Confederacy," *Emory University Quarterly* V (December 1949), 207-20. Also published in *The New Index: Journal of the Confederate Research Club*, London, I (1956), 45-47, 55-58, 59-61.

"Billy Yank and Abraham Lincoln," *Abraham Lincoln Quarterly* VI (June 1950), 103-20.

"Southern Reaction to Federal Invasion," *Journal of Southern History* XVI (November 1950), 491-510.

"Billy Yank Down South," *Virginia Quarterly Review* XXVI (Autumn 1950), 557-75.

"Billy Yank and the Brass," *Journal of the Illinois State Historical Society* XLIII (Winter 1950), 249-64.

"Billy Yank and the Black Folk," *Journal of Negro History* XXXVI (January 1951), 35-52.

"Boys in Blue," *Abraham Lincoln Quarterly* VI (December 1951), 415-30.

"Men in Blue: Some Types among the Union Rank and File," *American Heritage*, New Series, III (Winter 1952), 18-21, 81.

"Johnny Reb and Billy Yank," *Emory University Quarterly* VIII (March 1952), 1-6.

"Holy Joes of the 'Sixties: a Study of Civil War Chaplains," *Huntington Library Quarterly* XVI (May 1953), 287-304. Also published in *Military Chaplain* XXIV (October 1953), 17-22; and in *The New Index: Journal of the Confederate Research Club*, London, I (1956), 84-93.

"Historians and the National Register," *American Archivist* XVII (October 1954), 325-30. Translated in "O Registro Nacional de Manuscritos," Publicacoes Tecnicas do Arquivo Nacional, No. 15. Rio de Janeiro, Brazil (1960), 15-23.

"Origin of the World War II Historical Program," Office of the Chief of Military History, Department of the Army, Washington. Mimeographed, 1954.

"Civil War in America," *The Encyclopedia Americana* (1955) 6-22. Republished in each annual edition, 1956-1965 and 1967.

"A Time of Greatness," *Journal of Southern History* XXII (February 1956), 1-35. Also published in George Brown Tindall, ed., *The Pursuit of Southern History, Presidential Addresses of the Southern Historical Association, 1935-1963.* Louisiana State University Press, 1964.

"Southern Yeomen in the Civil War," in Earl Schenck Miers, ed., *The American Story, the Age of Exploration to the Age of the Atom.* Channel Press, 1956.

"Commemorating the American Civil War," *Emory University Quarterly* XIV (March 1958), 43-47.

"Letters of Warren Akin, 1861-1865," *Georgia Historical Quarterly* XLII (March, June, September, December 1958), 70-92, 193-214, 294-313, 408-27, and XLIII (March, June, September 1959), 74-90, 186-202, 281-301.

"Lincoln and the Plain People," U.S. Information Agency, Washington. Lithoprinted for overseas distribution, 1958. Also published in Henry B. Kranz, ed., *Abraham Lincoln: a New Portrait.* G.P. Putnam's Sons, 1959.

"Lincoln, Plain Man of the People," *Emory University Quarterly* XIV (December 1958), 195-206.

"Kent Roberts Greenfield: an Appreciation," *Military Affairs* XXII (Winter 1958-1959), 177-80.

"The Memorable War," *Missouri Historical Review* LIII (January 1959), 99-104. Also published in the *Congressional Record*, CV (April 23, 1959), A3317-18.

"Report of the Committee on Historical Activities," *Civil War History* V (December 1959), 374-81.

"Battle of Shiloh — April 6-7, 1862," *Battles of the Civil War, 1861-1865, a Pictorial Presentation.* Pioneer Press, 1960.

"Suggestions for Centennial Observances," *United Daughters of the Confederacy Magazine* XXIII (March 1960), 13-14, 30.

"The Role of the Archivist in the Civil War Centennial," *American Archivist* XXIII (April 1960), 131-42.

Why Georgia Should Commemorate the Civil War. Department of State Parks, Atlanta, Ga.

"The Soldier's Life, North and South, during the Civil War," *Life* (February 3, 1961), 64-77.

"Home Letters of Johnny Reb and Billy Yank," *Centennial Review* V (Winter 1961), 53-64. Also published in abridged form in *Army Information Digest* XVI (August 1961), 76-81.

"Robert E. Lee: an Appreciation," *Emory University Quarterly* XVIII (Winter 1962), 240-50.

Common Man in Crisis. Proceedings of a special meeting, Annual Convention, New Jersey Educational Association, November 8, 1962.

Kingdom Coming; the Emancipation Proclamation of September 22, 1862. Chicago Historical Society, 1963.

"A Story of Three Southern Officers," *Civil War Times* III (April 1964), 6-9, 28-34.

"The Collapse of the Confederacy," *Emory Alumnus* XL (May 1964), 4-8.

"Billy Yank and Johnny Reb in the Campaign for Atlanta," *Civil War Times* III (special Atlanta Campaign issue, June 1964), 18-22.

"Lincoln and Lee," *Congressional Record* CXI (May 4, 1965), 9079-82.

Lincoln and Lee. Clarendon Press, 1967.

"Jefferson Davis: an Appraisal," *Civil War Times* VI (April 1967), 4-11, 44-49.

"The Common Soldiers of the Civil War," *Congressional Record* CXIII (October 16, 1967), A5068-71.

"The Confederate Congresses," *Civil War Times* VII (April 1968), 22-24.

"Johnny Reb and Billy Yank Compared," *American History Illustrated* III (April 1968), 4-9, 44-47. Also published as "Johnny Reb and Billy Yank" in *Annual Editions: Readings in American History*. Bicentennial edition, Volume 1. Dushkin Publishing Group, 1975.

"Rebel Idea: Poison Gas via Balloons," *Civil War Times* VII (July 1968), 40-41.

"The American Civil War and the Common Man," in *From Jefferson to Johnson: Traditional Values in American Life*. Lectures given at American Studies Conference, Konigswinter, Germany, July 4-8, 1966. Mimeographed, Cologne, Germany, 1968.

"From Slavery to Freedom: Negroes in America, 1800-1865," Ibid.

"Johnny Reb and Billy Yank," in *The Boyd Lee Spahr Lectures in Americana, 1962-1969*. Volume 4 (Dickinson College, 1970).

"Life in the South," *Civil War Times* VIII (January 1970), 4-9, 44-47.

"The War's Impact on Slavery," *Civil War Times* IX (April 1970), 36-48.

"Slavery in the United States," *American History Illustrated* V (April 1970), 10-17.

"Get It Right," *Civil War Times* IX (May 1970), 30-31.

"The Library and Its Friends," *Emory Magazine* XLVI (November-December 1970), 10-13.

"Johnny Reb and Billy Yank at Shiloh," *West Tennessee Historical Papers* XXVI (Fall 1972), 5-12.

"Johnny Reb and Billy Yank in the Shiloh, Chickamauga and Chatta-

nooga Campaigns," *Perspective*, magazine of the Tennessee Valley
Authority (Winter 1972).

"The Common Soldier of the Civil War," *Civil War Times* XII (July
1973), 2-64.

"Women of the Lost Cause," *American History Illustrated* VII (December 1973), 10-23.

FOREWORDS AND INTRODUCTIONS TO BOOKS

The Segregation Decisions, papers read at a session of the 21st annual
meeting of the Southern Historical Association, Memphis, Tennessee,
November 10, 1955. Southern Regional Council, Atlanta, 1956. Foreword, 5-7.

As They Saw Forrest, Robert S. Henry, ed. McCowat-Mercer Press,
1956. Foreword, vi-viii.

Gunner with Stonewall: Reminiscences of William Thomas Poague,
Monroe F. Cockrell, ed. McCowat-Mercer Press, 1956. Foreword,
vii-viii.

Theodore Upson, *With Sherman to the Sea*, O.O. Winther, ed. Indiana
University Press, 1958. Foreword, vii-x.

Jefferson Davis, *The Rise and Fall of the Confederate Government*.
Thomas Yoseloff, Inc., 1958. Foreword, vii-xxii.

Irving A. Buck, *Cleburne and His Command*, T.R. Hay, ed. McCowat-
Mercer Press, 1959. Foreword, 7-8.

A Life for the Confederacy: the War Diary of Robert A. Moore, C.S.A.,
James W. Silver, ed. McCowat-Mercer Press, 1959. Foreword, 7-8.

Frederick H. Dyer, *A Compendium of the War of the Rebellion*. Thomas
Yoseloff, Inc., 1958. Foreword, v-vii.

Some of the Boys: the Civil War Letters of Isaac Jackson, Joseph O. Jackson, ed. Southern Illinois University Press, 1960. Foreword, vii-xv.

Florence Fleming Corley, *Confederate Augusta*. University of South
Carolina Press, 1960. Foreword, xiii-xiv.

Whipt 'Em Everytime: the Diary of Bartlett Yancey Malone, William
Whatley Pierson, Jr., ed. McCowat-Mercer Press, 1960. Foreword,
11-13.

Alice Hamilton Cromie, *A Tour Guide to the Civil War*. Quadrangle
Books, 1965. Introduction, xv-xviii.

John Worsham, *One of Jackson's Foot Cavalry*, James I. Robertson, Jr.,
ed. McCowat-Mercer Press, 1965. Foreword, vii.

Robert S. Henry, *First with the Most Forrest*, McCowat-Mercer Press, 1969. Foreword, 7-8.

Richard M. McMurry, *The Road Past Kennesaw: the Atlanta Campaign of 1864*. National Park Service, 1972. Foreword, i-iv.

N.B. The writing of book reviews has been a major bibliographical contribution by Bell I. Wiley. His reviews are too numerous to list here. By one count he had written 310 between 1939 and 1960. In addition to entries in such reference books as *Who's Who in America* and the *Directory of American Scholars*, a useful, illustrated, biographical sketch of Wiley was written recently by John Duncan, "An Interview with Bell Wiley," *Civil War Times Illustrated* XII (April 1973), 32-38.